The New Scots

The Story of Asians in Scotland

BASHIR MAAN

Foreword by Bruce Millan

JOHN DONALD PUBLISHERS LTD
EDINBURGH

© Bashir Maan 1992
All rights reserved. No part of this
publication may be reproduced in any
form or by any means without the
prior permission of the publishers,
John Donald Publishers Ltd.,
138 St Stephen Street, Edinburgh EH3 5AA.

ISBN 0 85976 357 9

Dedication

This book is dedicated to the people of Scotland
who have all been at a certain time in the history of
this country, the new Scots.

Publisher's Acknowledgement

The publisher would like to thank Strathclyde
Regional Council for their generous contribution
to the production of this book.

British Library Cataloguing in Publication Data
A catalogue record for this book is available from the British Library.

Phototypeset by The Midlands Book Typesetting Company, Loughborough
Printed in Great Britain by Arrowsmith Ltd., Bristol

DA
774.4
.A74
M33
1992

Foreword by Bruce Millan, Member of the Commission of the European Communities

The story of the Asian community in Scotland is a story of success. They are now a familiar part of the Scottish scene and an important element in our business life, from the corner shop to the wholesale trade and now increasingly also in the professions.

I can think of no one better qualified to give an account of Asian settlement in Scotland over the last 40 years than Bashir Maan. He himself has been with us for almost all of that time and an active and distinguished involvement in politics and community relations has given him a special insight into the problems and successes of this latest addition to Scottish society.

If he had confined himself to these last 40 years that would have been fascinating enough. But he has done more than that. He has gone back to the inter-war years and as a result of much research has provided the link between the small Asian community of these days and the much larger and more significant community of today. The Asian seamen and pedlars have become today's successful business men. In tracing this journey he has provided us with much valuable material not readily available elsewhere.

As a counterpoint to his account of the Asians in Scotland, Mr Maan has given us a history of the Scots in India which is particularly interesting to someone like me, born and brought up in Dundee, a city once dominated by the jute industry and the jute barons whose wealth came from the Indian sub-continent. He does well to remind us of how many Scottish fortunes had their origin, honest or corrupt, in India.

He also reminds us that there have been other migrations to Scotland and much of what he tells us of the Lithuanians and Poles, as well as the Irish, Jews and Italians, will be new to most Scots.

Differences in background, in language, religion and culture are a breeding ground for resentment, prejudice and discrimination and most immigrant communities have suffered at one time or another. When differences in skin colour are added to the distinctions between the new community and the old, the potential for mischief making by the ill-disposed is heightened.

Bashir Maan gives a fairly positive assessment of Scotland in this respect. Certainly we have been spared some of the uglier manifestations of racism which have disfigured English cities from time to time and it is good to know that the Asian Community itself has found Scotland on the whole more welcoming than England, so that there has been some internal movement in the UK from England to north of the border. However, anyone who believes that there is no problem at all of racism in Scotland is out of touch with reality. My own experience as a Glasgow Member of Parliament with Asians among my constituents was salutary, with too many instances of harassment and attacks on Asian shopkeepers to allow complacency. There is still need for an active policy of Community relations at all levels, local as well as national.

At least in the UK, we have avoided so far, and I hope will continue to avoid, the growth of powerful racist and fascist political parties such as we have seen in France and elsewhere and which is a particularly worrying feature of the present European political scene. If this healthier situation in Britain is a tribute to the political maturity of the British people, it is also a tribute to the Asian community itself — hard working and law abiding as it is. They have managed to become good Scots but have done that without losing their own cultural identity.

Bashir Maan's book deserves to be read by everyone in Scotland involved in community relations, in school, at work or in the wider community. Indeed it should be read by every Scot who wants to know more about the new Scots among us.

Brussels, 1992   B.M.

Contents

Foreword by Bruce Millan   iii
Acknowledgements   vi
Introduction   1

Chapter 1   The Makings of the Scots   5

Chapter 2   The Scots in India   37

Chapter 3   The Indians in Scotland   62

Chapter 4   The Indians Between the Two Wars   98

Chapter 5   World War II and After   149

Chapter 6   Cultures and Customs of the Newcomers   182

Chapter 7   Conclusions and the Future   201

Bibliography   208

Index   210

Acknowledgements

I am very grateful to Dr Robert Miles (who is Research Director of the Research Unit on Migration and Racism in the Department of Sociology at the University of Glasgow) for his encouragement, valuable advice and generous guidance throughout the five years of my occupation with this study. In spite of his very busy life at the university and his national and international commitments, he always found time to read, correct, comment and make constructive suggestions on my draft chapters. In fact, without his keen interest and unstinting support, I may not have been able to accomplish this project.

The Glasgow University Senate conferred upon me an Honorary Research Fellowship which gave me access to any book and every other source of information I needed. This facilitated my research on this difficult subject. I owe a debt of gratitude to the Senate for this favour and indeed this honour.

My sincere thanks to the staff of the Glasgow University Library and the University Archives, the Mitchell Library Glasgow, the Strathclyde Region Archives, the Edinburgh University Archives, the National Library of Scotland, Edinburgh, and the India Office Library and Records in London, for helping me by meeting my requests for books, records and documents so courteously and efficiently.

For the reproduction of illustrations detailed below acknowledgement is due as follows:

From *The Cornchest for Scotland: Scots in India* by Alex M. Cain. National Library of Scotland, 1986: 'William Hamilton's Funerary Inscription'; 'An Elaborate Hookah'; 'Alexander Gardner'; 'A Nautch Girl'. From *Raj: The Story of British India* by Michael Edwardes. Pan Books Ltd., 1969: 'Shah Alam'; 'A Dinner Party in the 1840s'. From *India in Britain* by K. Vadgama: 'The British Revenge'; 'Maharajah Dunleep Singh'; 'Munshi Abdhul Karim'; 'Two Nannies'. The back cover illustration depicting Queen Victoria with an Indian Servant, Mohammed Ismail, at Balmoral, is also reproduced from K. Vadgama's *India in Britain*.

The staff of Strathclyde Community Relations Council and several other people have encouraged me and helped me with suggestions, advice and time. I thank them all. Most particularly, I would like to thank all those individuals, only some of whom have been mentioned in this book, who were good enough to give me interviews. They patiently accepted each new set of questions that I posed and raked their minds again and again, each time providing me with immensely valuable and revealing information.

Lastly, I would like to record my gratitude to my daughter Rashda, her husband and their daughters, my daughters Hanna and Aalya and their mother and my son Tariq. They all took a very keen interest in this dissertation and gave me much needed moral and emotional support.

Glasgow, 1992   B. M.

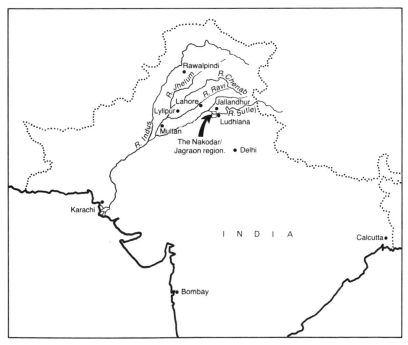

Northern India (1930): The arrow indicates the area detailed overleaf.

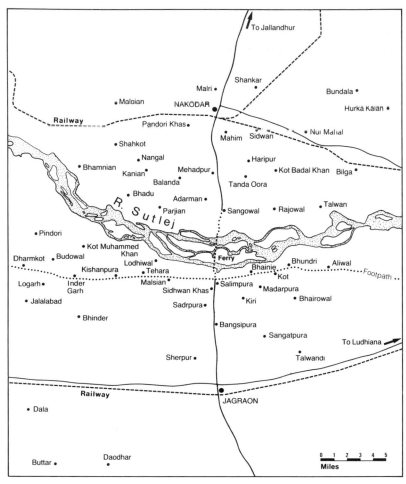

Villages in the Nakodar/Jagraon region from where the early migrants came.

Introduction

The origin of this book lies in an invitation offered to me twenty-five years ago. In early 1967, I was asked to write an 'Indian and Pakistani' column for a monthly local newspaper, the *Gorbals View*. The Editor, the Reverend John Harvey, wanted to present all points of view, including information about the 'dark strangers' who had become the new neighbours of many of the inhabitants of the Gorbals. During the 1950s and 60s, most of the Indo-Pakistani immigrants who settled in Glasgow lived in the Gorbals area. Hence, in a series of articles spread over a period of two years, I presented a picture of the culture, the history of migration from the subcontinent and the process of settlement in Glasgow of these immigrants from India and Pakistan.

By 1970, race relations had become a live issue in Scotland, much later than in England. Those involved in this subject who were looking for information about the immigrants in this part of the country located back issues of the *Gorbals View* in the libraries and found those articles useful. As far as I am aware, those articles were the only written information then available relating to the Indo-Pakistani community in Scotland. But this information was limited and concerned only those immigrants living in the Gorbals and in Glasgow. Friends and wellwishers involved in race relations, particularly the late Miss Stella Reekie, asked me therefore to expand on those articles in order to cover the whole of Scotland and to update the information.

Their argument was that, in the absence of correct information about these Asian settlers, their problems in Scotland were being interpreted in terms of the problems faced by the immigrants in England, and solutions were being sought on the basis of information and experiences derived from England. But these solutions seemed not to be working. In

1

part this was because, as will be explained in this book, the Asian community in Scotland was in many respects different from that of their compatriots in England. Furthermore, the Scottish legal system, the Scottish education system, and Scottish customs and culture are different from those in England. Consequently, there seemed to be a need for an in-depth study of the Asians who settled in Scotland in order to understand them and their problems. Throughout the 1970s and 80s, personal circumstances and many time-consuming commitments prevented me from giving attention to this matter. It was only at the end of the 1980s that I was able to begin work on the project which many people had urged me to undertake so long ago.

As soon as I began my research, it became clear to me that Scotland was a nation created from many different peoples. Scotland has been attracting invaders, settlers, immigrants and refugees throughout its history. The present Scottish nation, therefore, is a blend of many people. To put the recent immigration from the Indian subcontinent and other parts of the world in its proper perspective, I felt that this paramount fact ought to be reiterated. I have thus begun by referring to the various invaders and interlopers who settled in Scotland prior to the Union of Scotland and England in 1707. The age of invaders ends there, and from then on it is economic immigrants and political refugees who seek entry into Scotland, most of them white Europeans. They are all fully fledged Scots now, but in their own particular time, whether they came as invaders or immigrants, they were the new Scots like the present new Scots of Asian origin. I have traced their histories, concentrating on the circumstances which forced them to leave their respective countries, the problems they faced on their arrival, the level of discrimination and hostility they suffered during their settlement in Scotland, and how and when they achieved their integration or assimilation in this society.

This history I have dealt with in a summary fashion, whereas I have presented the history of the Asian migration to Scotland in a more comprehensive way. Perhaps the ordinary Scottish man and woman does not realise that it was hard-up Scots who first went to the rich and luxurious Indian subcontinent to make their fortunes, long before the Indo-Pakistanis ever even dreamt of coming to Scotland. To emphasise this point, I have started this part of the book with a chapter which documents the exploits of the Scots in India and the impact of the wealth they brought back on the economy of Scotland. This provided the context for the arrival of the first Indians in Scotland.

Scottish families returning to Scotland from India often brought with them their Indian servants, and then Indian seamen were employed on British ships as cheap labour. I also discuss the impact the visiting Indian princes and the Indian students made on this country and the impressions of Scotland that they took back with them. But most of these early migrants came to this country for a certain period or a specific purpose, and when that was achieved they returned home. The settlement of Indians in Scotland began in the 1920s when some of the unemployed seamen and abandoned servants became pedlars in order to earn a living, and developed during the period between the two wars. Few official records are available regarding this migration and settlement in Scotland. However, fortunately, a few of the pioneers who came in the 1920s and 30s were still alive, and I have used their memories and their case histories, along with contemporary press reports, valuation rolls and the register of pedlars' licences, to build up as accurate as possible a picture of this crucial period.

The period after the Second World War was relatively easy for me to record. I myself came to Scotland in 1953 when the Asian community was beginning to grow. Since then I have been a participant in the settlement, the development, and the integration of this most recent wave of immigrants to Scotland. Having been actively involved in race relations, politics and community work for the past 35 years, I know from direct experience their frustrations and their aspirations. I am aware of their limitations and their achievements. I have therefore based this part of the book on available records, case histories and my own observations and experiences. I discuss

3

the independence and partition of the subcontinent into the two separate states of India and Pakistan, and document the small but steady flow of newcomers to Scotland from the two new dominions in the late 1940s and early 1950s and then the sudden rush to beat the ban in the early 1960s. Thereafter, we see the Asian pedlars and bus conductors turn into successful shopkeepers and restaurateurs, and their success in turn attracts internal Asian migrants from England. The movement of more and more Asians into trade and commerce continues during the 1970s and 80s, and Asian-owned businesses spread to provincial towns and villages throughout the length and breadth of Scotland.

The concluding chapter deals with the current constitution of the Asian and other ethnic minority communities in Scotland. I discuss their vocations and professions, their problems and aspirations, their approximate numbers in the various regions and cities, their culture and customs and their varied religions, in order to present a complete picture of this recent addition to Scottish society.

CHAPTER ONE

The Makings of the Scots

> 'O, mankind! We created you from a single pair of a male and a female, and made you into nations and tribes, that you may know each other (not that you may despise each other). Verily the most honoured of you in the sight of God is (one who is) most righteous of you.' (*Al-Quran*)

The recent presence in Scotland of over 50,000 people of different colours and races has made us realise that this is now a multiracial multicultural society. It would, however, not be unhistorical to observe that Scotland has been, right from the dawn of history, a multiracial society. People of numerous tribes and several races and cultures have been entering and settling in this land for, at least, the last 2200 years. Every wave of newcomers must have faced problems of adjustment in their new environment and, at the same time, must have made their impact on the indigenous population. It is only natural that they would have preserved their identity and clung to their own culture and customs as long as they could. Eventually, however, they either became assimilated with the local inhabitants or, if numerous and strong enough, they absorbed or obliterated the natives.

To elaborate upon this aspect of the Scottish people and to be able to draw a comparison between the most recent immigrants and their so many predecessors we shall take a cursory look at the history of Scotland.

The first historical people to be found in this country were the Caledonians and the Picts, two branches of the Celtic stock. They most probably came over from Ireland in the second century B.C. Not much is known about the prehistoric natives who were then living in this land, nor what became of them.

In the ninth decade of the first century A.D. the Romans appeared in 'Caledonia', the name applied to this country in those days. They occupied southern, central, and north eastern parts of the country and held intermittent control of these areas for over 300 years. Incidentally, the Roman armies posted in this part of the Empire included black soldiers of African origin. It is, therefore, most probable that the first black people to have come to Scotland were those Roman legionnaires. The Romans, having left their considerable influence and many descendants, withdrew their armies and their authority from this land in the fifth century A.D.

In the early sixth century another Celtic tribe called the Scots crossed over from Ireland (then known as Scotia) and occupied the present Kintyre and Island of Mull and other parts of the region which is now known as Argyll. The newcomers called this part of the country Dalriada. It was these Scots who, a few centuries later, laid the foundations of this country as we know it now and gave it the name Scotland.

It ought to be noted that the Celtic people were inhabiting the central and western parts of Europe in the first millennium B.C. From there some of their tribes migrated to England and Ireland in the fourth century B.C. They came to Scotland from Ireland, in successive waves, over a period of 800 years (from 200 B.C. to A.D. 600). Most historians are of the opinion that the Celts were a branch of the great Aryan nation. The Aryans, it is believed, originally emerged from central Asia about 1500 B.C. Some of them went to India and others headed for Europe. The present-day Scots and the people from the Indo-Pakistan subcontinent, or at least many of them, therefore have common ancestors, as both are descended from Aryans.

The Angles made their inroads into this country in the later part of the sixth century. They were a German tribe who had invaded and occupied parts of England in the fifth century A.D. From England they moved north and colonised the Borders and south east of 'Scotland'.

In the eighth century the British, a Welsh tribe, overran south western 'Scotland' and took possession of the country from the Solway Firth to the Firth of Clyde. Near the end of

6

the eighth century the Norsemen started their raids on the 'Scottish' coasts, and in the ninth century they began to settle in the Hebrides and the Orkney and Shetland Islands, and also on the coast all around the mainland. By the end of the tenth century they were well entrenched in their 'Scottish' settlements.

Thomas B. Johnston, in his *History of the Working Classes in Scotland* p 19 draws the following picture of this country during the tenth century: 'Scotland, however, was still a land of independent clans owning a light, fitful and voluntary allegiance to any central authority, and there must have been in the Lowlands thousands of peasant proprietors, the descendants of Roman legionnaires who, retiring from the army at the age of 45, were given four acres of land in freehold. On the eastern seaboard were the Saxon colonists — most unpromising material they for exploitation; in the far north the sons of the wild rovers from "Norroway, Norroway, ower the foam"; on the west the Scots from Ireland; in Galloway the intractable Picts. Many a long day was to elapse ere all these would be welded together into one nation, acknowledging one King and suffering baronial tyrannies and plundership.'

In the fourth decade of the eleventh century, the Picts, the Scots, the Angles and the British were united under one King named Duncan. King Duncan belonged to the Scots tribe which had been the dominant force in the country for the past 200 years. The country from then on became known as Scotland.

In the second half of the eleventh century, when the Normans conquered England, the heirs of the former kings and an influx of English sympathisers took refuge in Scotland and settled mainly in the Lowlands. Throughout the middle ages intermittent conflicts and wars continued between Scotland and England with a corresponding flow of people from one country to the other.

The ravages of the medieval wars and the exploitation and oppression of the lairds and barons reduced the common man in Scotland to a state of abject misery. Slavery and perpetual servitude became the lot of many of the working classes during the middle centuries of the present millennium. Vagrants, unemployed and beggars swarmed everywhere. Parents sold their children to avoid starvation. Thousands of able-bodied Scots were sold as slaves to row the galleys or to work on the plantations in the West Indies. 'In 1665 Edinburgh merchants were given permission to transport the beggars and thieves to the plantations in Jamaica and Barbados.' (*Glasgow Herald*, 29 October 1988).

The feudal overlords and their cronies held sway in the land and controlled the destiny of the Scottish people right up to the close of the eighteenth century. They used legislation and every other trick in the book to rob and exploit the common people and to enslave the poor wretches either to sell them or to use them as unpaid labour. 'At Aberdeen, for example, a regular slave market existed from 1740 to 1746, a company of enterprising capitalists which included a bailie of the city and the Town Clerk Depute engaging themselves actively in kidnapping people in the rural districts and selling them to slavery to American plantations: no fewer than 600 men and women being thus shipped in six brief years from the Aberdeen slave market' (T. B. Johnston, *History of the Working Classes in Scotland* p 58). Such slave markets existed all over the country, and slave labour was used in the factories and works which were being set up by the rich barons during the seventeenth and eighteenth centuries.

The pace of industrial development quickened from the second half of the eighteenth century and at the same time there was a significant expansion in the agricultural sector in this country. These two factors created more employment and thus generated a degree of prosperity among the working classes. This welcome change resulted in a rapid transformation of the social set-up in Scotland. The feudal system started to crumble and the common people began to attain freedom, dignity and justice. The relative prosperity and growing demand for labour in the eighteenth and nineteenth centuries attracted, not any hostile invaders this time, but humble economic immigrants from across the Irish sea once again.

THE IRISH IMMIGRANTS

Communications between Scotland and Ireland have remained active since prehistoric times. As has been mentioned earlier, it was the Scots, the Irish colonists, who eventually unified this country in the eleventh century A.D. and gave it its name. It was also these Irish invaders who brought Christianity to this land. The Irish had been converted by the fifth century A.D. A number of missionaries, therefore, came over from Ireland, in the wake of the conquest of 'Dalriada' by the Celtic Scots, in the sixth century, to convert the native 'heathens'. Again, it was Ireland which gave the potato to Scotland in the eighteenth century, thus easing the food situation and changing the diet of the Scottish people. Yet again Ireland, as we shall see in the following pages, provided the most significant part of the manpower required for the accomplishment of the Industrial Revolution in Scotland during the eighteenth and nineteenth centuries. It was the ever available, 'wide framed', strong and hardworking Irish labourers who dug the canals, laid the railway tracks, constructed the roads, and built the harbours and docks which facilitated the industrial development and brought the resulting prosperity to this land. Scotland thus owes much to the Emerald Isle for the latter's contribution towards its national identity, its faith, its food, and its prosperity.

There has been a constant movement of people and ideas between the two countries which are separated by only 12 miles of water. At certain times though, due to some extraordinary circumstances, the movement of people from one country to the other increased considerably and became more noticeable. There were instances, particularly in the late middle ages, when people from Scotland moved to Ireland; but on the whole the flow has been mainly from Ireland to Scotland. This flow increased significantly in the second half of the eighteenth century and accelerated greatly in the nineteenth.

For centuries Ireland was treated as a colony by the British. Most of the land was owned by English and Scottish nobility

— the absentee landlords — who were only interested in the annual rent from their Irish estates. The estates were managed by the landlords' agents. These greedy and unscrupulous people oppressed and exploited the tenant farmers. There was no security of tenancy for the tenants as the agents evicted them at their whim. For the Irish peasantry there were no other job opportunities except farming. Eviction therefore meant starvation or migration. Naturally the poor peasants migrated to places where they hoped to avoid starvation.

Early in the eighteenth century new methods of farming were introduced in Scotland and the agriculture industry improved considerably. More land was brought under cultivation and the yield per acre also increased. The increase in production required more seasonal labourers to harvest the produce. Harvesting in Scotland, due to the vagaries of the weather, had to be accomplished in the shortest possible (opportune) time. To achieve this the farmers needed ready and reliable labour. However, from the middle of the eighteenth century, the farmers began to experience some difficulties in procuring the required number of seasonal workers, as more and more of the native workers were being engaged full time by other industries, which were being set up at this stage. The farmers were thus forced to turn to other sources to secure their required seasonal labour.

According to Dr Robert Miles (*Racism and Migrant Labour*), the Irish seasonal workers are on record as having been present in Scotland in the early eighteenth century. The Scottish farmers, therefore, out of necessity at first, engaged this migrant labour at harvest times. Soon, however, the farmers became convinced of the reliability and better performance of the Irish labour. Thus the demand for their labour increased and so did the number of Irish immigrants arriving every year to meet that demand. Some of the immigrants who had no attachments back home, or had no compelling reasons to return after the season was over, stayed on in this country doing odd or unskilled jobs. Thus an Irish community started to take roots and develop in Scotland during the eighteenth century.

These Irish settlers were perhaps the first people to come

to Scotland as economic immigrants. Others who had settled in this country before them had come as invaders, conquerors or adventurers. They possessed some power and authority, whereas the Irish were not only humble intruders, but also considered to be of an inferior race and alien faith.

The man in the street did not appreciate or comprehend the contribution of the Irish immigrants to the Scottish economy, especially the agricultural industry. The bigots and religious extremists spread myths and untruths and preached hate and violence against those Irish 'Catholic' immigrants. They were portrayed as heretics and undesirable intruders. The 1770s, therefore, saw the first open manifestation of enmity and resentment against the presence of Irish communities in the cities and towns of Scotland. There were serious riots and attacks on Irish people and their properties in many places. 'In January 1779, Catholics in Glasgow who had assembled as usual in the house of Donald McDonald, a combmaker residing in Blackstocks Land at the foot of the Saltmarket, to attend Mass, were assaulted and the house wrecked. ... At Dundee, Perth and Peebles there were also disturbances, but Edinburgh was the scene of the most violent outbreak.' (J. E. Handley, *The Irish in Modern Scotland* p 268–9).

The Irish were not, however, intimidated into returning to Ireland where they faced unemployment and starvation. As a matter of fact, in spite of the harassment and humiliation they had to put up with, more and more of the seasonal Irish workers kept staying on in Scotland after every harvest, and thus their numbers grew steadily. The Industrial Revolution was in progress by then, existing industries were expanding and new plants were being set up. Accordingly the demand for labour was rising sharply. This situation resulted in not only a greater number of seasonal workers coming to Scotland, in August of every year, but also in a continuous flow of Irish labourers throughout the year.

By the close of the eighteenth century 'there were about 30,000 Irish (Catholics) settled in various towns and cities of the lowlands' (R. Miles, *Racism and Migrant Labour* p 144). Some of the Irish settlers who had come over earlier as reapers and labourers had progressed to become successful shopkeepers, stallholders and pedlars. With hard work, determination and fortitude they had done well against heavy odds and thus set an example for their compatriots to follow them. Handley records 'From about 1790 Irish names begin to appear in the roll of Burgesses, in the first Glasgow Directory published in 1783 there are already a few Irish shopkeepers in the city' (J. E. Handley, *The Irish in Modern Scotland*, p 255). By the turn of the century then, small Irish communities had become well established in many towns and cities of central and southern Scotland.

By the beginning of the nineteenth century the Industrial Revolution was getting into full swing, and more and more jobs were being created. The highlanders who used to come down to reap the harvests and to work as unskilled labourers were, at this stage, emigrating to the New World in greater numbers than ever. Most of the available indigenous workers were now employed as skilled and steady workers. There were therefore not many able-bodied natives at hand to work as labourers or to take up the undesirable, servile or dirty jobs. The farmers were the worst hit in this situation. They had even more land under cultivation now, better crops and higher yields, but not enough labourers to harvest or reap their crops. They were thus forced to send advertisements to Ireland calling for labourers to take up the work.

The Irish responded with enthusiasm and came in greater numbers. They could not resist this opportunity as everything was against them in their own country. The legacy of the 1798 rising, lack of arable land patches, high rents, the uncertainties created by the Eviction Acts, and an atmosphere of perpetual and widespread unemployment, all contributed to the push factor. Scotland became their promised land where work was available and wages higher. The relative security of the permanent Irish settlements in Scottish cities and towns also lured relatives and friends to Scotland. The introduction of steamships between the two countries early in the nineteenth century made the crossing from Ireland to Scotland cheaper, quicker and safer. The new arrivals, in contrast to their

12

predecessors who had to live rough in the open till they found employment and accommodation, were now put up and looked after by their relatives, friends or contacts in Scotland. They were also helped and guided in finding work.

The rapid growth of Irish communities in Scotland in the first quarter of the nineteenth century resulted in the establishment of more Catholic institutions such as chapels and schools, and also in the formation of Irish welfare associations and other social organisations. In the 1820s, for example, between one fifth and a quarter of the population of Glasgow was Irish or of Irish descent, and certain districts of the city had been transformed into Irish colonies in the preceding twenty or so years. All this, with competition for jobs, aggravated the situation further and created an atmosphere of intense hostility towards the Irish settlers. The contemporary media, with rare exceptions, played a significant part in spreading the myths and fabrications, denouncing and degrading the Irish and thus fanning the flames of racism, resentment, prejudice and bigotry. The Irish were now being blamed for overcrowding, lack of sanitation, and for lowering the moral and living standards of the natives. They were portrayed as dirty, lazy, criminals, scavengers and paupers. They were accused of lowering wages and of working to break strikes. 'The newspapers of the districts where the immigrants were numerous were naturally the chief purveyors of this kind of lampoonery. Anecdotes rebounding to the discredit of the Irish race and their religion filled their columns. The Irishman's alleged gullibility, naivety or, where it suited, cunningness, was woven into stories of elephantine skittishness. Seldom were the protagonists of these stories indicated . . .' (J. E. Handley, *The Irish in Modern Scotland*, p 271).

The Church also, at this stage, became active in the campaign against the Irish. Religious and sectarian leaders saw a challenge to Protestantism with the influx of Irish Catholics. The ever-increasing number of Irish settlers was thought to be a serious threat to the political and religious dominance of the kirk. The Church ministers fulminated in their pulpits and did their utmost to stir up hate and hostility against the immigrants. Rallies and assemblies were held which were addressed by demagogues and racist agitators, and leaflets accusing the Irish of every hardship and every ill in the country were distributed freely. 'The Irish' they claimed 'were directly responsible for both the material and moral deterioration of the Scottish working class' (R. Miles, *Racism and Migrant Labour*, p 140). This anti-Irish propaganda was being blasted from so many quarters and with such a ferocity that soon the Irish men, women and children were being subjected to insults, abuse, harassment, and physical violence all over the country.

The widespread exposure of the shocking crimes of Burke and Hare in 1829 further intensified the resentment and animosity against the Irish settlers and immigrants, not only in urban conurbations, but also in rural Scotland. 'For many a day after the trial an Irish pedlar dare not show his face in a Scottish village with impunity, and a new bitterness was fused into racial quarrels in the industrial towns' (J. E. Handley, *The Irish in Scotland*, p 251). Incidents of physical violence against individuals increased and there was an upsurge in premeditated attacks on Irish communities and their properties through the length and breadth of the country. 'A mob of Edinburgh labourers making common cause of their resentment against pugnacious immigrants marched to Irish haunts of Cowgate, Cannongate, Grassmarket, Westport, Lawnmarket and High Street, and beat every Irish they could find on the streets . . . the shops owned by the Irish were wrecked, the doors and windows of the Irish houses were shattered, next week the houses which had escaped were demolished' (J. E. Handley, *The Irish in Modern Scotland*, pp 241–2).

Glasgow manifested its own unique brand of hostility towards the Irish immigrants. Whenever a boat arrived at Broomielaw, the ruffians and youngsters of the city gathered at the quayside and hurled taunts and abuse at the disembarking newcomers, and then pursued them to their destinations in the city mocking, jeering and insulting the petrified strangers all the way. James Handley records another wicked peculiarity of

Glasgow of those days: 'For many years after the commence-
ment of Irish immigration to the city, the Glasgow mob, in
addition to showing its displeasure in other ways, staged an
annual demonstration against the immigrants. This was the
sport of 'Hunting the Barney' — 'Barney' being the nickname
bestowed by the citizens on Irishmen. The game formed the
pièce de résistance of the annual Fair. No Irishman was
permitted to approach the Fair with impunity. If he ventured
too near he was hustled by the crowd into the quadrangle
formed by the booths and belaboured with bludgeons. Sus-
pects were forced by a hastily formed committee on elocution
to submit their pronunciation of such words as 'peas' and
'tea' for criticism. 'Paze' and 'tay', as phonetic interpretations,
sounded the doom of the unfortunate performers. When sport
lagged for lack of victims stray Irishmen were rounded up,
clubbed and kicked by the bullies at the Fair. As a final
episode to the hilarities of this holiday week the hooligan
element, armed with clubs, rooted among the warrens of
the Saltmarket, where immigrants sought uneasy shelter,
and found hearty expression for their conception of rich
fun by breaking doors and windows, clubbing Irishmen out
of their homes and ducking them in the stream of the
Molendinar, which flowed into the Clyde at this point. This
annual demonstration ceased only when proper policing of
the Fair was undertaken and when the number of Irishmen in
the district had grown sufficiently large to lower the odds for
their attackers.' (J. E. Handley, *The Irish in Modern Scotland*,
p 270–1).

On the other hand, there were people in Scotland, such as
industrialists, contractors, builders, etc., and, of course, the
farmers, who appreciated the presence and availability of Irish
labour and who valued the contribution of these immigrants
towards the industrialisation and development of the country.
Scottish farmers everywhere welcomed the sturdy Irishmen
with open arms. The Irish on their part 'put their powerful
frames and their strong right arms' freely and cheerfully at
the disposal of their employers. 'The Irishman is too much the
object of ridicule ... but on a moment's reflection every one

must see that his presence could not, in reality, be dispensed with at the harvest season. But for the presence of these Irish reapers, how much of the finest produce of the land must have this season wasted in the furrows (*The Glasgow Courier*, 6 September 1834).

According to the 1841 census, the number of Irish people in Scotland (excluding those of Irish descent) was 126,321 out of a total population of 2,620,184. Glasgow housed the bulk of the immigrants and a quarter of the city's population was now of Irish origin. Like any other immigrant who had come to earn a living and had the responsibility of maintaining dependants back home, the Irish lived as frugally as possible in order to save money, either to send it to their dependants or to provide for a rainy day. They therefore always looked for the cheapest accommodation which naturally was only available in neglected and undesirable properties. The Scottish neighbours distanced themselves from the Irish and in most cases left the neighbourhood. This exodus of the natives resulted in many localities, in cities like Glasgow, becoming Irish dominated. Such concentrations in certain areas offered many advantages to the immigrants. They were better able to organise themselves and to set up their own religious, educational and social institutions and organisations. Also, such areas provided security from harassment and persecution which were, as we know, common in those frightening days. Their dominance in certain districts further encouraged those who had entrepreneurial tendencies to go into various businesses. With the guaranteed patronage of their compatriots, all such businesses flourished and gave a good start to many a future magnate and commercial baron.

The Catholic temperance movement started by Father Mathews in the 1830s bore fruit in the 1840s. Thousands of Irish took the pledge of total abstinence. Brawls and fights among the Irish, and with the local people, disappeared in certain areas of the cities. Many Irish people transformed themselves into peaceful, law abiding and orderly citizens of their new country. This new and temperate image of the Irish brought them a degree of acceptance and respect from some sections of the Protestant majority. Irish and Catholic festivals and celebrations which had previously been shunned and condemned by the Scots started to attract mixed gatherings. More and more Irish-owned businesses were appearing in the high streets and markets places of the Scottish cities and towns. There were Irish grocers, tailors, fishmongers, drapers, second-hand clothiers, furniture dealers, shoemakers, wine and spirit sellers, pawnbrokers, etc., making their contribution to the trade and commerce of the country. The directories of that period indicate that the Irish were engaged in every kind of trade by then.

The potato famine of late 1840s was a catastrophe of great magnitude for Ireland. In six years from 1845 to 1851 Ireland lost two million people. One million starved to death and one million migrated to various countries. Scotland received its share of the Irish exodus. The number of Irish-born people in Scotland according to the 1851 census rose to 207,367, i.e. over 7% of the total population. 'The number of Irish immigrants in the decade 1841–1851, the second half of which covered the famine years, was about 115,000.' (J. E. Handley, *The Irish in Modern Scotland*). The total number of people of Irish descent, however, must have been over 300,000 as the census figure did not include those born of Irish parents who were now in many cases third or perhaps fourth generation. This modified figure means that they formed over 11% of the total population of Scotland in the early 1850s.

Their numerical strength gave the Irish a sense of security and made them bold and politically active in urban areas. Associations were formed to express their nationalism and their loyalty and support for Ireland. The Fenian movement became popular among the Irish and quite active in Scotland. In the 1860s Fenianism caused a great scare when rumours of an uprising by the Irish in Scotland and the imminent landing of Fenians from abroad were taken so seriously that the authorities took precautionary measures.

This unfortunate episode, accompanied by many more myths and misstatements, gave a fresh impetus to the ever-present hate and hostility towards the Irish community. A new and more vicious wave of violence and destruction engulfed the country. Irish houses, businesses and chapels were attacked, destroyed and in some cases burned down. Attacks and assaults on people of Irish origin increased. In many places and on many occasions Irish families had to flee from their houses and even their localities. Belligerent and hysterical crowds forced many employers to sack their Irish employees. Even local authorities and Government departments were persuaded to dismiss their loyal and faithful employees of long standing because those unfortunates happened to be Irish or of Irish descent. The period from 1850 to 1880 was perhaps the most troublesome and most violent for Irish settlers in Scotland. During these three decades there were anti-Irish riots in nearly all the industrial towns and cities, and also at most of the building sites, factory gates and pitheads all over Scotland. In 1875 there was a major riot in Partick, Glasgow, which lasted for several days. In short, perhaps more atrocities and brutalities were inflicted upon the Irish in these thirty years than ever before or after.

The number of newcomers from Ireland during this period, though not as great as during famine years, was still quite high. The persecution and violence prevalent in Scotland did not deter them. In the period 1851 to 1861, about 45,000 Irish immigrants came over and just about the same number arrived in the next decade. Their numbers, however, rose to about 54,000 in the following ten years from 1871 to 1881. After that the immigration from Ireland to Scotland started to decline and the figures for the decades 1881 to 1891 and 1891 to 1901 were 27,445 and 10,484 respectively. (J. E. Handley, *The Irish in Modern Scotland.*)

The decrease in the flow of newcomers from Ireland, along with other factors such as the arrival of Jewish immigrants in Scotland, resulted in the easing of resentment and ill-will towards the Irish. By the end of the 1880s serious incidents of violence and riots against the Irish in Scotland had also ceased. At this stage the Irish settlers in Scotland became very active in the Irish Home Rule Campaign. The Irish National League of Great Britain became very powerful in Scotland and controlled Irish opinion. The Irish vote became a strong force in Scottish politics and the Irish National League used it to advance the cause of Irish Home Rule. The Irish communities also became politically conscious and started to field candidates for elections to local authorities.

By the close of the nineteenth century most of the intolerant elements and, more importantly, most of the Scottish press had changed their attitude from one of open antipathy to that of resigned apathy concerning the Irish. However, 'At a Municipal Election in Glasgow in which an (Irish) immigrant candidate took part, a local minister declared from the pulpit that it would be the everlasting disgrace of the ward if the electors allowed papists or atheists to be returned as their representatives' (J. E. Handley, *The Irish in Modern Scotland*). This was perhaps the last full blast of bigotry in a rapidly changing world. Soon after, in 1897, Patrick O'Hare from Springburn ward was elected a Glasgow city councillor. O'Hare was probably the first Irish Catholic councillor in Scotland and the first Irish bailie of the city, when he was elevated to that office in 1903. Incidentally, the late minister, provided he has not changed his views in the hereafter, would be, not turning, but birling in his grave, at the reality of so many councillors, provosts and members of parliament of Irish descent and of Catholic faith in Scotland today.

The beginning of the twentieth century saw the Irish community well settled, tolerated and involved in the mainstream of life in Scotland. There was still widespread prejudice against them but no persecution. Discrimination, the evil offspring of prejudice, existed in its ugly and flagrant forms until a little after the middle of the present century; even in the 1950s some advertisements, announcing vacancies, appeared in the press and other places, with a note at the bottom saying 'Catholics need not apply'.

Conditions improved rapidly after the Second World War, and the remnants of old hostility and any remaining resentment against the Irish disappeared quickly. The most important factor which helped bring about this improvement was, without any doubt, the profuse involvement of Irish-descended Scots in the politics of this country. It is mainly due to their participation in the process of policy-making and their presence in the corridors of power, at local and national levels, that people of Irish descent are now accepted as equals in social, political and commercial fields. But one must not forget that it has taken a long and torturous span of about 200 years for the Irish to achieve their proper place in this society. Such was the intensity of the racial, religious, political and economic prejudice against them that even this span of two centuries has, so far, only managed to eliminate the overt and blatant forms of discrimination and prejudice they were subjected to in Scotland. As far as religious prejudice and covert discrimination is concerned, regretfully it still persists, in rather subtle forms though, in some spheres and some circles, even in this the last decade of the twentieth century.

THE JEWS

As mentioned earlier, Jewish immigrants appeared on the Scottish scene in the 1880s. These Jews were fleeing from the Czarist pogroms in Russia and Poland. The economic and religious persecution inflicted upon these unfortunate people compelled them to leave their ancestral homes to seek refuge in other lands.

There has been a Jewish presence in the British Isles since, perhaps, the eleventh century A.D. However, in the thirteenth century, Jews were banished from England by King Edward I, and only allowed back, by Cromwell, in the seventeenth century. Some probably came to Scotland from England in the eighteenth century. During the Napoleonic Wars a few Jewish families arrived from the Continent and settled in Edinburgh and Glasgow. In 1812, Issac Cohen became the first freeman of Jewish origin in Scotland.

There were, therefore, a number of Jews living happily in Scotland before the arrival of these refugees in the 1880s. According to James Cleland (*Enumeration of the Inhabitants of the City of Glasgow*), the Jewish population of Glasgow in 1831 was 47. There were a few families in Edinburgh and also a couple of families in Dundee. The total number of Jewish people in Scotland at the beginning of the fourth decade of the nineteenth century, therefore, was just about 100. Their numbers, however, were increasing steadily as a result of the arrival of Jewish merchants and businessmen from Holland, Germany and Poland. By the late 1850s there were about 300 Jewish people in this country. 'There were 26 Jewish families in Glasgow in 1858, when they consecrated their new, elegant and commodious synagogue at 240 George Street' (J. Brown, *The Religious Denominations of Glasgow*). Edinburgh had about 20 families then and they also had their own small synagogue. The Glasgow and Edinburgh communities had both already acquired their own burial plots. The first interment in the plot at Glasgow was that of a Mr Levy in 1833.

By 1880 the number of Jews settled in Scotland had risen to about 900. This small community had succeeded in developing amicable and harmonious social and commercial relations with the natives. They were all engaged in various businesses, and had become a prosperous and somewhat influential community. The degree of their influence and their acceptance in Scottish society can be assessed by the fact that in 1883 Michael Simon, who had come in 1849 as an immigrant, was elected a councillor to Glasgow City Council. He was the first Jewish elected representative on a local authority in Scotland.

The Eastern European Jews who began to arrive in the 1880s were from rural areas, of poor working-class backgrounds, and Yiddish speaking. Many of them had boarded ships intending to go to America, but had disembarked at Scottish ports believing that they had reached their destination. Others broke the journey to get another boat to America but then somehow stayed on in Scotland.

By the year 1900 an estimated 10,000 Jewish refugees had come to this country. The local Jewish community took it upon itself to help the poor refugees. Societies and organisations were formed to assist the newcomers, morally, materially and spiritually. Hostels were set up for temporary accommodation, until houses and flats could be found for the refugees. They were helped to find jobs, and in every other way to enable them to stand on their own feet as soon as possible. Weekend and night schools were set up by the Jewish community to teach English, and also certain trades and crafts to those who lacked any skills.

There was, of course, the usual hue and cry against the influx of Jews into the United Kingdom. The media became very involved in the issue, and the press and certain politicians encouraged anti-semitism and hostility against the Jewish community. In Scotland, however, there were no serious incidents of violence, nor was there widespread resentment against the Jews. The reason for this indifference lay perhaps in the role played by the Scottish Jewish community in relation to the reception, the settlement and the general welfare of the refugees. The affluent Jews of Scotland themselves bore the cost of helping their persecuted and penniless co-religionists. There were no calls on local social services for material help. The refugees did not, in most instances, compete with the Scots in the labour market, as many of them were absorbed by the Jewish-owned works and establishments, while others were helped to set up their own small businesses. All these factors contributed to keep the calm and prevent the spread of serious hostility against the refugees and the Jewish community.

By 1905, when the Aliens Act was introduced to curtail immigration to Great Britain, the Jewish population of Scotland had increased to about 15,000. Those who had come in the 1880s and 90s were well settled by this time. Jewish communities had sprung up beyond the industrial cities in towns like Falkirk, Dumfries, Greenock, Ayr, and even Inverness, where they were running tailor shops, shoe repair services, tobacconists, and furniture stores. Jewish pedlars travelled to rural areas and mining villages all over the country to sell their wares. In 'cities like Glasgow the Jews owned many stores, factories and sweatshops. A newspaper for the Jewish community, owned and edited by a Jew, had also appeared soon after the turn of the century. In 1902 a 27-year-old Scottish-born Jew, Frank Israel Cohan, was elected as a councillor for Springburn to Glasgow City Council. Michael

Simon, the other Jewish councillor who was elected in 1883, was appointed a bailie of the City of Glasgow and a Deputy Lieutenant to His Majesty the King in 1905. This was indeed a great achievement for such a small community in such a short time, and shows the degree of acceptance which the Jewish community obviously enjoyed in Scotland.

There was no significant increase in the numbers of Jews after 1905. This allowed the Jewish welfare and relief agencies to concentrate their efforts on social, religious and educational matters. The communities by now had become concentrated in certain inner city areas, thus creating certain localities of Jewish dominance. This situation facilitated the opening of Jewish butcher shops, dairies and bakeries to provide Kosher food for the adherents of the Jewish faith. Every such locality founded its synagogue and religious school where children were taught religion and Yiddish in the evenings and at weekends.

At the outbreak of the First World War a number of Jews joined the armed forces. Quite a few, on the other hand, were interned as enemy aliens, particularly those who had migrated from Germany. A year or so later, however, they were released and allowed to return to their communities.

After World War I, many Jewish families left for America in search of greener pastures. The Jewish community, by its hard work, financial scruples and determination, was doing rather well here also, better in many ways than most of the native Scottish population. The 1920s were hard times but the Scottish Jewish community managed to avoid any disasters. As a matter of fact, there was a degree of internal Jewish migration from England to Scotland in this period. In 1922 another landmark was reached in the history of Scottish Jewry. The first Jewish member of parliament from Scotland, Emmanuel Shinwell, who later on became a cabinet minister and then a peer, was elected from the constituency of Linlithgow, which did not perhaps have even a single Jewish vote.

The 1930s witnessed another wave of Jewish refugees, fleeing this time from the Nazis in Germany. Scotland received its share of about 1,000. Again the Jewish relief and welfare agencies became active and took good care of these new-comers. The Jewish community by this time had become well integrated and active in Scottish society, contributing to the arts, music, sciences, literature, politics and commerce of the country. Most of them were quite affluent and some were very rich. The poor Jews (and there were poor Jews) were always helped and looked after by the community and particularly by their welfare organisations. There was also a trend among second and third generation young people to enter the professions or white collar jobs instead of following their fathers in trade and commerce. A few hundred had already qualified as teachers and doctors before the start of World War II.

At this stage the Jewish community also started to concen-trate in two cities, Glasgow and Edinburgh. Small communities moved there from provincial towns where they found it difficult to stay without compromising their cultural and religious values and traditions. In the same period their concentrations in these cities also started to break up as rich and well-to-do Jews moved out to the suburbs and better areas. This process continued during World War II and accelerated after the war. By the mid 1950s, there were no Jewish colonies or quarters left in Glasgow or Edinburgh. The Jewish communities had gradually dispersed to the affluent and modern residential areas of their respective cities.

The Jews clung to their religion, preserved their culture and traditions and yet became an integral part of Scottish society. They have set a fine example of integration without assimilation. They have demonstrated how to keep one's identity and still be part and parcel of society at large. During the process of their settlement in Scotland they did suffer discrimination in employment, prejudice in trade and commerce, abuse and harassment in schools and streets, and all the other humiliations which become the lot of uninvited immigrants and refugees in any country, but surprisingly the Jews did not fare as badly as the Irish before them.

Their transition from Jewish immigrants to Scottish Jews was definitely far easier and a lot smoother.

THE ITALIANS

The forefathers of many of the recent Italian immigrants came to Scotland in the first century A.D. as Roman conquerors. They were, however, forced to leave after about 350 years and their descendants eventually were absorbed by the indigenous people. 1100 years later, in the sixteenth century, we find a few Italian minstrels and entertainers attached to the court of Scottish sovereigns. The eighteenth century witnessed the astounding rise in popularity and patronage of Italian arts and culture throughout Europe. The Scottish aristocracy were also affected by this phenomenon and a number of artists, musicians and teachers of music and of the Italian language were attracted to Edinburgh, the cultural seat of Scotland. From the aristocracy the craze for Italian music spread to the middle and lower classes. The nineteenth century therefore saw a rise in the number of Italians in Scotland as more and more street musicians and entertainers came over to meet the demand. As communications and contacts grew between the people of Scotland and Italy, pedlars also started to accompany the troupes of entertainers. The musicians and entertainers amused the crowds in the streets, in halls or at fairgrounds while the pedlars sold the wares they had brought from Italy.

The first census held in 1861 recorded the presence of 119 Italians in Scotland. By 1891 this had grown to 1,025. From then on their numbers increased rapidly as the pedlars and entertainers were replaced by ice-cream vendors. Soon the 'hokey-pokey' man, as these Italian ice-cream vendors were called then, became a familiar sight in the streets of all the major towns and cities of Scotland. Ice-cream became very popular and the Italians did well in this trade. Word spread back home of their success, and more and more relatives and friends came over to escape the poverty and deprivation they were experiencing in their villages in Italy.

Most of these pioneers, like the Irish immigrants before them, were poor illiterate peasants and farm labourers from rural and deprived areas with a tradition of migration. Many walked all the way from Italy to Scotland as they could only afford the fare. Once in Scotland they were helped by their friends and relatives who provided them with lodgings and ice-cream barrows. The language, or the total lack of it, did not present any major problems. They were taught a few necessary words and phrases of English and, more importantly, were very well familiarised with the local currency to enable them to sell the ice-cream, charge the proper price and give the right change.

By the year 1900 a few Italian restaurants and ice-cream parlours had appeared in Edinburgh and Glasgow. Those who had done well in peddling or ice-cream vending were now expanding and aiming higher. By 1914 the number of Italian restaurants in Scotland had gone up to about 300 and the number of Italians to about 5,000. There were no new arrivals from Italy during the World War I years, but as soon as the hostilities ceased immigrants were on the move again. The British Government at this stage brought in another piece of legislation called the Aliens Act 1919. This was an attempt to stem the rush of post-war migration to the United Kingdom. The Italians were also affected by this legislation and the flow of new immigrants from Italy was curtailed substantially.

The number of Italians in Scotland, however, had reached about 6,000 by 1930. This small community was now well on the road to integration. Most of them were in major cities, but a few were drifting to smaller towns such as Port Glasgow, Greenock, Irvine, Falkirk and Stirling. More social and cultural organisations were being formed to look after and cater for the social needs of the Italian community. The Fascist movement also became popular among Italians living in Scotland and gained a number of adherents. The inter-war years were very hard times but, like the Jews, the Italians also managed without any serious hardships.

By the mid 1930s not many Italian ice-cream vendors were left in the streets, as more and more of them were opening up ice-cream parlours and restaurants. The number of Italian restaurants had gone up to 700 by the year 1931. (B. Kay, *Odyssey.*) At this time there was some hostility towards the Italians because they opened their restaurants on Sundays and also because young people were allowed to meet freely in the ice-cream parlours. It was alleged that the Italians were breaking the Sabbath laws and lowering the morals of the nation by providing facilities for the young people to meet and mix under dubious conditions.

There was, however, no serious resentment or hostility against the Italians in the economic field as they did not compete with local labour for jobs, etc., and thus could not be blamed for taking away jobs or lowering wages, the two most common allegations against the Irish and the Lithuanian immigrants. The Italians were a hard-working close-knit community. They created their own jobs, and provided jobs for their compatriots. Like the Jews, they assisted the newcomers financially and helped them in starting up their small businesses. This assistance to the newcomer was usually obligatory and traditional, as most of the earlier arrivals were either related to or were the friends of the newcomers.

A great majority of the early Italian immigrants to Scotland belonged to two specific regions of Italy. Most of those who settled in Glasgow and its surrounding areas came from a town called Barga and its neighbourhood in the Province of Lucca in northern Italy, and a majority of those settled in and around Edinburgh came from the village and the district of Picinsco in the Province of Frosinone south of Rome. This shows that the coming of these Italians to Scotland was a classic case of chain migration.

The relative happiness and ease of the Italian community was suddenly shattered on 10 June 1940. On this fateful day Italy joined Germany and was thus at war with Great Britain. As soon as this news was broadcast resentment, anger and violence errupted against the Italians living in this country. The short night falling between 10 and 11 June became the longest and most dreadful night for the Scottish Italian community. Their shops, restaurants and even some houses were attacked, vandalised and burnt down. Next day was even worse as all the Italian adult males were rounded up to be interned as enemy aliens. Children and females were put in camps for their safety and state security. In just two days the Italian community suffered its economic ruination and the most heartrending family splits.

It was not until 1944 that the internees were set free from wherever they were and allowed to return to their families. They had to make new starts, which they promptly set to do soon after they returned to their homes. With hard work, long hours, patience and determination they achieved their economic recovery and regained social acceptance. The resentment and hostility towards them vanished quickly after the war and their ice-cream parlours, restaurants, cafés, and fish and chip shops were again patronised in even greater numbers by the Scottish people. Their rehabilitation and their re-integration were speedy and amicable.

The post-war economic boom forced the British authorities to recruit labour from abroad for industries with acute labour shortages. This brought another wave of Italian immigrants to Scotland in the 1950s. Most of these migrant workers stayed on in Scotland after their contracts expired with their respective employers. Thus the Italian community has been growing at a steady pace since the end of World War II, and more so since Britain's entry into the European Economic Community. Their present strength in Scotland (in 1992) is about 20,000.

The infusion of new members to the settled community here has not only kept alive links with the home country, but has also revived dormant or broken links. More and more Scottish Italians are going to Italy for their holidays, and their relatives are coming to Scotland. Thus the families on both sides are in touch with each other and relations and communications among them are improving. This is helping the Italian community to retain its identity and in many cases to remain bilingual. In the absence of these connections the Italians might have been completely assimilated into Scottish society. The first generation prevented their assimilation by avoiding intermarriage with the Scottish people. The second and third generations, however, have not been constrained in this way. They are marrying Scots, they have developed close relationships with the Scottish people and they feel Scottish. Under these circumstances there is no other barrier to their complete assimilation except for the Italian connection. As long as this connection remains active, the community will remain conscious of their Italian heritage and identity.

The second and third generation Italians were not willing to work long hours and late nights as their fathers did. They are, like the Jews, going increasingly into the professions, the civil service and vocations with social hours, prestige and good wages. Their fish and chip shops, cafés and restaurants are being take over by the latest wave of immigrants to Scotland, the Asians.

THE LITHUANIANS

The Lithuanians arrived in Scotland mainly in the 1890s and in the first five years of the twentieth century. It is not known for certain how the Lithuanians happened to come to Scotland or what prompted them to head for this country. There were no obvious connections or communications between this country and Lithuania at the time of the arrival of these immigrants. Lithuania, a Baltic state, was under Czarist rule and going through a repressive stage of Russification in the latter part of the nineteenth century. Lithuanians were of the Roman Catholic faith, while their rulers belonged to the Orthodox Church. They therefore experienced widespread religious persecution. The main occupation of the people was agriculture. In the absence of large-scale industries, the bulk of the population depended upon the land for eking out a living with primitive farming methods. Excessive taxation by an oppressive government further aggravated the destitution of the populace.

Like the Eastern European Jews, most of the Lithuanian Christians left their country to go to America. Some, however, mistakenly disembarked at the Scottish ports of Leith and Dundee, when their ships called there en route to America. Others intended to use Scotland as a stepping stone, but just stayed here. It is probable that some of these entrants knew Jewish immigrants who had come from the same neighbourhoods a few years earlier and were now living in Scotland. There is abundant evidence that Latvian and Lithuanian Jews did settle in Scotland in the last two decades of the nineteenth century. It might have been this connection, therefore, which brought the Lithuanian Christians to Scotland.

Once in Scotland the Lithuanians were either guided to, or just attracted to, the industrial and mining areas in search of work. There was plenty of work available in such parts of the country. The bulk of the Lithuanian immigrants, therefore, found jobs and settled in the Lanarkshire industrial belt and the Lothian and Fife mining areas. Normally accommodation or housing was provided with such jobs, and this suited the migrants very well as their lack of English language, lack of finance and lack of local contacts would certainly have made it very difficult for them, if not impossible, to find suitable habitats in a new and somewhat hostile environment.

The Lithuanian pioneers were mostly single men. Once they found work and realised the potential of a better life in Scotland, they sent for their families and friends to join them. The community started to grow by this process of chain migration and by the end of the first decade of twentieth century their numbers had gone up by about 4000 in Lanarkshire and possibly 7–8000 in the whole of Scotland.

On their arrival and during their settlement in Scotland they went through the usual phases of hostility and prejudice from the natives. They were blamed for all the ills befalling the Scottish workers. They were accused of lowering the wage rates by working for less and for stealing the jobs of the local workers. These accusations to some extent were true, as some of the unscrupulous employers did engage the desperate immigrants on lower wages, while others used them to break strikes. The Lithuanians, however, soon learned from their exploitation by the employers, and by 1910 most of them had become good trade union members.

Like other immigrants in a strange land, the Lithuanians also felt secure within their own community. They therefore created little colonies by living next to each other near their places of work. They were thus able to preserve and practise their traditions, their culture and their language. The first generation settlers did not know English. Their Scottish-born children grew up to be bilingual, learning and speaking English in school and outside, and Lithuanian inside the house. On many occasions and in many a situation the children interpreted for their parents. Weddings and other happy occasions were celebrated in Lithuanian tradition, according to old customs. Like the Jews and the Irish, the Lithuanians opened up their own shops in their localities to cater for their particular tastes. They had their own clergy who held services and ceremonies in the Lithuanian language. Two weekly newspapers in Lithuanian had also appeared by 1914.

After World War I immigration from Lithuania came to an end. The first generation of Lithuanians had avoided intermarriage with Scottish people. Nearly all the young or unmarried immigrants brought over their marriage partners from Lithuania. The second generation, however, were not as strict, nor as keen to limit their choice of a partner to the old country. The period between the wars, therefore, saw the gradual assimilation of the Lithuanians into the indigenous population through intermarriages, dispersal and education. Being of the same faith and the same colour of skin, there were no strong barriers between the Scottish and Lithuanian peoples. Once the language barrier was broken by the second generation, there was not much which could induce them to remain isolated or even to retain their identity. The first generation did their best to pass on their customs, their culture and their language to their children, but the second generation had none of the first generation's enthusiasm to cherish and retain them.

Serious cracks had begun to appear in the cohesion and the insulation of the community during the 1940s. After World

War II the process of assimilation gathered pace. Second and third generations were growing up as Scots, and behaving and feeling like Scots. The first generation were now dying out and disappearing from the scene. By the year 1980 there were only a few of the community who could speak the language and take pride in their Lithuanian heritage. With the fourth generation now grown up, no significant vestige of the Lithuanian community is left in this country except for one or two of their struggling social and cultural organisations. It is only a matter of time before the descendants of the Lithuanian immigrants are absorbed into Scottish society, and any reference to their Lithuanian origin becomes just a matter of academic interest.

THE POLES

Polish refugees and immigrants have been present in Scotland since at least the beginning of the nineteenth century. When, in 1795, Poland was occupied and partitioned among Austria, Prussia and Russia, many Polish soldiers and politicians left their country and some sought refuge in Britain. In 1830 the Poles made an attempt to free their homeland. It failed and most of the activists had to flee to save themselves from the wrath of the occupying powers, many again coming to the British Isles.

We learn about the presence of Polish refugees in Scotland in the 1830s from a report of the Council of the Literary Association of Friends of Poland, presented at their annual general meeting held in London in 1837. It states 'There are few branches of trade, art or profession in which there are not some refugees creditably occupied. ... Mr Baxter has employed several Polish soldiers in excavating a canal in Scotland, and Mr Kirkman Finlay has five in his employ as foresters in his estate near Glasgow, and Mr Charles Tennent, also of Paisley, has two officers constantly occupied making baskets.' (J. Zubrzycki, *Polish Immigrants in Britain*, pp 33–4). A number of Polish Jews came to Scotland in the last two decades of the nineteenth century, but here our interest is in Polish Christians. Perhaps a few Christian Poles also found their way to Scotland in the same period.

At the beginning of the twentieth century the total number of Poles living in Scotland was under 100. Some authors have, however, erroneously given a figure of thousands. This is due to the mistaken Polish identity applied to Lithuanians by the local people, the local newspapers and even in the official records of those times. Lithuanians, as we have already seen, came here between 1880 and 1910. They numbered about 8000 in 1914 and were wrongly called Poles by everybody in Scotland. The Lithuanian spokesmen always protested against this mistake, as they did not like to be referred to as Poles. The *Glasgow Herald* published a statement on 14 October 1914 from a Polish representative, pointing out this error and stating that there were at that time only about 60 Poles living in Scotland compared to 7–8000 Lithuanians. Unfortunately the records have never been corrected and some researchers and authors are still being misinformed on this subject.

Few refugees or immigrants from Poland came to Scotland between the two world wars. Their numbers, therefore, remained virtually static until 1939 when Germany and then Russia invaded Poland. After the defeat and occupation of their country, a great number of Polish soldiers and civilians managed to escape. They assembled in France where they set up a Polish Government in exile and reorganised the remnants of the Polish armed forces. Soon after, France also collapsed and the Polish Government in exile, its soldiers and civilians, all sought refuge in Britain. The soldiers were sent up north to Scotland, to be trained and reformed. Huge camps were set up in 1940 along the east coast of Scotland to accommodate the Polish army. A section of that coast was allotted to this army to be patrolled and protected by them. Scottish Polish associations were set up to promote good relations between the Polish soldiers and the Scottish people. A number of Polish soldiers married Scottish girls and a Scottish Polish Wives Society was also formed in Dundee in early 1940s. These associations succeeded in their objectives initially, and relations were good for some time between the population near the camps and the camp dwellers. However, this honeymoon did not last long.

In July 1941 an agreement was concluded between Russia and the Polish Government in exile. Under the terms of this agreement all Poles who had been deported to Siberia and other places, since the occupation of Eastern Poland by Russia in 1939, were freed and assisted to join the Polish forces under British command. This swelled the Polish ranks in Britain.

The Polish army was fighting beside the allied armies on the understanding that after victory the Allies would assist the Poles in the recovery of their country. This did not materialise. On the contrary, the Allies recognised the Russian-formed communist regime in Poland at the end of the war. The Polish exiles were opposed to the Russian dominance of their motherland and would not accept or recognise that Polish Government. Animosity grew between the commissars in Poland and the Poles abroad. The expatriates, both soldiers and civilians, were thus reluctant to go back home for fear of reprisals or oppression. Realising the dilemma of the Polish refugees in Britain, the British Government allowed all those who did not wish to return to settle in Britain. Legislation and regulations were introduced to facilitate their settlement.

In Scotland, hostels were set up throughout the country to provide lodgings for Polish workers. The unskilled males among them were encouraged to take up employment with farmers, in coal mining, quarrying and brick-making industries. The females were engaged in the textile industry and hospital services. Initially the trade unions opposed the recruitment of Polish workers. In addition to the same old allegations of lowering the wages and bringing down standards, the Poles were collectively labelled as Fascists by the trade unionists. As Catholics they were also accused by some of being 'Papist spies'. So, like other refugees and immigrants, they also went through a period of prejudice, discrimination and resentment, but fortunately for the Poles this period was very short. The reasons for this are as follows.

The Poles were political and not economic refugees. They fought and laid down their lives to uphold the freedom of Britain and many other countries. The Polish community in this country was predominantly male. There were very few Polish women with them. Most of the Polish males, therefore, married Scottish girls. These mixed marriages integrated them quickly into families and through families into communities. Finally, as early as 1950, the Poles began to leave their employments and set up small businesses of their own. Once they were not competing for jobs with the local workers, hostility against them disappeared rapidly.

By the early 1950s Polish communities had penetrated nearly all the major towns of central and eastern Scotland. Between nine and ten thousand of them settled in this country. The businesses they set up included launderettes, especially in Glasgow and Edinburgh, watchmakers, jewellers, cobblers and grocers. They also formed their own associations and societies to look after the interests of their communities and to keep in touch with each other. Some of these societies are still very active, particularly in Glasgow, Edinburgh, Falkirk, Perth, Dundee, Kirkcaldy and Galashiels. Social clubs and Sunday schools are run by these societies where the Polish language, history and culture are taught to the ever-dwindling number of pupils. Naturally, not very many children of second generation mixed marriages, where the mother happens to be Scottish and the father himself a product of a mixed marriage, would have any strong persuasion to go to these Sunday Schools.

The Polish community, having already passed the integration stage, is now being fast assimilated into Scottish society. Some have even changed their Polish surnames, perhaps to lose their identity. The recent political developments in Poland, however, may change the situation. Communism is on the wane and democratic forces are emerging fast to replace it. The fears and suspicions are disappearing, and old soldiers are renewing and repairing the broken links with their families and friends in Poland. Some have already returned to pass their remaining days in the surroundings and environment in which they were born and brought up.

The second and third generations here are now getting to know their relatives in the old country. This establishment of communications will probably help to prolong the memory and manifestation of Polish heritage among the Scottish Poles.

The Poles were the last of the major migrant groups, before the arrival of the Asians, who settled in Scotland in the nineteenth and twentieth centuries. There were, of course, other smaller groups of European immigrants such as the Hungarians, Ukranians, Greeks, etc., who came to this country during the same period in order to escape persecution or destitution in their respective countries. But their numbers were so small, their arrivals so unnoticeable and their settlements so uneventful that we cannot learn much or at least anything new from a detailed study of them. Therefore we move on to the Asians who, after the Irish, are the largest immigrant group to settle in Scotland. However, to understand fully the factors and the reasons behind the coming of the Asians to Scotland, we must study first the role of the Scots in establishing communications and connections with the Indian subcontinent and other South Asia Countries. As we know it was the Scots who went to India first, we therefore begin with an account of the Scots in India.

CHAPTER TWO

The Scots in India

It is most probable that Scotland had trade links with India many hundreds of years before the discovery of the sea route to the fabled 'Indies' by Vasco da Gama in 1498. Whether any Scottish merchants visited India in those days is not clear, but it is evident that Indian products such as spices, textiles and other artifacts were being brought to Scotland. The recent discovery of a set of ivory chessmen on the island of Lewis also points to some connection between the two countries which conveyed this ancient game from India to Scotland, sometime in the first millennium A.D.

Trade with India and other eastern countries was carried out by the overland route before the rise of the Ottoman Empire. When the Turks captured Constantinople in 1453, they blocked this route, thus denying the European nations this indispensable and lucrative trade. Hence the desperate search for an alternative trade route to the East Indies and the ultimate discovery, 45 years later, of the sea route round the Cape.

The first official contact between Scotland and India was established in the second decade of the seventeenth century. It was in the year 1615 that Sir Thomas Rowe presented his credentials, along with presents from King James VI of Scotland (James I of England), as Ambassador from the United Kingdom of Scotland and England, at the court of the Mogul Emperor Jahangir at Agra. This was the beginning of the long and eventful relationship between the two countries thousands of miles apart.

The legendary riches of India, its indigo, silks, spices, gems and textiles had been attracting European and other foreign traders since time immemorial. The East India Company was founded in England in 1599 to capture a share of the highly profitable trade with the 'East Indies'. Queen Elizabeth I granted the charter to this company on the last day of the last year of the sixteenth century. Her successor, King James, renewed the Company's charter and, in order to lend his Government's support to the ventures of the Company, appointed Sir Thomas Rowe as his envoy to the court of the Emperor of India. The East India Company had started its commercial dealings with India in the first decade of the seventeenth century and by 1611 had established two factories (warehouses) on Indian soil.

The East India Company was purely an English concern, and Scots were not involved in it as shareholders or otherwise. Realising the potential of trade with the East, efforts were made by some Scottish entrepreneurs to form a Scottish East India Company. Stiff and effective opposition, however, from vested interests in England brought these efforts to naught. Therefore, very few Scots, if any, reached India in the seventeenth century.

The beginning of the eighteenth century heralded momentous changes for both India and Scotland. The Act of Union was given the royal assent by Queen Anne in March 1707. Under this Act the Kingdoms of Scotland and England were united. In India, coincidentally, in the same month of the same year Aurangzeb, the last great Mogul Emperor, died. The Act of Union gave the Scots the privileges of free and equal trade opportunities throughout Great Britain and its dominions. To the Scots this opened the doors of the East India Company, its cherished service, its lucrative trade and, at a later stage, even its control. The death of Aurangzeb was followed by the rapid decline and decay of the Mogul Empire, eventually creating a situation demanding the presence of British troops in India to protect the Company's interests. This necessitated the raising of new Scottish regiments to be sent to India, and the acceptance of more and more Scots by the Company for service in India. By the beginning of the second half of the eighteenth century, therefore, a considerable Scottish presence had been established in India.

Of those few Scots who were accepted for service in India by the Company in the early eighteenth century, William

Hamilton of Dalzell is perhaps the most noteworthy. He went to India in 1711 as a surgeon in the service of the East India Company. From 1711 to 1714 he served as a member of the Embassy to the court of the Mogul Emperor Farakh Siyar, where he successfully treated the Emperor for an infectious disease. The Emperor was very pleased and rewarded Hamilton generously, granting him 'an elephant, a horse, five thousand rupees, two diamond rings, a jewelled aigrette, a set of gold buttons and models of all his instruments in gold'. More importantly, however, the Emperor granted to the Company the coveted right of free trade in Bengal, Behar and Orissa, the richest and most populous provinces of the Mogul Empire. He further awarded to the Company 38 villages (probably covering more than 300 square miles of area and with about 20,000 inhabitants) near Calcutta. William Hamilton thus achieved for the Company and his country far more than any other individual had until then in India. D. G. Crawford, the historian of the Indian Medical Service, writing about Hamilton states: 'He is certainly the one who has been the greatest benefactor of his country'. Hamilton died in India in 1717 and is buried in Calcutta (Cain, *The Corn Chest for Scotland*).

By the middle of the eighteenth century the political situation in India had become chaotic. The vast Mogul Empire was disintegrating fast. The provincial governors, princes and petty chiefs were all in open rebellion against the now weak and impotent King at Delhi, while at the same time feuding and fighting among themselves. The East India Company also became involved in these local feuds and fights and, because of the better performance of its trained and disciplined troops, emerged as an influential political and military power in South India.

In 1757, the victory at Plassey gave the Company virtual control of Bengal, and the victory at Buxar, seven years later, made them the undisputed rulers of the Provinces of Bengal, Behar and Orissa, a rich territory with more people and a larger area than Scotland and England put together. The Commander-in-Chief of the Company's forces at Buxar, incidentally, was General Sir Hector Munro, a Scotsman from

Novar in Ross-shire. General Munro returned to Scotland soon after, with his fortune, and became the Member of Parliament for Inverness.

A few Scottish businessmen and planters had also reached India during the first half of the eighteenth century. The Company's military successes, resulting in their control of huge, populous and rich areas, had brought its employees, British planters, free traders and adventurers, certain highly favourable privileges. They had absolute power over millions of people in extensive and prosperous territories; they had monopolies allowing them to buy and sell without any price controls or reviews; they were exempt from taxes or customs duties; they had the final say in what should be produced or manufactured and where, and what wages, if any, should be paid to the native workers; they had the authority to make or break the native rajahs and chieftains. All this power and privilege in an alien land, together with human greed, resulted in their gross abuse of authority. There followed an era of scandalous oppression and exploitation of helpless natives, rich and poor, high and low. It was also a period of unscrupulous corruption and graft. With rare exceptions, everyone, from the lowly clerk to the Governor General, from the planter to the trader, and from the free booter to the regular soldier, tried to amass as much wealth as they could by very little fair and mostly foul means.

This deplorable state of affairs had started soon after the battle of Plassey and lasted until the close of the eighteenth century. Robert Clive, the victor of Plassey, returned home from India loaded with jewels and gold. The *Scots Magazine* of July 1760 reported 'It is supposed that Mr Clive can realise £1,200,000 in cash bills and jewels, and his lady has a casket of jewels which are estimated to be worth at least £200,000. So that he may with propriety be said to be the richest subject in the three kingdoms.'

This was the period which produced the *nouveaux riches,* the 'nabobs', 'the men who had made incredible fortunes in India "out of trade" (sic) and came back red in the face with their fiery curries and enough gold and rubies to lord over the traditional Scottish country gentry' (Cain, *The Corn Chest for Scotland*, p. 13).

India at this stage was a rich and prosperous country, whereas Scotland was poor and impoverished. Thomas Johnston records: 'Before the coming of steam-power and the Industrial Revolution, the current wars, famines, and dearths produced a great army of migratory starvelings who maintained themselves in their itinerances upon the charity and generosity of the settled, though scarcely less starved, peasantry. In 1723, for example, we are told that no fewer than 1000 mendicants — some of them from Ireland — attended the funeral of an Earl of Eglinton for a share of charity money — £30 — distributed at the obsequies; and in the time of Fletcher of Saltoun it was estimated that no less than one fifth of our total population was vagrant.' (Johnston, *History of the Working Classes in Scotland, p. 290*).

With so much poverty at home, the astounding tales of the fortunes which were made and could be made lured the impoverished Scots to opulent India. Appointments were secured by fair means or foul and many Scots, some as young as 12 or 13, left for Hindustan to return with rank and riches. 'There were so many who embarked for India with wet eyes and a lump in their throat and thought of the day when he would return from the "Injy" with money enough to buy a farm and settle in his native place.' (C. Grey, *European Adventurers in North India*).

Those who survived the rigours of the journey and the Indian climate did return with a lot more than enough money. 'John Johnstone of Westerhall, and founder of the House of Johnstone of Alva, pursued wealth with an enterprise and ruthlessness which gave him a fortune probably second only in size to that of Clive. He is estimated to have had a fortune worth £300,000 when he returned to Scotland around 1765, where he bought three estates — Alva, Handingshawe and Denovars' and, of course, acquired a parliamentary interest. (Cain, *The Corn Chest for Scotland* p. 14.) 'Another Scottish "nabob", Colonel Charles Campbell, reputedly spent £17,000 in acquiring his (parliamentary) seat at Stirling. William Young (the natural son of Lord Elibank) seems to have cleared his £100,000, Peter Murray (MacGregor of Glencarnaik) reputedly amassed £200,000 . . . . Highlanders appear to have predominated among the Scottish gentry in India, though there was a fair sprinkling from elsewhere, such as Brodie from Forres, Balfour of Balbirnie in Fife, the Dalrymple brothers from East Lothian and Bogle of Daldowie near Glasgow.' (G. J. Bryant, 'Scots in India in the Eighteenth Century', *The Scottish Historical Review*, April 1985.)

The wealth brought back from India had a rejuvenating effect on the economy of eighteenth-century Scotland. 'Thomas Somerville recorded in 1813, looking back over his life as a minister in Jedburgh, Roxburghshire, that the wealth brought back from the East over the previous fifty years had been so great and had ". . . been so generally applied to the purchase of estates, that the property thus acquired bears a great proportion to the whole landed property in Scotland", adding that in his own area no less than eight valuable estates had been bought by Indo Scots'. And 'A Glasgow banker believed, after the Scottish banking crisis of 1772, that ". . . were two or three nabobs to take up their residence amongst [us], matters would soon revive"' (G. J. Bryant, 'The Scots in India', *The Scottish Historical Review,* April 1985). Such was the impact of these nabobs and their riches! This wealth also played a major part in accelerating the progress of the Industrial Revolution in Scotland, which had started in the first half of the eighteenth century.

Over and above the wealth, the Scots also acquired the local virtues and vices during their stay in India, particularly in the eighteenth century. The British had gone to India initially as traders, and to be successful traders they had to establish good communications and amicable relations with the indigenous government officials and the people. To achieve this they learnt Persian, which was the official language of the subcontinent during the Muslim rule, and also the Hindustani tongue for dealings with the ordinary people. They adopted the local dress and many local customs and habits to be able to mix and socialise with the Indian gentry and thus win favours from them. The East India Company encouraged its servants, both soldiers and civilians, to marry native women, mainly to save the expense and trouble of bringing over and maintaining their European wives in India, but also perhaps to foster closer relations with the natives. They did not in the seventeenth and eighteenth centuries exhibit any racial superiority or express any arrogance or prejudice towards the Indian people. On the contrary, they were awestruck by the magnificence and richness of the Indian culture and civilisation which was far superior to anything they had ever experienced in Europe. It was the Indians who disliked the *Farangi*, as they called the Europeans, for their deviousness, their drinking, swine eating and other strange and 'uncivilised' customs and habits. D. Kincaid observes 'Nor was the drunkenness the only accusation levied against the foreign merchants, for from Terry we learn that the "natives, who are very square and exact to make good all their engagements, used the word Christian as a synonym for cheat".' (*British Social Life in India,* p 18). The English merchants, therefore, did all that was required of them to appease the local opinion and cultivate good relations with the natives.

Consequently, when the Scots arrived on the scene in the early eighteenth century they followed the trend and the traditions set by the English. They also adopted local customs and developed local tastes. Like their English cousins, they also married Indian wives or kept native mistresses or 'bibis' as these 'ladies' were called euphemistically, and sent their sons (in some cases daughters, too) to Scotland for education. They wore expensive native clothes, smoked hookas, enjoyed Indian music and dance (nautch) and chewed *pan* and betel nut. They pursued indigenous sports like cockfighting, hawking, pigeon racing and hunting. They drank a lot but often 'arrack', a native alcoholic drink. In fact while in India most of them became Indianised.

With the wealth at their disposal and the power and authority they were gaining so rapidly in the second half of the eighteenth century, they vied with the decadent Mogul nabobs and Rajput rajas of the country in leading fantastic and even more luxurious lifestyles. P. Speirs wrote the following quite comprehensive sketch of a day in the life of a typical Scottish/English 'nabob' residing perhaps in the rich provinces of Bengal or Behar. 'About the hour of seven in the morning, his durwan (doorkeeper) opens the gate and the viranda (gallery) is free to his circars (clerks), peons (footmen), hurcarrahs (messengers or spies), chubdars (a kind of constable), houcca-burdars and consumahs (stewards and butlers), writers and solicitors. The head bearer and jemmadar (head servant) enter the hall and his bedroom at eight o'clock. A lady quits his side and is conducted by a private staircase, either to her own apartment, or out of the yard. The moment the master throws his legs out of bed, the whole force is waiting to rush into his room, each making three salaams, by bending the body and head very low, and touching the forehead with the inside of the fingers and the floor with the back part. He condescends, perhaps to nod or cast an eye towards the solicitors of his favour and protection. In about half an hour after undoing and taking off his long drawers, a clean shirt, breeches, stockings, and slippers are put upon his body, thighs, legs and feet, without any greater exertion on his own part than if he was a statue.'

The 'nabob' has thus risen and after being waited upon and dressed by over a score of servants he is now ready to go through his other routine morning ceremonies. 'The barber enters, shaves him, cuts his nails, and cleans his ears. The chillumjee (basin) and ewer are brought by a servant whose duty it is, who pours water upon his hands and face, and presents a towel. The superior then walks in state to his breakfasting parlour in his waistcoat; is seated, the consumah (butler) makes and pours out his tea, and presents him with a plate of bread or toast. The hairdresser comes behind, and begins his operation, while the houccaburdar (hooka attendant) softly slips the upper end of the snake or tube of the houcca into his hand; while the hairdresser is doing his duty the gentleman is eating, sipping and smoking by turns. By and by his banian (treasurer) presents himself with humble salaams and advances somewhat more forward than the other attendants. If any of the solicitors are of eminence, they are honoured with chairs. These ceremonies are continued perhaps till 10 o'clock.'

Our lord 'nabob' is now ready to face the day, to go to his office perhaps, or to his work: '... attended by his cavalcade, he is conducted to his palanquin, and preceded by eight to twelve chubdars, harcarrahs and peons, with the insignia of their profession and their livery distinguished by the colour of their turbans and cummerbunds (a long muslin belt wrapt round the waist) they move off at a quick amble; the set of bearers, consisting of eight generally, relieve each other with alertness and without incommoding their master. If he has visits to make, his peons lead and direct the bearers; and if business renders his presence only necessary, he shows himself, and pursues his other engagements until two o'clock when he and his company sit down perfectly at ease in point of dress and address, to a good dinner, each attended by his own servant. And the moment the glasses are introduced, regardless of the company of ladies, the houccaburdars enter, each with a houcca, and present the tube to his master, watching behind and blowing the fire the whole time. As it is expected that they shall return to supper, at four o'clock they begin to withdraw without ceremony, and step into their palanquins; so that in a few minutes, the man is left to go into his bedroom, when he is instantly undressed to his shirt, and his long drawers put on; and he lies down in his bed, where he sleeps till about seven or eight o'clock, then the former ceremony is repeated and clean linen of every kind as in the morning is administered; his houccaburdar presents the tube to his hand, he is placed at the tea table, and his hairdresser performs his duty as before.'

Between eight and nine o'clock in the evening then, our young gentleman is ready for his nocturnal pursuits. Let us, therefore, to round off his day, see how he passes his late evenings and his nights: 'After tea he puts on a handsome coat, and pays visits of ceremony to the ladies; returns a little before ten o'clock; supper being served at ten. The company keep together till between twelve and one in the morning, preserving great sobriety and decency; and when they depart our hero is conducted to his bedroom, where he finds a female companion to amuse him until the hour of seven or eight the next morning. With no greater exertions than these do the Company's servants amass the most splendid fortunes.' (Cited in P. Speirs, *The Nabobs* pp. 43–5).

The wholesale plunder, extortion and exploitation being practised so blatantly by the East India Company's employees and other British people in India soon attracted the attention of upright and fair-minded people and the press both in Great Britain and some other European countries. The conduct of the British in India was deplored and condemned in very many written and spoken words. The following comments in the *Scots Magazine* of September 1782 on the 'Evidence of our Transactions in the East Indies' by Mr Parker, Lincoln's Inn, are both revealing and damning. 'The substance of the evidence appears to be this: the provinces of Bengal, Behar and Orissa were in the year 1757 in the state of great fertility and plenty as any country in Europe; and inhabited by about 50 millions of people, under the government of a prince called Seraja Dowla, who had lately succeeded his grandfather .... That from the beginning of our first war in 1757 to the year 1771 it is acknowledged or proved that the Company and its servants received between 29 and 30 million pounds sterling from the princes of India and their subjects, besides a sum not known arising from the exclusive trade which the Company's civil and military servants took to themselves after they had obtained all the power. ... There can be no position more clear than that avarice was the governing motive of the Company and its servants, and that a tyrannical force was the means employed by them to gratify that unsatiable passion .... He is more concerned to describe and ascertain the principles which governed and directed the proceedings of the servants of the Company. These he reprobates in the strongest terms, and it appears as the result of his enquiries that the most wanton oppression, and the most open and flagitious cruelties, have been committed and perpetrated by the British in Hindostan.'

The Parliament in London also took notice of this widespread 'wanton oppression' and the 'most open and flagitious cruelties'. The politicians resolved to stop this corruption and exploitation and to put an end to the illicit fortunes being amassed by the British in India. Parliament assumed supremacy over the Company. Warren Hastings was appointed new Governor General of the Company's Indian possessions in 1773 with instructions to stop the rot. Hastings himself was a scholar of Persian, and he encouraged the study of Persian and Sanskrit among the employees of the Company, for a better understanding of India. He introduced many reforms and achieved a degree of success in the fight against corruption and maladministration. Thus the change for the better started, in a rather sluggish way, in the mid 1770s.

Henry Dundas, Viscount Melville, had been appointed Solicitor General for Scotland in 1766. As a powerful man in the Government in London, he had been using his power and influence to introduce more Scots into the service of the Company to be sent to India. The Scots, therefore, were penetrating into every branch of service and every part of the Company's territories in India. 'An even higher proportion of Scots was to be found among the royal troops who were intermittently sent to the East. Of the fourteen royal regiments which served in India between 1754 and 1784, seven had been raised in Scotland, amounting to some 4000 to 5000 men.' (G. J. Bryant, 'Scots in India in the Eighteenth Century', *The Scottish Historical Review,* April 1985)

In 1784, Dundas was appointed Senior Commissioner of the Board of Control which was set up by the Government to oversee the affairs of the Company in India. This gave Dundas in collaboration with David Scott of Dunninald, another Scot who was on the Board of the East India Company, an even better chance to promote and sponsor many a young Scot for appointments in India. From then on proportionally far more Scots were sent to India, and the Scots began to play a major role in the affairs of the Company in that country. 'He Scotticised India, and Orientalised Scotland. The second

Earl of Minto ... told Lord Stanhope that there was scarcely a gentleman's family in Scotland ... that had not at some time received an Indian appointment or some act of kindness from Dundas.' (A. M. Cain, *The Corn Chest for Scotland p. 16*)

The rapid growth in their numbers in an alien land prompted the Scots to form their own sociocultural organisations in order to practise and preserve their distinct customs and traditions. Thus a number of Caledonian societies and St Andrew's Associations sprang up in the penultimate and the last decade of the eighteenth century throughout the British possessions in India. Scottish festivals and other national events were celebrated by these organisations in authentic Scottish fashion. An account of the St Andrew's day celebrations in Calcutta in the year 1794 is as follows: 'On Monday last the anniversary of St Andrew was celebrated by a respectable and numerous company of gentlemen ... and upward of two hundred guests had assembled by five o'clock, when the joyous sound of bagpipes summoned to the festive board .... The exhilarating tone of the bagpipes lent its aid and diffused much joy over every Caledonian countenance as to affect by sympathy the whole company .... The bottle had rapid circulation, the room resounded with loyalty and every nerve vibrated with joy' (*Calcutta Gazette,* 4 December 1794).

By 1790, therefore, the presence of Scots had become quite obvious in India. General Sir David Baird of Newbyth, East Lothian, Sir Robert Abercromby from Clackmannanshire, Lt Col James Stuart of Culross, Sir John Malcolm, a borderer, Thomas Munro a Glaswegian, the brothers William and James Kirkpatrick of Closeburn Dumfriesshire, Mountstuart Elphinstone of Elphinstone in Stirlingshire, and Lt Col Hercules Skinner of Montrose are some of the better-known Scots who made their careers and fortunes in India. They contributed significantly to the conquests and consolidation of the huge Indian territories in the closing years of the eighteenth and the opening of the nineteenth centuries.

After the death of Tipoo Sultan in 1799, the British became the dominant power in India. By 1810 the whole of India except Punjab and Sindh was under the direct or indirect rule of the East India Company. More administrators and more soldiers were required to administer and protect the fast growing Empire. Also, there arose now unlimited opportunities for British entrepreneurs in a captive market in extensive conquered areas. More and more Scots, both high and low, from crofts and castles, from the highlands and the lowlands, and from the towns and villages, were being drawn to India. India had become the great job opportunity for Scotland as acknowledged by Sir Walter Scott in 1821 when he wrote 'India is the corn chest for Scotland where we poor gentry must send our younger sons as we send our black cattle to the south' (A. M. Cain, *The Corn Chest for Scotland*).

Scots did very well in trade and commerce also. In 1813, in spite of the trading monopoly of the East India Company, there were fourteen private Scottish merchant houses in Calcutta compared to only ten English concerns, and the picture was somewhat similar in Madras and Bombay. John Gladstone, who was a native of Leith and father of the future Prime Minister of Britain, made his immense fortune from trade with India. James Finlay and Company opened their offices in Calcutta in the eighteenth century and are still there today. Hamilton the Jewellers, famous throughout India, was founded by an Edinburgh man early in the nineteenth century. It is still trading and has branches all over India.

In the 1830s someone, a Dundonian most probably, hit upon the idea of shipping jute to Dundee — a town with a substantial weaving industry. Bengal is the home of jute and the fibre stripped from the plant had been woven there on hand looms into cloth and other articles since time immemorial. In Dundee, spinning and weaving was done on machines. The antiquated hand looms of Bengal were unable to compete with the sophisticated power looms of Dundee. When the Dundee-manufactured goods came on the market, hundreds of thousands of Bengal weavers lost their trade and their livelihood with it. But Dundee prospered and thousands of Dundonians found employment in the jute industry.

In the second half of the nineteenth century jute mills were set up in Bengal with machinery manufactured in Dundee.

The labour for these mills was recruited locally as it was far cheaper, but the management and maintenance staff were sent from Dundee. Dundee thus monopolised the jute trade, and Bengal became a home from home for the new breed of Dundonian nabobs. Hence the adage 'Dundee made jute and jute made Dundee'.

There were also other rather dramatic Scottish nabobs in the nineteenth century who had fallen in love with India and had made that country their home. They adopted Indian culture and customs, or those which suited them of course, so thoroughly that they were referred to as eccentrics by their compatriots, who were now in the process of discarding every aspect of the Indian way of life. One of them was Sir David Ochterlony, an Angus man. After a distinguished army career he was appointed resident at the court of the now titular Mogul Emperor of Delhi. The Emperor bestowed upon him the grand title of Nasir-ud-Dowlah (helper of the state). Sir David lived like an eastern prince. He married thirteen Indian wives and gave every one an elephant for her conveyance, as well as a symbol of social status. Sir David died in India in 1825.

William Fraser, a soldier and diplomat, was another colourful Scot in India. He was one of the Frasers of Reelick in Invernesshire. He admired Indian culture and developed an understanding and a taste for Indian ways of life. He was a scholar of oriental languages and always felt more at home with Indian nobles and scholars than with his own countrymen. He had seven Indian wives and many children by them.

'Hamish McGregor McPherson of Scotland, killed in battle at the head of his regiment while fighting against the Dewan Mool Raj at Siddhoosam near Multan on the 1st July 1848.' So reads the inscription on the tomb at Ahmedpur built by a Bahawalpur woman Begum Murad Bakhsh, widow of the deceased. Hamish McPherson probably deserted his Scottish regiment and entered the service of the Amir of Bahawalpur in 1828. He rose to become the commander of the Bahawalpur Infantry, probably became a Muslim and married the daughter of a Muslim noble. He was killed in action after 20 years of distinguished service to his master.

Alexander Houghton Campbell Gardner, the son of a Scotsman and an Irish mother, was an adventurer who entered the service of Ranjit Singh, the Sikh ruler of Punjab, in 1832. He married an Afghan lady and after her death took a Kashmiri wife. He rose to the rank of colonel. After the collapse of the Sikh kingdom he joined the service of Ghulab Singh, the British-appointed Rajah of Kashmir, where he subjugated the Kashmiris for the new Rajah. He was so proud of his Scottish heritage that he usually wore a tartan uniform, made by native tailors, with a tartan turban graced by an egret's plume. He died at Jammu in January 1877 and was buried at Sialkot three days later.

The period of understanding and cordiality between Indians and the British, however, had begun to run out rather quickly after the close of the eighteenth century. There were two major reasons for this transition. The East India Company or in other words the British had become the rulers of India, and they were not now merely the obsequious traders of the seventeenth or early eighteenth century. A feeling of superiority and authority was descending upon every member of the ruling nation. Secondly, with improved communications between India and Britain, more and more British women were travelling to India to join their husbands or to be married. Family units were being established and, with their numbers increasing, these families were creating their own British way of life and their own social circles of European friends at their stations in India. The intermarriages between British men and Indian women which were encouraged in the seventeenth and eighteenth centuries were now denounced and looked down upon.

Indian ways and customs had started to disappear slowly from the British community in India during the last quarter of the eighteenth century, and this process gathered speed in the first quarter of the nineteenth century. The smoking of hookas, enjoying Indian dances and music, the wearing of Indian clothes and pursuing native sports, etc., were nearly all discarded by 1850. The smoking of hookas, being a habit-forming trait, had become so popular that its use lingered on, in some cases, for another two decades. Some returnees brought their hookas with them to Scotland. Writing in the 1880s, the authors (Yule and Burnell) of *Hobson Jobson* recorded their own interesting recollections: 'Going back some 12 or 15 years it was not very uncommon to see the use of the hooka kept up by old Indians after their return to Europe; one such at least, is the recollection of the elder of the present writers in his childhood, being a lady who continued its use in Scotland for several years. When the second of the present writers landed at Madras in 1860 there were perhaps half a dozen Europeans at Presidency who still used the hooka; there is not one now.'

Eventually all social connections were broken with the natives and the Indian way of life. Commodious, imposing houses in planned surroundings were provided for British administrators and soldiers at a distance from the native settlements, thus ensuring physical separation between the rulers and the subjects. In most cases Indian servants were the only natives left after 1850 who had any links with the British families. Servants were indispensable and every family was obliged to keep enough of them, according to their status and their needs, to maintain a highly comfortable and aristocratic standard of living. It was not uncommon to find 50 and even up to 100 servants employed by certain families of high rank. These hordes of servants further added to the sense of superiority of the British. Soon, therefore, racism and prejudice replaced respect and cordiality. The activities of the Christian missionaries also contributed to the deterioration of communications and relations between the Indians and the British. Many of these envoys of the 'Prince of Peace' condemned the natives, both Hindus and Muslims, as heathens, contemptibles, 'irredeemably corrupt' and so on.

This contempt for a conquered, 'inferior' and 'unbelieving' people, and everything dear to them, was propagated and preached openly by the rulers and their spiritual guides. A sample of the feelings of the new breed of British rulers for their Indian subjects is presented here from the pages of *Curry and Rice* by G. F. Aitkinson: '... for niggers — orientals, I mean, have that peculiar faculty which characterises the ape and the kangaroo; they can only stand erect on an occasion, let a nigger alone and down he drops on his hams spontaneously, with as much joy as the wretched monkey in our streets when his polka is accomplished'.

There were exceptions, of course, and the Scots rated very high in these exceptions. They were friendly and gregarious, not as overbearing and as lordly as their English cousins. But for an ordinary Indian subject there was no way of knowing a Scot from an English officer. He did not know that Scotland was another country and the Scots were another nation. They were all sahibs to him. A sympathetic and condescending master was a kind sahib, whereas an arrogant and intimidating master was a hard sahib. Phillip Mason states: 'The Scots were always to form a core to the service, sons of the manse, younger sons of the big house, sons of doctors and crofters, more industrious than the English, less aloof, hard-headed but emotional, more romantic at heart, but to the Indian indistinguishable' (*The Men Who Ruled India*).

There were Scots and some English too, particularly academics, who continued to take an interest in Indian culture and literature. Some even worked hard for the general welfare and uplift of the Indian masses. For example, the first professor of Arabic and Persian at Fort William College, Calcutta, was John Baillie from Inverness, and John Borthwick Gilchrist of Edinburgh was a lecturer in Urdu at the same institution. David Hare co-founded with Rajah Ram Mohan Roy the Calcutta Hindu College; John Anderson from Galloway founded a mission school in Madras which later became the Madras Christian College. John Robert Ballantyne was the Principal of Sanskrit College at Benares. Dr John Login from Orkney initiated and supervised many charitable works at Lucknow and persuaded the King and his nobles to build hospitals, roads and bridges for the benefit of the native people. Sir Charles Aitchison founded the Punjab University while he was Lt Governor of that province. Flora Annie Steel, the wife of a Scottish civil servant, opened many girls' schools in the Punjab and actively encouraged female education. She motivated many local philanthropists to open schools for girls when she became the first female Inspector of Schools for the province of Punjab.

The Scots made their greatest contribution in the medical field in India. The present Medical Universities of Calcutta, Madras and Bombay all grew from Medical Schools started by Scots in the nineteenth century. Dr Alex Duff, a missionary from Perthshire, was instrumental in the founding of the Medical School at Calcutta, the first such institution in the subcontinent. Grant Medical College, Bombay, owes its existence to Charles Moorehead, an Edinburgh man.

It was a Scottish Member of Parliament, Charles Grant from Inverness, who argued for the first time in the British Parliament during a debate in 1833 that the British Government had an obligation to promote and actively encourage western education in India and to improve the state of the people of that country. And the brothers Sir David and Sir William Wedderburn, baronets of Balindean, encouraged Indian nationalism during their service in India. They lamented the poverty of Indian peasants and blamed the system for that. Allan Octavion Hume, another Scotsman, was the moving spirit behind the birth of the Indian National Congress, the political organisation which ultimately won the independence of India from Britain in 1947. Hume advocated, as early as the 1880s, that Indians ought to be given a say in the running of their affairs and their voice should be heard and given due consideration.

Scotland also produced its fair share of men who ruled India as Governors, Governor Generals and Viceroys. The first Scottish Governor General (from 1785 to 1786) was Sir John McPherson of Skye. He was 'best remembered for singing ballads with equal verve in Gaelic, Spanish and Hindustani'. He was in the battle of Culloden on the losing side. At the age of 40 he arrived at Bombay as a clerk in the Company's service and rose to become the Governor General. Lord Cornwallis, his successor, described his tenure as a 'system of the dirtiest jobbery'.

Gilbert Elliot, the Earl of Minto, was Governor General of the East India Company's possessions in India from 1807 to 1813. He belonged to the well-known Scottish Border family of Elliots. He resisted demands from Christian missionaries for the conversion of Indians as he believed in and maintained the policy of non-interference in and toleration of the Indian religions.

John Adam from Kinross went to India at the age of 16 in the last decade of the eighteenth century and became the Acting Governor General for a short period of six months in 1823. He was the first Governor General to be so considerate as to 'grant public money, one lakh of rupees (approximately £10,000), in favour of public education'. (A. M. Cain, *The Corn Chest for Scotland*)

James Andrew Broun Ramsay, Lord Dalhousie, of Coalstoun in East Lothian was the Governor General of India from 1847 to 1856. He pursued a deliberate policy of expansion, and annexed the Kingdom of Oude and a number of other princely states on one pretext or the other. After the collapse, in 1849, of the Sikh Government of Punjab, the only independent state left in the Indian subcontinent, he also added that vast territory to the possessions of the Company and thus completed the conquest of India. His high-handed policies in dealing with the Indian princes contributed more towards the disaffection of the Company's rule and the eventual uprising which is known as the Indian Mutiny of 1857. On the credit side, however, Lord Dalhousie introduced to India the 'three great engines of social development', i.e. the railways, the telegraph and a uniform system of postage. He also took a keen interest in public works and ordered the repairs of the roads, irrigation works and canals built by the Moguls but fallen into disrepair due to lack of maintenance since the breakdown of the Mogul administration.

It was the Scottish engineers like Sir William Patrick Andrew, an Edinburgh graduate, who repaired the old and built new roads and railways. And it was the Scottish engineering firms such as Sharp Stewart and Company, the North British Locomotive Company, P. W. McLellan, all of Glasgow, and J. A. S. Gooodwin of Motherwell who supplied the materials and the locomotive engines for the Indian railway system. The railway network set up by the Scots facilitated the transportation of cotton and other raw materials from the hinterland to the Indian ports, from where it was shipped to Glasgow, Leith and Dundee. The goods manufactured from that raw material were then sent back to Indian ports from Scotland, and conveyed again by the railway to the markets and bazaars frequented by the peasants who had toiled to produce the raw materials.

It ought to be mentioned here that India led the world in the cotton and the textile industry till nearly the end of the eighteenth century. It was the highly sought-after Indian textiles, among other products, which attracted the European traders to India in the middle ages. The Indian handloom weavers, however, were unable to compete with the powerlooms and weaving machines of Glasgow, Paisley and Dundee. In the late eighteenth and early nineteenth centuries, therefore, the Indian textile industry was finished off by the combined onslaught of the Lanarkshire, Renfrewshire, Dundee and, of course, the Lancashire and Yorkshire cotton and textile mills and factories.

Scots were also involved in establishing the telegraph network, restoring waterworks and building new canals, all commenced by Lord Dalhousie. William Brook O'Shaughnessy, a graduate of Edinburgh University, supervised the installation of the telegraph system as Director General of the Indian Telegraph Department. Col Richard Baird Smith, who was educated at Lasswade and Dunns, was the Superintendent General for Irrigation for the Government of India.

All these innovations and restorations brought great benefits to the peasants and other people of India. None the less, these measures contributed further to India becoming a gigantic reservoir of resources for the United Kingdom. Scotland along with England obtained most of its raw materials, at very cheap prices, from India and sold most of its manufactures at arbitrary prices back to India. Also, all the machinery and material for public works and other development projects were bought for India from Scotland and England, thus generating more work and more wealth for the people of this country. Scotland benefited far more than England through its trade, service and other links with India because the Scots had been such a dominant force in that country from the last quarter of the eighteenth century until nearly the end of the Raj; so naturally Scottish interests were favoured and patronised.

Dalhousie bid farewell to India in 1856, after a controversial as well as a progressive reign of nine years. The ominous clouds of discontent, however, were gathering on the horizon before his departure. The political changes and reforms which had been introduced by Dalhousie and his predecessors during the last 30 years had created a sense of misapprehension and unease in the minds of Indian people. So, less than a year after his departure, the thunderbolt struck and the Indian subcontinent submerged into a spate of violence and bloodshed it had seldom experienced before. The sepoys, the Indian soldiers of the Company, rebelled against their British officers and in many cases killed them. The 'Mutiny of 1857' had started and there was a complete breakdown of law and order in vast areas of central and northern India. The sepoys, however, lacked leaders, discipline and distinct ideals. The British, therefore, with the help of the loyal Indian forces and other collaborators succeeded in suppressing the disorganised uprising against them in a few months.

However, the barbarity and brutality which was practised by the British — the English as well as the Scots — during and particularly after the so-called mutiny is incomprehensible and inexcusable. Throughout India, a reign of terror, tyranny and indiscriminate slaughter and plunder followed in the wake of the 'mutiny', to destroy the morale of and to coerce and humble the entire Indian nation into abject submission and servitude. In their vengefulness and madness, the British completely ignored the glaring facts that in the year 1857 there were only 47,000 of their troops in India, scattered all over the huge country, among 200 million Indians; that the ordinary people did not manifest any significant hostility towards them or their authority; that had it not been for the loyalty and the help of their Indian troops and other sympathisers, not one of the British would have been able to escape alive. None the less, all over India the victors in their vindictiveness killed in droves and hanged in scores some 'guilty', and countless innocent. Moreover, as a long-term and rather sinister legacy of the failed uprising, the British rulers, disregarding completely the loyalty and assistance rendered to them in their hour of dire need by the majority of the Indians, developed hostile feelings of distrust and rancour towards the whole native people.

As a minor consolation though, the violent events of 1857 brought about an overdue change. The authority of the East India Company was replaced by the British Crown in 1858, and the administration of India was taken over by the British Government in London. The Governor General of India who, so far, was an agent of the Company and accountable to it, became the Viceroy, the representative of the British Monarch and accountable to the British parliament.

The first Scottish Viceroy of India was James Bruce, the eighth Earl of Elgin and Kincardine. He was appointed in 1862. His tenure lasted for only 18 months, a short but critical period following the horribly vengeful aftermath of the 'mutiny'. He tried to make amends and restore the confidence of the terrified and shaken people of India. But unfortunately, he did not have much time at his disposal as he died in November 1863, at Dharmsala, a hill station in Punjab.

Victor Alexander Bruce, the ninth Earl of Elgin and Kincardine was the Viceroy of India from 1894 to 1899. He encouraged the extension of the railway network to the remote and outlying towns and districts for the benefit of the populace of those areas. The atmosphere at this stage in India was in complete contrast with the times of the viceroyalty of the eighth Earl of Elgin, the father of the present Viceroy. Indians were speaking out now and standing up for their rights and privileges. Indian nationalism was gathering pace and Indians were talking of Home Rule and aspiring for independence.

Lord Minto, Gilbert Elliot, the fourth Earl of Minto was appointed Viceroy in 1905. He was the great grandson of the first Earl of Minto who was Governor General of India from 1807 to 1813. His reign would always be remembered for the introduction of the Indian Council Act of 1909 and the Morley Minto Reforms which laid the foundations for Home Rule or self-government for India.

The last Scottish Viceroy was Victor Alexander John Hope, the Marquess of Linlithgow. He was appointed in 1936 and held that regal office till 1943, longer than any other viceroy. The first general elections in India were held in January and February 1937 with the blessings of Lord Linlithgow, who stated that he wanted to see 'the full and final establishment in India of the principles of parliamentary government'. However, when World War II broke out in 1939, he declared India at war without even informing, not to mention consulting, either the central or the provincial legislatures. In spite of that, India's contribution to the war effort was tremendous, far greater than in the first World War. About two and a half million Indians joined the armed forces without conscription, 'the largest voluntary recruitment ever recorded in history'. Indian soldiers served with distinction on all fronts and made significant contributions towards allied victories against Italians, Germans and Japanese. 'Out of the 1,000,000 troops engaged in the final Allied victory of the war, the defeat of the Japanese in Burma, 700,000 were provided by the Indian army' (*Encyclopaedia Britannica*). About 36,000 Indian soldiers lost their lives during the war, nearly 65,000 were wounded and about 80,000 were prisoners of war. The economic contribution of India was even greater, as soon after the start of the war India developed such a comprehensive and effective industrial network which was able to produce and supply nearly all the military requirements needed at home (in India) and by the British forces in North Africa and the Middle East.

Lord Linlithgow left India in October 1943. Less than four years later all the Scots and English bade goodbye to India as its rulers and masters. In August 1947 two independent countries emerged from British India — India (Bharat) and

Pakistan. The British Raj came to an end. After nearly two centuries of subjugation, the people of the subcontinent were masters of their destiny once again.

The signs of the Scottish presence in India and Pakistan and the testimonials to their deeds still exist in the two countries in the shape of institutions, buildings, irrigation works, roads, railways and towns founded and built by them during the 200 years of the Raj. Thousands of Scots lie buried in various places in Pakistan and India. Many place and street names like Campbellpur, Fort Munro, McLeod Road, etc., still revive the memory of bygone days when the Scots and English ruled the subcontinent. The Scottish influence will linger on for a long time to come. As long perhaps as the schools and universities founded by them remain the founts of knowledge and learning, and as long as the whirls and skirls of the bagpipes — which have become so popular in both India and Pakistan — keep enchanting and exciting the people of these two countries.

Scotland gained far more from its 'association' with the Indo-Pakistan subcontinent. The wealth brought back from India, especially in the eighteenth and nineteenth centuries, transformed the economy of Scotland. Firstly, this wealth played a major role in the development of Scottish industry and commerce. Secondly, the huge captive market for Scottish products in India sustained and helped to further develop and strengthen the Scottish economy. It would therefore not be incorrect to say that the industrial development which took place in the last two centuries, and the resulting prosperity of Scotland, was largely due to the injection of wealth which came from India and Pakistan.

Scots also gained from the culture and customs of India during their stay in that country. Numerous new words were added to their language. For example, words like bungalow, cot, curry, cummerbund, chutney, jungle, mogul, nabob, pyjamas, pundit, shampoo and many more are all Hindustani words which are now part of the English vocabulary. Many textile patterns were borrowed from India. The famous 'tear drop' design from Kashmir was copied by the Paisley manufacturers and is now renowned the world over as Paisley Pattern.

On both sides, therefore, the influences and the effects of the mingling of the two people are obvious. But the most obvious contemporary product of this connection or association is the presence of about 35,000 Pakistanis and Indians in Scotland. Had this association not existed, had there been no Empire, and had Scots not gone to the Indian subcontinent, the arrival of the Pakistanis and Indians in Scotland would have been most improbable and their presence here perhaps impossible.

CHAPTER THREE

The Indians in Scotland

THE DOMS

In A.D. 1505 certain foreigners appeared at the Court of King James IV of Scotland. The King received them well, bestowed presents upon them and gave to one described as 'an earl of little Egypt' certain letters of recommendations. An item in the Lord High Commissioner for Scotland's records for the year 1505 reads 'items to the Egyptians by the Kingis command, vii lib'. During the reign of King James V in the year 1540, the Privy Council of the Kingdom of Scotland issued a writ in the name of the King recognising the Gypsy Kingdom of 'little Egypt' under its monarch Johnnie Faa (Source: the *Glasgow Herald*, 11 February 1989).

Gypsies in those days were assumed to be people of Egyptian origin, and hence the name they were given. However, we now know that assumption was fallacious and that these people came from India. It was a Scotsman by the name of Francis Irvine who, during his stay in India at the beginning of the nineteenth century, noticed the close relationship between the gypsy and the Indian languages. This breakthrough ultimately led to the establishment of the true identity of these people. It is now an historical fact that the 'gypsies' belong to a tribe called Doms which inhabits northern parts of India (now mostly Pakistan). Until recently the Doms were mostly a nomadic people, being musicians and ropemakers by profession.

A section of this tribe migrated from India, for reasons not known, sometime near the end of the first millenium A.D. They remained in Persia for roughly two centuries and then in the thirteenth century, perhaps to flee from the onslaught of the invading Mongols, moved westward, reaching the Balkans in the fourteenth century. From there they marched to central Europe and entered into many countries. By 1500 they had crossed the Channel and arrived in England. From England they travelled north, perhaps at the very beginning of the sixteenth century, and thus we find them at the court of the Scottish Sovereign in the year 1505.

The patronage they acquired and the reception they were accorded at the Scottish Court was perhaps reflected in the tolerant attitude and the friendly behaviour of the Scottish people towards them. This happy situation seems to have encouraged more of these persecuted stateless nomads to flock to Scotland. Certainly their numbers in Scotland by the year 1540 must have been considerable to justify the recognition of the Gypsy Kingdom of 'Little Egypt' by the Scottish Privy Council.

These Doms, alias gypsies, have been in Scotland now for the last five hundred years. Most of them, like their relations they left behind in India about ten centuries ago, have recently abandoned their nomadic lives and settled down in the various cities and towns of this country. They have acquired the creed, the customs and the language of this land. Having lived in this country for so long, and through intermarriages, they have become nearly indistinguishable from the indigenous Scots. After five centuries they have at last reached the stage where they are poised for total assimilation in the local society. History will, however, remember them as the first people of Indian origin who came to live in Scotland.

The next people of Indian origin to visit Scotland were the Indian seamen serving on the East India Company's ships and the Indian servants brought over by returning Scottish families in the eighteenth century. It was these seamen and servants who at a later stage began to settle in this country and thus set the trend and lay the foundations for the settlement of the present Asian community.

The seamen and servants were followed by more important and distinguished visitors such as princes and students in the nineteenth century. The nabobs, the maharajahs, and the other Indian noblemen came to Scotland for pleasure or on official business. The students came in pursuit of knowledge. The princes went back to their states and their domains in India after seeing Scotland and broadening their outlook, and the students returned home after gaining skills and knowledge which were not available in their own country. In the following pages we shall discuss in depth all these Indian visitors to Scotland, starting with the princes. We shall explore the marks and memories they left behind, and the impressions and images they formed of this country and its people.

PRINCES AND OTHER VISITORS

India was the land of princes, hundreds of them. Some were fabulously rich, others just rich. Some possessed more territory than the whole of Scotland. Though the guardians of the Raj in India did not always like it, most of the princes were very keen to come to Britain. And starting from the middle of the nineteenth century many came, some only once, but others very often. They always created great excitement in this country and were looked upon with great admiration and awe by the populace and the polity. A few are mentioned here, as a sample, to illustrate the impact they made, the reception they acquired, and the interest they aroused in Scotland.

The first Indian nobleman to set foot in Britain was perhaps Mirza Abu Talib Khan. He kept a journal of his visit which he published in Persian on his return to India. His chronicle aroused such interest that from Persian it was translated into English and published under the title *The Travels of Mirza Abu Talib Khan*. In this fascinating book Mirza tells us that he was encouraged to come to Britain by his friend 'Captain David Richardson, a Scotchman who perfectly understands both the Persian and Hindustani languages' and who undertook to teach him English during the voyage and provide for all his wants. He arrived in London on 21 January 1800. The news of his arrival spread quickly and his presence in the city excited great interest in all circles, especially in high society.

He records 'A few weeks subsequent to my visit to Mr Dundas, I had the honour of being introduced to the King and on the following day to her most gracious Majesty Queen Charlotte. Both of these illustrious personages ... commanded me to come frequently to court'. He further states '... the nobility vied with each other in their attention to me ... I may perhaps be accused of personal vanity but my society was courted ...'.

His friendship was sought by politicians and peers; by high-ranking civil servants and rich merchants. But Mirza emphasises 'for be it known that of my European friends, many more of them are Scotch than English'. He found Scottish people cordial and more compatible, 'quite different than the other Europeans'. Lady Winifred Constable of Edinburgh met Mirza in London and became a great admirer of him. When Lady Winifred was returning from London she asked Mirza to accompany her to Edinburgh. He rendered his apologies then, but promised to follow her in a couple of months. When Mirza was ready to come to Scotland he 'received the melancholy tidings of her death'. It saddened Mirza to have lost a sincere friend and also to have missed the opportunity of seeing Scotland, as soon after he resumed his journey back to India.

Maharajah Duleep Singh was the first Indian prince to come to Scotland. He was the son and successor of the famous Ranjit Singh, the ruler of the Sikh Kingdom of Punjab. Duleep Singh ascended the throne in 1843, at the age of five. In March 1849, after the defeat of the Sikh armies, the East India Company's Governor General in India, the Marquis of Dalhousie, annexed the Kingdom of Punjab and Duleep Singh lost his throne at the age of ten. Dr John Login, a Scot from Stromness on Orkney, was appointed Governor of the Citadel 'Killah-ki-Malik' of Lahore, the capital of the Sikh Kingdom, and also the guardian of the young Maharajah. Millions of pounds worth of gold, silver and jewels, including the famous Koh-i-Noor diamond, and other precious contents of the Lahore Treasury were expropriated by the occupying British forces. The priceless Koh-i-Noor was dispatched to London as a 'gift' from the 'loyal' subjects of Punjab to Her Majesty Queen Victoria.

A few weeks after his eleventh birthday, Duleep Singh was forced to leave the royal palace he was born in, and exiled to Fatehgarh, a town outside his former kingdom and about five hundred miles away from Lahore. The East India Company allowed him to retain the title of 'His Highness the Maharajah' and granted him an annual pension for his maintenance. Dr Login accompanied the titular Maharajah as his tutor and guardian. At Fatehgarh the education of the royal ward was begun in earnest. Dr Login was a kind and patient tutor but also a dedicated Christian. Soon, therefore, the pupil started to develop an antipathy towards his Sikh religion, and considerable sympathy for his teacher's faith. Moreover, after learning so much about England and Scotland, he became obsessed with a desire to visit these countries. The inevitable consequence was not delayed for long and within a couple of years the young prince was formally 'allowed' to renounce the Sikh faith. His long unshorn hair was cut, symbolising his physical break with Sikhism and, in March 1853, when he was just fourteen years old, he was 'welcomed' into the Christian creed to the delight of everybody from Dr Login to Lord Dalhousie. Ironically though, the royal convert was baptised by the sacred water of the Ganges, and not of Jordan, perhaps in deference to his past religion.

Once the ceremonies of conversion were over, arrangements were finalised for the deposed Maharajah's visit to Britain. Accompanied by about half a dozen Indian servants and a couple of teachers, and of course Sir John and Lady Login, 'His Highness Maharajah Duleep Singh Bahadur' arrived in London in May 1854. Although he had abandoned his faith, the Maharajah had not given up wearing his Sikh court dress with the diamond-studded turban, in which he looked like a fairytale prince. Therefore, his youth, his looks, his robes and his jewels all together, created quite a stir in London society and the royal court circles. Queen Victoria, perhaps because of her compassion or compunction, took an immediate liking to this exiled young king and manifested great interest in his welfare.

The following year, the Maharajah was brought to Scotland by the Logins, and Castle Menzies in Perthshire was leased from Sir Robert Menzies to serve as his Scottish residence. Over the years, among the Scottish gentry, he became one of the most prominent and picturesque figures in Scotland. Amongst the ordinary folk of the country, he was better known as the 'Black Prince'. He developed cordial relations with most of the Scottish noble families, particularly those owning estates in his neighbourhood of Perthshire. His shoots and his lavish receptions and entertainments became so popular and so famous that even now, more than a century and a quarter later, people living around Loch Tay and other parts of Perthshire talk of the 'Black Prince' and his shooting parties.

His best friends in the area were the Marquis of Breadalbane, the Duke of Atholl and Harry Panmure Gordon of Killie Chassie. With each of these families he had established very close and caring ties. It was 'the Duke of Atholl who persuaded the Maharajah to adopt the kilt for shooting on the moors and undertook the ordering of one for him from his own tailor'. The Maharajah perhaps did not need much persuasion as he had admired the highland dress right from the first day he set his eyes on it at Lahore during his childhood. In a letter from Punjab to his wife, Dr Login says: 'When I was with Duleep Singh at the garden fête given to the soldiers by Lawrence, the boy's fancy was much taken by some highlanders in full dress. Lord Dalhousie said, "Login, tell him they are my countrymen."' (Lady Login *Sir John Login and Duleep Singh,*). Seeing that highland dress so suited their master, the English servants of the Maharajah also adopted the 'exotic' outfit.

Of his Indian servants, Kashee, Sowdagar and Buland are known to have attended their master in Scotland. Pundit Nehemiah Goreh, 'a young and learned Brahmin convert to Christianity', also came with the Maharajah as his tutor in Oriental languages. The Pundit had become an earnest and a true Christian; his vast academic knowledge combined with a strong faith had a profound influence on the educational progress of the young Maharajah. During his stay in Scotland he attracted considerable attention and admiration from the

Scottish friends of Duleep Singh for his piety and his learning. In 1857 he went back to India to resume his missionary work.

The Maharajah also had a great love for hawking. He was a member of the British Hawking Club and was considered to be one of the best falconers of his time. He had indulged in the sport in his childhood, and in Scotland he found the opportunity of enjoying that passion again. He secured the services of first-rate falconers like John Barr, the famous Scottish master of that sport. His hawking parties also became big occasions and attracted much attention and curiosity.

When the lease of Castle Menzies expired in 1858, the shootings of Auchlyne, near Killin on Loch Tay, were rented from Lord Breadalbane and for the next couple of years Auchlyne remained the autumn retreat of Duleep Singh in Scotland. In 1860 the Maharajah left for India to see his mother, from whom he had been separated when his kingdom was occupied in 1848. In his absence Sir John Login, who was seeking to acquire an estate for him in Scotland, found one ('Grandtully' probably) and wrote to him in India about it. Duleep Singh was so excited and so delighted at the possibility of owning an estate in Scotland that he wrote back: 'Oh it is too cruel of you to write me, so soon after coming here, about an estate in Scotland, for now I cannot make up my mind to stay a day longer than is necessary to see my mother. Your letter has driven me wild, so you may expect to see me back sooner than I thought of when I left'. This shows the degree of his infatuation with Scotland.

In July 1861 the Maharajah returned from India, bringing his mother, the once beautiful Maharani Jindan Kaur, and her retinue with him. But the young Maharajah and his still headstrong old mother, who had only known her son when he was a child, were incompatible. Duleep Singh responded by acquiring a suitable residence for his mother in England. He then turned his attention to his new estate and within a short time 'converted his Perthshire estate of Grandtully into a first class grouse shoot (indeed the record for grouse being shot over a set of dogs was held by the Maharajah shooting on his Grandtully estate).' (J. G. Ruffer, *The Big Shots*)

The Maharani became seriously ill in August 1863. Duleep Singh was in Scotland at Loch Kennard Lodge at that time, and was sent for. He reached his mother's bedside only a few hours before she died. Two months later Sir John Login also died. With the death of Sir John, it seems that the Maharajah not only lost his most trusted friend but also his strong bond with Scotland. From then on he started to spend more and more of his time and energy at Elveden, his English estate in Suffolk, which he had bought in the year of the deaths of his mother and friend. He built there as his residence a spacious and graceful mansion in Indian style. He carried on with his shooting parties and prodigal receptions at his new estate and became 'a giant of the shooting history' of Britain. His extravagance eventually led him to financial troubles in the 1880s and he died a broken man in 1893.

Rajah Bhagwat Sinhjee, Thakore Sahib of Gondal, was another visitor to Scotland. He arrived at Edinburgh on 18 July 1883 and stayed with Mr and Mrs Nutt 'in their pretty mansion called Grange House'. The Lord Provost of Edinburgh entertained the Prince and arranged for him to visit the Castle, Holyrood Palace, St Giles' Cathedral, the Royal Infirmary, the Medical School and other places of interest.

The Rajah left for Glasgow on 22 July, where he was received by the Lord Provost of that city. During his stay in Glasgow, the Rajah and his suite resided at the St Enoch Hotel. The city chamberlain, Mr Nicol, conducted the distinguished visitor to see the shipyards in Glasgow as well as the Scottish beauty spots of Loch Lomond, Loch Katrine, the Trossachs and Callander. He was also taken to Aberfeldy and then to Pitlochry from where he was able to tour Killiecrankie pass, Blair Atholl and other beautiful places in Perthshire. The Rajah admired the beauty nature had bestowed upon Scotland and lauded the hospitality of its people. In his journal he wrote 'Scotland is a very beautiful country, pleasanter to live in than England', and noted 'the people are remarkably hospitable'. He developed such a soft spot for Scotland that he became a regular visitor and made many friends. In 1877, he was awarded the honorary degree of LL.D by the University of Edinburgh. He sent his three sons for education to Scotland. One qualified as a doctor and the other two as engineers.

Not all Indian visitors were from noble families. B. M. Malabari, a journalist, visited Britain in 1890. Not being a dignitary and thus not being conducted to 'selected' people and places, he was able to penetrate all classes and study all sections of British society. He noted the gross disparity between the rich and the poor and was shocked to find so much poverty and deprivation among the working-class people living in the congested parts of major British cities. He describes what he saw in parts of Glasgow and other places as follows: 'Men and women living in a chronic state of emaciation, till they can hardly be recognised as human, picking up as food, what even animals will turn away from; sleeping fifty, sixty, eighty of them together, of all ages and both sexes, in a hole that could not hold ten with decency; swearing, fighting, trampling on one another; filling the room with foul confusion and foul air. This is not a picture of occasional misery; in some places it represents the everyday life of the victims of misfortune .... And side by side with such heart rending scenes of misery one sees gorgeously dressed luxury flaunting in the streets'. (B. M. Malabari, *The Indian Eye on English Life*)

In 1897, many Indian princes came to Britain to take part in Queen Victoria's Diamond Jubilee celebrations, but few ventured up to Scotland. The two who are reported to have come up north were Rajah Ajit Singh of Khetri, and Rajah Kumar Singh of Shakpura. They visited Scotland 'to extend their knowledge of Britain'. They were entertained to a luncheon by the Lord Provost of Glasgow and 'waited upon by the city magistrates in their hotel'. They also made excursions to Oban, Edinburgh and other places of interest. (Source: The *Glasgow Herald,* 19 August 1897.)

His Highness the Yuvarajah (heir apparent) of Mysore paid a visit to Scotland in August 1913. His first port of call was Oban, from where he travelled to Glasgow. The Acting Lord Provost took him on a tour of Glasgow harbour on a yacht. In the evening the Prince was entertained to a dinner in the City Chambers. Bailie Paxton, the Acting Lord Provost, in proposing a toast to the honoured guest said 'the intercourse of Glasgow with India was of the most intimate and far-reaching description, and much of the prosperity and development of Glasgow was closely allied to the resources and products of the country of which their distinguished guest was an illustrious representative' (the *Glasgow Herald,* 22 August 1913). Next day the Prince and his party were taken on a sight-seeing tour of the Trossachs and the surrounding country. The party came back very pleased with the trip and were impressed by the beautiful scenery of Scotland.

The Indian Home Rule movement had gathered pace after the end of the First World War. Official delegations were sent abroad by the Indian National Congress to win support for their cause. One of these high-powered delegations, led by Mr R. G. Tilak, President of the Congress, visited Scotland in September 1919. They addressed a large gathering in St Andrews Halls, Glasgow, on 26 September. In his speech, the Hon. V. J. Patel (a member of the Supreme Legislative Council of India) said that after 150 years of British rule India from being one of the richest countries of the world was today the poorest. The material wellbeing of the Indian people was being neglected by the British rulers. He concluded by stating that they did not wish separation from the British Empire, but wanted self-government. Mr R. G. Tilak and Mrs Sarojni Naidu also addressed the meeting. (Source: the *Glasgow Herald,* 27 September 1919.)

The Maharajah of Jodhpur was a guest of Lord Belhaven and Stenton at Wishaw House in August 1925. Accompanied by Lord Belhaven and Lord Raglan, he visited a local coal mine and a couple of confectionery factories in Motherwell during his stay at Wishaw House. The Maharajah was pleased to learn that some of the raw materials for the manufacture of confectionery and jams came from India, and part of the production of the factories was destined for the Indian market. The next day his hosts took him on a sight-seeing tour of Edinburgh and the Palace of Holyrood. A few days later

71

the Maharajah moved on to Inverness, where he indulged in fishing in the river Spean for a week or so. This was the time when the trial was going on in Glasgow of the accused in the case of the murder of the Indian pedlar, Noor Muhammed, and the press were reporting it daily. It is doubtful, however, if either His Highness took any notice of the troubles and trepidations of the Indian community in Scotland, or the community displayed any interest in the Maharajah's royal pursuits.

In comparison with other Scottish cities, Edinburgh, being the official as well as cultural capital of Scotland, had succeeded in establishing stronger official, civic and academic links with the subcontinent. During its long association with India, the city honoured a number of Indian dignitaries by bestowing upon them the distinction of 'the freedom of the city' and conferring upon them honorary degrees of its University. One of the recipients of such an honour was the Hon. the Maharajahdhiraja Bahadur of Burdwan, G.C.I.E., who received the freedom of the city on 24 November 1926.

The Maharajah attended the ceremony held in the Usher Hall dressed 'in his picturesque native costume'. The Lord Provost of Edinburgh referred to the Maharajah as 'our distinguished representative from our great Indian Empire' and welcomed him as the head of one of the states which had given much loyal service to the King Emperor. The Maharajah responded by saying 'I wish to convey my deep appreciation of the great honour you have conferred upon me and I will conclude by addressing your great city in the name of Burns, "Edina, Scotia's darling seat, I am proud to belong to you today."' (*The Scotsman,* 25 November 1926).

On the same afternoon, after a civic luncheon in the City Chambers, His Highness was whisked away to Edinburgh University, where he was to receive yet another honour, an honorary degree. Before the capping ceremony, Professor Mackintosh, who was Chancellor of the University, introduced the Maharajadhiraja Bahadur of Burdwan as 'a great prince, a scion of a line of illustrious rulers'. Thus this Indian prince bagged two great honours in one day from the generous city of Edina.

Sir Feroz Khan Noon, a nobleman and the High Commissioner for India in London, travelled to Scotland in September 1937 to launch the Scindia Steam Navigation Company's pilgrim ship El-Madina. Most of the vessels operated by the Indian shipping companies were built on the Clyde. The El-Madina was built at the Clydeholm yard of Barclay Curle and Company, Whiteinch, and launched on 22 September. According to Indian custom, Sir Feroz Khan used a coconut instead of a bottle of wine for the launching ceremony.

One of the last Indian princes to visit Scotland before the end of the Raj was perhaps Colonel H. H. the Maharajah of Nawanagar. He was the Indian representative on the war cabinet in London during World War II. He visited the Indian Army contingent stationed in Scotland and inspected the mule companies in various camps. On 23 September 1942, he toured the Clyde shipyards and in the afternoon had tea with the Lord Provost of Glasgow. The Maharajah told the Lord Provost that he had found Scotland most hospitable on this his first visit to the country and it was a revelation to him to see how cheerful of spirit the people were in spite of the war conditions. He then left for Edinburgh and spent the next few days visiting army establishments in that part of the country.

The British Raj came to an end in 1947, and with that ended also the romantic era of rajahs and maharajahs.

STUDENTS AND ACADEMICS

The earliest students to come to Scotland from India were the children of Scotsmen who had gone there in the eighteenth and nineteenth centuries and who had either taken their Scottish wives with them, or had married or taken Indian women as mistresses. All those students bore the Scottish names of their fathers, and so it is almost impossible to identify those of mixed parentage, using presently available school or university records. There are, however, a few cases where references to the colour or parentage of some of these students have been recorded for a specific reason. Only in such cases, then, can the true identity of an Indo-Scottish student be established.

The first Indo-Scottish child that we know of was brought to Scotland in 1803. She was an eight-year-old girl by the name of Jane Cumming Gordon. Jane was the natural daughter of George Cumming and a 15-year-old Indian girl whom George had taken as a mistress in India. George Cumming was the eldest son of Lt Col Alexander Penrose Cumming of Altyre. Following the tradition of his family, he had gone to India in 1792 in the service of the East India Company. He died there aged 26, but before his death he had informed his mother about his little daughter. His mother, Lady Helen Cumming Gordon arranged, somehow, for the child to be brought to Scotland. She kept Jane with her for a few months at her mansion, the Gordonston (now housing the famous expensive private school), and then in 1804 placed her in a boarding school at Elgin, where Jane remained for the next five years.

In 1809 Lady Helen moved to Edinburgh and Jane, who was now 14 years old, was transferred to a girls' school in the city to be near her natural grandmother. During her stay in the school, Jane and some other pupils accused their two school mistresses of an indecent relationship. These accusations turned into a big scandal and Jane, along with her grandmother, became involved in prolonged law suits. It is for this reason that there is a record of Jane Cumming Gordon who was described as 'a dark-skinned girl, a native of India'. After the litigation was over Jane lived the rest of her life in Scotland, probably in oblivion. (Lillian Faderman, *Scotch Verdict*).

John Campbell, however, did go back to India after finishing his education in Scotland. He was the son of a Bengali mother and a Scottish father. John was brought 'home' to be educated at Tain and Aberdeen University. He returned to India around 1830 as a missionary, to work at the Bhowanipore Institution, a mission school in Bengal run by the London Missionary Society.

By the 1850s there were over fifty students from India, studying in all four Scottish universities. Edinburgh alone had about 30 in the 1850–1 session. However, not one of them was a native Indian, they were all the descendants of Scots serving in India. There were certainly among them some of mixed parentage and we know of at least one. He was Josiah Dashwood Gillies who came to study medicine at St Andrews University in 1855. He returned to India after obtaining his M.D. degree and being admitted a member of the Royal College of Surgeons. He became a medical officer in the service of the East India Company but suffered a lot of racial prejudice and discrimination from his white cousins in the medical profession in India.

The first indigenous Indian student to come to Scotland was most probably Wazir Beg from Bombay. He is listed as a second-year medical student in the records of Edinburgh University for the session 1858–9. Perhaps he came in 1857. From then on there were one or two admissions to that institution nearly every year until the 1880s, when the numbers of native Indian students coming to Scotland started to increase. Glasgow University probably received its first Indian student in 1869. He was Gopal Chandra Roy from Bengal who obtained his M.D. degree in 1871.

In the early 1880s, Edinburgh and Glasgow both had about half a dozen indigenous Indian students each. Most of these young men came to Scotland to read medicine. They may have been influenced to come to these well-established and well-known institutions by their Scottish teachers in the Indian medical schools, as there were far more Scots in the medical field in India than Englishmen. Moreover, almost all the medical schools and colleges in India were conceived and founded by Scots. It is therefore not surprising that a large number of medical students from the Indian subcontinent have always been drawn to Scotland. Engineering was the other field which attracted students from India.

The first Indian students' society in Scotland was founded at Edinburgh in 1883. The Edinburgh Indian Association, as it was named, is still alive and thriving. In the light of the growing number of students from India, the founding pioneers formed this Association to meet social and cultural needs, and to look after the wider interests of their fellow students. In its first year the Association had only six members. Its membership started to grow steadily from the mid eighties and increased very rapidly during the nineties as more and more indigenous scholars from India sought admission to Edinburgh University and other colleges. Around 1900, the membership of the Association had reached about 200. (Source: *The Edinburgh Indian Association Magazine 1883–1983*).

Early in the first decade of the twentieth century it was felt that, with such a large membership, the Association ought to have its own premises where the members could get together to pursue their social and cultural activities, hold meetings and debates, and above all be provided with Indian meals. A fund-raising campaign was started for this purpose under the patronage of the Prince and Princess of Wales. With the active support and full cooperation of many members of the Scottish aristocracy and public, a bazaar was held in December 1907 in the Music Hall, George Street. The campaign raised almost £6000. Donations also came from India; the Maharani of Vizianagram sent £3365 — the largest single contribution. The Association soon after rented spacious premises at 11 George Square. 'The premises contained a debating hall for 100 people, a dining-hall serving Indian dishes, a library, a billiard room with two full-sized tables and one ping-pong table ...' (*The Edinburgh Indian Association Magazine 1883–1983*). The Association operated from these premises until the building was demolished for redevelopment in the late 1950s.

Glasgow did not attract as many students from India as Edinburgh, and St Andrews and Aberdeen Universities only received an odd one now and then. More of those who came to Glasgow pursued engineering studies and the rest mainly medicine. Otherwise the pattern was similar to that in Edinburgh. Their numbers grew quickly after the mid eighties and went up to about seventy in Glasgow University and colleges around 1900. The Glasgow Indian Union was established in 1911 to look after the welfare of its members.

Its membership was open to Burmese and Ceylonese students as well as to Indians.

Some of the Indian medical students after qualifying as doctors started their practices in Scotland. Dr Pulipaka Jagannadham from Madras was perhaps the first to set this trend. Having received his M.B., C.M. from Edinburgh in 1891, he started his practice in 1892 from 13 Rillbank Terrace, Edinburgh, and by the turn of the century there were at least half a dozen Indian doctors practising their medical skills in this country. Their numbers grew considerably in the first decade of the twentieth century and between the two world wars. But most of them normally returned to their native land after gaining a few years' experience in medical practice, and perhaps obtaining another one or two postgraduate degrees or diplomas during their extended stay.

Scotland attracted proportionately far more Indian students than England, especially during the period 1890 to 1910. This was probably due to the stronger presence of Scots in the Indian academic world. By the opening years of the twentieth century there were, on average, about 300 Indian students in various Scottish colleges and universities, out of a total of just 'over 700 of them in the whole of the United Kingdom by 1910'. (Rosina Visram, *Ayahs, Lascars and Princes*, p 178). Their numbers, however, started to decrease slowly in Scotland from the beginning of the second decade of the twentieth century. The reasons for this were probably that, firstly, many excellent western-style educational institutions were now fully functional in the Indian subcontinent. These were manned by British and British-trained staff. There was, therefore, no need for Indian students to come to this country when the qualifications and courses were available in their own country. Secondly, the First World War disrupted the flow of students for about five years. Thirdly, provincial English universities such as Leeds, Birmingham, Manchester, etc., also started to attract Indian students. Last, but not least, the appeal made later on in 1921 by Mr Gandhi, urging the Indians to boycott British universities as well as British goods, also had its effect, and stopped many a prospective student from coming to Britain. Even then the Scottish share remained higher. In 1930 there were 1895 Indian students in Britain and of those nearly 250 were in Scotland; and in 1935 out of a total of 1387 about 200 were in Scottish universities and colleges.

With the Home Rule movement gaining momentum in India, the Indian students in Scotland also became active in this field. Edinburgh became the centre of such activities in Scotland. Meetings were held in the offices of the Edinburgh Indian Association, in the University, and in other places in the city to promote the Indian cause and to win the support of the Scottish people. At one of these meetings held on 14 January 1906, in the Shepherd's Hall, Victoria Street, Edinburgh, a radical student, Pandurang Mahadev Bapat, read an essay on 'British rule in India' which he subsequently published and distributed freely. The Indian Government did not like the tone or the tenor of this pamphlet and considered it mischievous and seditious. Bapat had come to Edinburgh University in 1904, on an Indian Government scholarship. To punish him for his disloyalty, his scholarship was forfeited. Bapat left Britain without completing his studies in 1907 and joined the Indian radicals' group in Paris. In 1908 he returned to India where he became better known in the freedom movement as 'Senapati' (commander) Bapat.

The Indian students in Scotland established contacts and communications with their compatriots in other universities in the U.K. Delegates were received from and sent to other cities to represent the Scottish Indian students' fraternity. Students from Edinburgh attended 'the 51st commemorative anniversary of the National Rising' (the 'Indian Mutiny') held in London in 1908, where 'tributes were paid to the memory of martyrs — Emperor Bahadur Shah, Nana Sahib and Rani Lakshmibai, leaders whom the British labelled "traitors and rebels"' (Rosina Visram, *Ayahs, Lascars and Princes*).

The second decade of the twentieth century was occupied by the advent, the course and the aftermath of World War I. Soon after the signing of the armistice, however, political activity and agitation for Home Rule started again in India. On the fateful day of 13 April 1919, a public meeting was held in a park enclosed by high walls, called Jallianwala Bagh, at the Sikh holy city of Amritsar, to protest against the arrest and deportation of two nationalist leaders. The authorities had banned such meetings, and the citizens were thus defying the law. The British Army Commander of the area, General Dyer, was furious at this insolence, and 'wanted to teach a lesson to the Indians'. He therefore went personally to the meeting place with two armoured cars and 90 Indian soldiers. He blocked the only entrance to or exit from the park with his armoured cars and then without warning ordered the soldiers to open fire on the thick crowd. Altogether 1605 rounds or bullets were fired and 1,579 people were killed or wounded. Because of the restrictions imposed on reporting, or perhaps because of the connivance of the press, it took some time for the correct and complete report of this macabre massacre to reach the public and the Indian students in this country.

The magnitude of this ruthless slaughter and the arrogance with which it was inflicted upon peaceful unarmed citizens stunned the Indian community in Great Britain. The Indian students in this country were the first to raise their voices against this monstrosity. The Government tried to pacify the protesters in Britain and in India by removing General Dyer from his command and by promising to set up a commission of inquiry. The students calmed down, but it took the Government six months to fulfil its promise, as the commission was not appointed until October 1919.

The Indian students in Scotland kept this issue alive in their meetings and debates, and continued to express their condemnation and abhorrence of this evil deed. Their frustration at the commission of inquiry's unsatisfactory pronouncements, and their disappointment at the Government's inaction, however, forced them to adopt a stronger course of action. At a stormy meeting in Glasgow on 28 December 1919, it was resolved that a mourning day be observed, 'in view of the "most horrible" and inhuman massacre and cold-blooded butchery of Indians at Amritsar'. The mourning day was duly kept on Saturday, 10 January 1920. 'A fast was observed during the day, and in the evening a meeting of protest was held at the Christian Institute ... A resolution was passed expressing great horror and indignation at the treatment accorded to the defenceless and unarmed citizens of Amritsar and other parts of India by the high-handed action of General Dyer, Sir Michael O'Dwyer and others, which it was stated had greatly prejudiced the faith of Indians in the British custodianship of India. An appeal was made to every member of parliament to establish justice and righteousness in India by securing proper punishment of those responsible. The meeting also resolved that until satisfaction was obtained the Indians in Glasgow should observe a day of mourning in April every year.' (the *Glasgow Herald,* 12 January 1920)

In 1920, there were about 180 Indian students in Edinburgh. Provision of accommodation for so many students had been a chronic problem since the 1890s. Those who adhered strictly to their dietary and hygiene customs found it very difficult and indeed frustrating to lodge with landladies or to live in privately run boarding houses. The Indian students' department of the Indian High Commission in London had been looking into this predicament for some time. With the cooperation of the Edinburgh city council and the assistance of the University, they succeeded in acquiring a building suitable for a hostel at 5 Grosvenor Crescent, Edinburgh. In this building the much needed Indian hostel, providing accommodation for 38 students, was opened in the winter of 1920. There were also ambitious plans for the opening of a hostel to accommodate 60 students in Glasgow. Mr J. S. Aiman, the joint secretary of the Indian Students' Union, came to Glasgow in November 1923 to explore such a possibility. However, in view perhaps of the smaller number of Indian students coming to Glasgow, the plans were shelved.

By 1925, political agitation had calmed down in India and as a result Indian students in Scotland were not involved in any major extra-curricular activities in the mid and late twenties. They were quietly pursuing their studies and participating in sports and other social ploys. Edinburgh Indian students were better organised and better equipped, as they had their own premises, or 'local habitation' as it was then called, where '... debates were held weekly on Fridays throughout the winter session (and sometimes on weekdays as well), helping no doubt to establish a firm grounding in the practices of western parliamentary democracy'. Indoor games like billiards, table tennis, cards, etc., were arranged at the premises, and outdoor sports were also organised. 'The Association also had a very active sports wing which was particularly noted for its cricket, tennis and hockey teams. The cricket and tennis teams were consistent winners of the much coveted Public Park Trophies and the hockey team was one of the finest in the whole of Scotland.' (*The Edinburgh Indian Association Magazine, 1883–1983*). In the Edinburgh University Sports held in May 1925, Jay Singh, a relatively thin and small-built Indian student, caused a sensation by beating well-built and towering Scottish students in winning the putting the weight contest.

By 1930, the number of Indian students at Edinburgh University had fallen to 138. In Glasgow, surprisingly, it had gone up to 83 (probably the highest ever) in that odd year, while St Andrews University had nine students from India. In 1940, however, there were just over 100 Indian students in Scotland, 64 at Edinburgh and 38 at Glasgow University. After the Independence of the subcontinent in 1947, the number of students from India and Pakistan rose again, and during the 1950s and 60s there were some 250 of them attending the various Scottish universities annually. The recent extraordinary increase in the fees for overseas students, however, has substantially curtailed their numbers again, perhaps forever.

SEAMEN AND SERVANTS

After the Doms, the Indian seamen serving on the East India Company's ships were perhaps the next people from the subcontinent to set foot on Scottish soil. The East India Company had started recruiting seamen from Indian ports as early as the beginning of the seventeenth century. Though

there were restrictions imposed by the British Government
on the employment of Indian seamen on British ships sailing
west of the Cape of Good Hope, these restrictions were often
ignored in order to fill the vacancies created by deaths on
board and desertions or call-ups during the European wars.
Moreover, Indian or other eastern seamen were far cheaper
to hire and maintain on ships than the Europeans. The Indian
seamen, or lascars as they were better known, were paid
between 15 and 25% of the wages of the European sailors, and
the cost of their feeding and upkeep was also similarly lower
than that of the European sailors. Shipowners and masters
therefore recruited as many Indian or Chinese sailors as they
safely could to boost their profits.

It is likely therefore that, after the Union of Scotland and
England in 1707 when the Scots also started to participate
in the East India Company's trade and traffic with India,
some lascars were taken aboard a Scottish merchant ship
and brought to Scotland. In the second half of the eighteenth
century, returning Scottish families would also have brought
Indian servants with them, like their English counterparts.
We have discussed in an earlier chapter how pompous and
conceited British families used to become during their stay
in India. Every comfort was available to them and everything
was done for them by the multitude of servants in every
household. On returning home after service in India, many
felt compelled to bring with them at least a few of their
scores of servants to carry on the luxurious style of life
they had become accustomed to, and which they could now
well afford in Britain with their wealth amassed in India. J.
Hecht confirms this and states: '... high civil and military
officials who had acquired wealth in the service of the East
India Company returned home to establish themselves in
luxury and splendour; and carried native servants with them'
(*Continental and Colonial Servants in the Eighteenth Century*,
p 50). However, there is a lack of recorded evidence of the
presence of both the Indian servants and sailors in eighteenth-
century Scotland.

There is, though, the narrative of a mysterious character

by the name of Secundra Dass, 'a gentleman of India', in *The Master of Ballantrae* by R. L. Stevenson. In 'late March or early April 1764', Secundra Dass appears in the House of Durrisdear at Ballantrae 'with his kind friend or good master (whichever it was)', James Durie the Master of Ballantrae. James Durie had been adventuring in India in the 1760s. On his return he brings Secundra Dass with him. Secundra Dass stays at Ballantrae for a few weeks and then departs to America with his 'friend or master' James Durie.

Now, if Secundra Dass is purely a fictional character and only a product of the fertile imagination of the author, then it is of little importance to us. On the other hand, if there is any substance in the events surrounding Secundra Dass, or if the author got his inspiration from a real Indian character who was brought to Scotland by a returning family, then we have some evidence of the presence of Indian servants in Scotland in the later half of the eighteenth century.

Also, there is a satirical article in *The Lounger* (8 October 1785, Edinburgh) in which the author, a Marjory Mushroom (obviously a pseudonym) states: 'My brother, who, as Mr Homespun has informed you, is returned home with a great fortune, is determined to live as becomes of it, and sent down a shipload of blacks in laced liveries, the servants in this country not being handy about fine things, though to tell you the truth, some of the Blackamoors don't give themselves such trouble about their work'. The brother referred to could have returned from India, or perhaps the West Indies, with his fortune and his servants. Most probably he came back from India, but the important thing is that in each case there is circumstantial evidence of the import of black servants into Scotland.

The lack of definitive and direct evidence in this period could be due to three reasons. Firstly, fewer servants came or were brought to Scotland as there were far fewer Scots, particularly in this period, than English people in India. Secondly, most of those who came here may have returned home. Thirdly, those who remained here were perhaps nearly all converted to Christianity as it was common in those days and given new christian names. Thus they lost their nomenclatural identity and became absorbed into the indigenous people, the evidence of their presence here vanishing with their eventual demises to the hereafter.

Moving to the nineteenth century, there is increasing evidence of the presence of Indian seamen, servants and other visitors to Scotland. Joseph Salter (*The Asiatics in England*), writing in the 1870s, states: 'Even in Scotland Asiatics are to be found, specially in the autumn months. They have been met and spoken to at Dundee, Glasgow, Perth, Greenock and Edinburgh ... In the Autumn of 1869 I went in charge of a crew of 22 men to Dumbarton to man a steamer on the Clyde ... From this Scotch town my tour commenced in search of the wandering Asiatics. Passing a short time in Glasgow, Stirling, Leith and Edinburgh I passed on to Sunderland ... On this journey I met and spoke to 81 Asiatics. At Stirling I had an interesting conversation with a native who had come from Aberdeen, where he had seen others.'

The lascars were not only very poorly paid but also very badly treated on board ships by the white officers. The most insensitive and humiliating abuse and insults were heaped upon these meek and helpless creatures. Floggings and other brutal punishments were the norms of a sea voyage. 'Salter met lascars who had been flogged; one had his teeth missing after being hit with a chain, another could not walk straight. The most gruesome story concerned nine lascars who died because of wounds inflicted by the captain, their bodies having been thrown overboard. Others arrived in England in a state near to death. In court the sad tale of Abdullah was narrated; he had been flogged, tied to the windlass and doused with salt water. Abdullah died.' (Rosina Visram, *Ayahs, Lascars and Princes*)

No wonder then that many of those who survived, and could not take any more of the barbaric savagery they were subjected to, deserted as soon as they could. Such deserters were normally destitute, as they usually jumped ships without their belongings and their wages to avoid suspicions. They therefore had to survive by begging or doing odd jobs in port cities such as Glasgow, Edinburgh, Dundee, etc. After their ship sailed away they sought employment with other ships going to India from any Scottish port. Failing that they tramped all the way down to Manchester, Hull, Liverpool or London in the hope of finding a ship which would take them back to their country. However, many died of cold before they could get a return journey, as they did not have suitable warm clothes or proper shelter for protection from the extremes of the British weather.

Those of the lascars who stayed with their ships were paid off by their captains as soon as they docked at their port of destination. This was done to avoid paying wages while the ship was laid up in port. When the ship was ready to sail again some of the previous crew were taken on, but often on reduced wages for the return journey.

Not only were these hard-working oppressed people exploited and humiliated on board ships, they were also abused, robbed and ill-treated on shore in British port cities where they had to wait for re-engagements to get back home. 'They were cheated, given spurious coins. Some women ... prostitutes and thieves ... made their living by plundering coloured sailors of their money and clothes' (Rosina Visram, *Ayahs, Lascars and Princes*).

The British Government did introduce certain rules and regulations, at the beginning of the nineteenth century, to persuade the shipping companies to look after and provide for the lascars while on shore and to treat them humanely on their ships. But such edicts were ignored too often by those concerned, and no significant improvements were achieved. In spite of all that, Indian sailors continued giving their sweat and blood for nearly another hundred years to bring the wealth of so many nations and so many countries to the shores of Great Britain.

Due to desertions from ships and long waits for re-engagements, colonies of lascars sprang up in major British port cities in the nineteenth century. Some smart and experienced hands from amongst them rented cheap old properties and set up boarding or lodging houses for their compatriots.

These houses became known to the Indian fraternity all over the country. The lascars from the ships in the ports and from other cities, and the Indian servants in the vicinity frequented these houses and these colonies. There they could meet with each other, talk to their countrymen in their own tongue and hear news from their country and perhaps get news of their own families. Some of the servants came there not only seeking comfort in a strange land but also looking for help and advice from their compatriots after being dismissed by their employers or being turned out after the death of their master. Servants in such situations were usually unprovided for and desperate to find another placement or, somehow, to get back home. They thus waited for their chance with their own kind.

These colonies, therefore, harboured both seamen and servants, long-term residents and those in transit. Some of them found work as odd job men or unskilled labourers. Others hawked in the streets and a few through their resourcefulness created their own jobs to earn a living. Here is a typical case as narrated by Joseph Salter: 'Roshan Khan is a well-known character, and long resident at the Scotch capital. He has long enjoyed the fame of supplying savoury pipes to the lovers of smoke; and he attends at High Street, near the Castle Hill, every Friday for that purpose. He had returned from Musselburgh races when I first accosted him in the Hindustani tongue, which made him smile as though he had seen a long-lost friend. He had no objection, like most of his countrymen, to salvation by the cross and approved of it as God's arrangement to save lost sinners. I entered his room one September evening ... and call it a room only because he was found there, for it was occupied by twenty others as destitute as himself.' (J. Salter, *The Asiatics in Britain*)

Joseph Salter was a missionary to the Asiatics and Africans, and in this role he travelled all over the country in the second half of the nineteenth century 'to proclaim the gospel of the redeemer' to the 'heathen' Asians and Africans visiting or living in various cities of the United Kingdom. Salter had learnt the Hindustani language and preached the gospel to the Indians in their tongue. He writes 'At Edinburgh and Leith I found Shaik Roshan and Meer Jan, and two others, the latter had not long come over from the Isle of Man ... My periodical visits are probably the only occasion on which these wanderers hear the word of life in their own tongue, and as I might not see them again for many years, I brought as earnestly as I could, the subject of salvation before their notice again'.

The efforts of missionaries and evangelists were successful and there were many conversions from the Indians, both Hindus and Muslims. Following is an interesting tale: 'I was born in Calcutta, and was Mussulman ... but Christian now. I have been in dis contree ten years. I come first as servant to military officer, ... I lived wit him in Scotland six, seven mont. He left Scotland saying he come back, but he not, and in a mont I hear he dead and den I come London ... I wish very often return to my own contree where every thing sheap ... I suffer from climate in dis contree ... I have no flannels no drawers, no waist coat, and have cold upon my chest ... I try get service, but no get service ... I put up many insult in dis contree. I struck sometime in street ... De boys call me de dis or de oder ... I not beg in street. So I buy Tom Tom for 10s ... and I start to play in streets for daily bread ... I had den wife, Englishwomen and dis little boy ... She servant when I mary her. De little boy make jump in my contree way when I play Tom Tom ... he too little to dance ... he six years. Most of my contreemen in street have come as lascar, and not go back for bosen and bosensmate and flog'. This is the life story of 'a very handsome man, swarthy even for a native of Bengal, with his black glossy hair most picturesquely disposed ... accompanied by his son' given to Henry Mayhew (Mayhew, H. *London Labour and London Poor* p. 188). This account epitomises so poignantly the life of those whom fate had brought over to this land as servants or sailors.

Salter relates the story of another native of Calcutta, a Jhulee Khan who came to Britain in 1841 as a lascar. He left his ship and earned his living mostly in the tap rooms of Scotland and England, playing hornpipes on the fiddle and singing English songs. He was converted in 1857 and given the name of John Carr. He married here and had five children.

It is, therefore, obvious that there were Indian sailors and servants in nearly every major city in Scotland in the nineteenth century. They had their small colonies in Glasgow and Edinburgh and possibly in Dundee, the three major port cities. These colonies served as bases for all the others who were scattered in other towns and other parts of the country.

Later in the nineteenth century, troupes of Indian entertainers and performers of various arts started to come to Britain. They were in most cases sponsored by British entrepreneurs who brought them over as a commercial venture and arranged their performances in cities and towns all over the country. These ventures did not flourish as the Indian performers and entertainers were not appreciated by British audiences. The sponsors, having suffered losses, abandoned this idea soon after.

The last quarter of the nineteenth century witnessed the arrival of royal servants from India. Indian servants were recruited for the Royal Household after the proclamation of Queen Victoria as Empress of India in 1877. 'Two of them, Muhammed Bux and Abdul Karim, arrived for service at Balmoral soon after the Golden Jubilee in 1887. Sir Henry Ponsonby, the Queen's Secretary, commented that 'she was excited about them as a child would be with a new toy'. Muhammed was large, bearded and quite dark; Abdul Karim on the other hand was much lighter, tall and with a fine serious countenance. He was only 24 years old. Dressed in scarlet and gold in the winter and white during the summer, Muhammed and Abdul Karim waited on the Queen at table, standing motionless behind her chair.' (Rosina Visram, *Ayahs, Lascars and Princes*).

Abdul Karim was an educated and intelligent young man. He made a very good impression on the Queen and was soon promoted to be a 'munshi' (a teacher) to Her Majesty to teach her Hindustani. The Queen made good progress in her lessons and was soon able to speak a few sentences to her servants, and to greet the visiting Indian princes and their consorts in

Hindustani. The Empress of India became very fond of her Indian teacher and in 1890 engaged the famous Von Angeli to do a portrait of him. In 1894 the Queen promoted Abdul Karim to the position of her Indian secretary. Soon after he was made a Companion of the Order of the Indian Empire. That was not all. To reward her munshi in India, Her Majesty wrote to the Viceroy of India, Lord Lansdown, 'for a suitable grant of land for her "really exemplary and excellent young munshi who was a confidential servant" (she does not mean in a literal sense, for he is not a servant). He was most useful to her with papers, letters, books, etc.' (Rosina Visram, *Ayahs, Lascars and Princes*)

This lavish royal patronage of an Indian munshi, however, did not go down very well in court circles. The members of the Royal Household, the India Office and the Government of India 'all resented the social status and the official position accorded to Abdul Karim in court circulars and on all occasions by the Queen and snubbed him wherever possible'. Every effort was made to discredit the munshi in the eyes of the Queen. Assistance and information were sought and received from India to damage the credentials and the credibility of the Queen's 'really exemplary and excellent young munshi'. Abdul Karim's adversaries eventually succeeded in their campaign and the munshi lost his former status in the royal court. Soon after, though, the Queen died and Abdul Karim returned to Agra, his native city in India. He died there is 1909.

Another notable Indian resident in Scotland was Aziz Ahmed of Lucknow. He came to Glasgow in the early 1880s. Being a convert to Christianity, he was brought over or came over to train as a missionary to work in his native land. He did go to a university or perhaps a religious educational institution in Scotland but failed to take a diploma or degree. He settled in Glasgow and married a Scottish wife by whom he had three children. He supported himself by lecturing on 'Mohammedanism and kindred subjects', appearing at lectures in his native dress.

He was brought to the attention of Glasgow police by the India Office who wanted him investigated for alleged anti-British activities. The Glasgow police found him a quiet and respectable man, living with his family at 36 Bank Street, Hillhead, 'but a disappointed man who felt very sorely that he was not appointed a missionary in India to his own people'. He was kept under observation for three years and the last report forwarded to the India Office by Glasgow police was on 10 January 1900, stating that he was still living quietly at the same address.

Aziz Ahmed contributed regularly from Glasgow to many Indian newspapers published in Lahore and Amritsar, and consequently he received many letters and newspapers from India. It was these articles published in India which aroused the suspicions of the authorities there and led to the investigations into his activities. He also had contacts with the local colony of lascars who, according to the police report, visited him regularly. Being an educated person, perhaps he helped these uneducated and exploited people with their problems and other requirements. (I am grateful to Rosina Visram for letting me have a sight of her research notes on Aziz Ahmed.)

In 1888 the International Exhibition was held in Glasgow, and a number of Indian craftsmen and other personnel came over to represent India in that spectacle. The committee organising the Exhibition had sent their emissaries to India in 1886 to interest the Indian Government in participating. The Indian Government responded positively and collected all sorts of artifacts and other curiosities from all over India and shipped these to Glasgow. In the Exhibition three courts were allocated to the Indian section in which Indian textiles, jewellery, pottery, metal manufactures, furniture, stone carvings, armour and weapons, etc., were displayed in an impressive fashion. Life-sized models displayed aspects of native life, character and dress. White-clad Indian cooks prepared real curries and chapaties and 'the crowd fell on these new and exotic delicacies'. Nine native artisans demonstrated their skills in various crafts.

The following is a contemporary account of the Exhibition's Indian section. 'Here are five rooms or workshops, measuring each about 6 feet in depth by 9 feet wide. In each is seated a native workman, busily engaged in plying his particular craft by the aid of those primitive tools which have been used by his predecessors for generations. When the cramped space in which they work and the nature of the instruments they handle are taken into consideration, it seems almost a miracle that without the aid of machinery such beautiful specimens of workmanship can be turned out. The end "shops" are occupied by potters, those next to them by wood carvers, while in the centre is a native jeweller. The floors of the shops are raised considerably above the level of the Exhibition flooring, an arrangement which affords a good view of the operations of the occupants.' (*Maclaren's Guide to the Exhibition*). The Indian section of the International Exhibition thus presented for the first time to millions of Scots and other visitors a real and comprehensive view of Indian life, culture, arts and crafts.

In the same year, as many of the Scots were admiring the splendid artifacts and fabulous riches of India displayed in the Exhibition at Glasgow, some Scots in Greenock were being lectured (in English of course) and perhaps pleasantly surprised, by the eloquent Mr Krishan Lal Datta from Bengal. Mr Datta was an Indian nationalist leader who was invited to address a public meeting, held in Greenock Town Hall, on the subject of Home Rule for Ireland. Scottish Irish nationalists and Indian nationalists were obviously supporting each other in their Home Rule campaigns.

Indian oculists or eye surgeons were another group of adventurers who came over to practise their skills in Britain. In 1892, three of them came to Scotland and settled in Edinburgh. They were Munshi, son of Mustakim, aged 37, Nabi Bakhsh, son of Faiz Bakhsh, aged 30, Din Mohammed, son of Nathu, aged 20, all from the village of Mehadpur in the Sub Division Nakoder, District Jallundher, Punjab. They were hereditary oculists and had been practising their profession in East Africa prior to coming to this country. In Scotland, however, they did not do very well. Soon they ran out of money and eventually became so destitute that they were admitted to a poorhouse. A few months later they were assisted with their passage back home by the management of the City Parish Chambers, Edinburgh (India Office Records, L/P&J/6/322 No. 991).

The year 1892 produced the first Indian Member of Parliament to sit in the British House of Commons. Dada Bhai Naoroji stood as a Liberal Party candidate for the Finsbury constituency in the General Election of that year and won the seat. Although this constituency was in England, very keen interest was evinced in this extraordinary affair in Scotland. Whereas many of the politicians and the press in England were bitter and resentful at the election of 'a fire worshipper' (Naoroji was a Parsi by faith) from Bombay to the Imperial Parliament, Keir Hardie, the famous Scottish Labour Leader, expressed his delight at Naoroji's victory. Moreover 'The *Scottish Leader* (a daily newspaper) was thankful that the electors of Finsbury were "free from the stupid and illiberal prejudice of colour" and had elected an Asian to Parliament' (Rosina Visram, *Ayahs, Lascars and Princes*). It is also interesting to note that before Naoroji was adopted as a candidate by central Finsbury, he was advised by his English wellwishers 'to try a Scottish seat as the Scots had the reputation of being "more liberal than the English Liberals"'.

The closing years of the nineteenth century brought the ravages of famine upon many parts of India. Scotland had built up very close commercial and service links with India over the last hundred years. The success of Scottish commerce and industry and the prosperity of the nation depended upon the Indian market. The Scottish people, therefore, felt concerned about the plight of the victims and relief funds were launched in many places to raise money for the help of the famished Indians. In Glasgow, a public meeting was called by the city's Lord Provost on 14 January 1897 to discuss the situation in India. The meeting was very well attended, especially by those connected with India. A fund was launched and the sum of £12,000 was raised from firms and individuals at that meeting. More donations came in and a total of £58,000 was reached by May when the fund was closed and the proceeds from Glasgow sent to the authorities in the affected areas.

Before leaving the nineteenth century, we should discuss

indentured labour, the factor which actually established the tradition of emigration from India. During the nineteenth century, starting from the 1830s, Indians were encouraged and in fact induced to go to other parts of the Empire as indentured labourers. After the abolition of slavery in 1834, the British colonists and planters in the various colonies found it impossible to recruit labour. Emancipated African slaves, having suffered violence and oppression during their enslavement, refused to work for their late masters. The colonists, desperate for labour, turned to the East India Company and obtained their approval to recruit Indians as indentured labour. These labourers were recruited in India and transported to the respective colonies. This process continued for about 80 years and was finally abolished by the Indian Government in 1916. During this period, however, Indian people were transplanted into almost all the British colonies all over the world. In the same period and even up to the Independence of India, Indians were employed by many British colonial governments to serve in their police forces, civil services, railways and even in the armed forces. Most of these employees and almost all of those who had left as indentured labourers did not return to India after their term of service expired. They decided to settle where they were. The open-door policy prevalent throughout the Empire made it possible for all British subjects to move with the minimum of restrictions from one part or country to another. The families and friends of the emigrants, therefore, had often no difficulty in joining them in whichever colony they were. Once the families were united the camp followers from back home converged upon them. Thus Indian communities started to emerge and grow in many parts of the Empire as early as the middle of the nineteenth century. These communities kept growing not only by natural multiplication but also by the continuous arrival of relatives and friends of the settlers from India.

By the beginning of the twentieth century so many Indians had migrated and settled in the new countries that some of these were transformed from indigenous to Indian-dominated, e.g. Mauritius, Fiji and parts of the West Indies. In other countries like Uganda, Kenya, South Africa and Malaya, their presence became quite obvious and their influence considerable. They also penetrated Canada, Australia and New Zealand. This tradition of migration and wanderlust eventually became so well-established and so well-accepted in the subcontinent that it still lingers on, and even now (near the close of the twentieth century) many Indians and Pakistanis are obsessed with the desire to go abroad to work or to settle there.

The white-dominated new dominions of Australia, New Zealand and Canada, wary of the influx of Indian immigrants, introduced legislation to control the flow of newcomers to their respective countries. Thus the open doors of the components of the Empire started to close in the first decade of the twentieth century. Soon after, other colonies started to tighten their immigration controls and slowly the free and unrestrained movement of British subjects from one part of the Empire to the other came to an end.

Great Britain, the mother country, however, did not close her door to her subjects. They were at liberty to come and go as they pleased. Some Indian labourers and fortune seekers, therefore, finding their entry restricted to the colonies, reluctantly perhaps at first, started to come to Britain. They were reluctant because not many of them in those days had any relatives, friends or contacts in the United Kingdom to whom they could come. Also they were overawed and in a way afraid of the British people whom they had known only as their rulers and masters, and with whom they had never experienced any social relationship. The language barrier and the cold weather were perhaps other elements which initially discouraged the Indian wanderers from heading for Britain. But those who did come found refuge, help and advice in the Indian colonies set up by the lascars in the major British cities.

The opening years of the twentieth century, therefore, saw a steady increase in the number of Indians in Scotland. Their small colonies started to grow bigger as more of the lascars and other wanderers joined them to seek their fortunes in the industrial towns and busy ports of Scotland. It was difficult for them to find work, but there were employers who were willing to engage them as 'cheap labour'. The Indians did not mind accepting lower wages for they were glad to find work. Those who were not fortunate enough to find employment sold trinkets in the city streets or did odd jobs and even begged to survive.

The presence of Indian labourers, it seems, had become quite obvious in the west of Scotland by the beginning of the second decade of the twentieth century. The indigenous workers and their trade unions became restive and started to resent the employment of Indian labour. Political agitation for the removal of Indian workers started and soon became serious and gained momentum. 'A demonstration in further-ance of the agitation against the employment of Asiatic seamen was held last night in the City Hall, Glasgow, under the auspices of the Clyde district committee of the National Transport Workers' Federation. The attendance numbered about 2000. The chairman, Councillor F. G. Stewart, said that their objection to Indian and Chinese labour was not because these men were of different race but because they lowered the standard of life for white men. Councillor Turner moved a resolution expressing alarm at the increase in the employment of cheap Asiatic labour and pledging the meeting to use every influence, constitutional or otherwise, to bring about their removal. The resolution was seconded and passed unanimously.' (The *Glasgow Herald*, 21 April 1914).

The Workers' Federation, ironically, did not have to wait long for the implementation of their resolution. Only a couple of months after the passing of this resolution, in July 1914, the First World War started. The workers and indeed the whole British nation were, then, more than glad to welcome gratefully instead of removing forcibly all the 'cheap Asiatic labour' they could get, not only in Scotland but also throughout Asia. Every available hand, Asian, African or European, black, brown or white, was desperately needed to fight the war. The Indians living in Scotland enlisted as sailors, soldiers and munition factory workers to contribute towards the war

95

effort. Their colonies became deserted and remained deserted during the war.

Back in India, over a million and a quarter enlisted and offered their services to fight for Britain. 'India's total contribution to the war effort was 1,302,000 men; casualties amounted to 106,594 ... Punjab was the chief recruiting centre and provided roughly 300,000 fighting men, Moslems, Sikhs Dogras and Jats, of whom more than one-half were Moslems' (*Encyclopaedia Britannica*). Indian regiments were deployed in France, Belgium, Greece, Turkey, Palestine, Mesopotamia, Egypt, Sudan and East Africa. At every front the Indian soldiers acquitted themselves with valour and honour. About 40,000 of them gave their lives fighting for Britain. Their services were gratefully acknowledged on many occasions by the King and the country. The following are just a sample of the tributes paid to the Indian soldiers. 'The departure of the Indian troops from the western front and the King's gracious message of thanks for the services they rendered to the Empire mark an epoch in the history of the Indian Army and in the relations between Great Britain and India ... Apart altogether from the great and important services rendered by the Indian troops at the battlefields of Flanders, at a time when we were in desperate need of men, the moral effect of the arrival of reinforcements from India was of incalculable value to Great Britain and its allies.' (The *Glasgow Herald,* 1 January 1916)

Mr Chamberlain, the Secretary of State for India, made the following statement on 12 September 1916: 'No one would understand the contribution India had made to the defence of our common interests unless they understood the effort in Mesopotamia, great as it had been, but one of many undertakings to which India had contributed, one of many campaigns in which her troops had borne a glorious share ....'

On 25 October 1918, the Lord Provost of Glasgow enter-tained a party of Indian journalists visiting Great Britain. Welcoming the journalists at a luncheon in the City Chambers, the Lord Provost paid tribute 'to the sympathy and support which the Indian people had given to Great Britain in its hour of need'. Responding to the Lord Provost, Mr Mahboob Alam, Editor of the *Paisa Akhbar,* Lahore, said 'India hoped that in future the people of Scotland and England would try to understand her better and reciprocate her good intentions'.

India's contribution towards the war effort also included materials of every sort. Its mineral, agricultural and industrial products, and each and every one of its other resources were put at the disposal of the Empire and made full use of during the war. 'India's financial contribution was no less remarkable. At its own request it bore the expense of its overseas forces and, in addition, made a free gift of £100,000,000 to the Imperial exchequer. By means of war loans in 1917 and 1918, a sum of £73,000,000 was raised. India's immense wealth of raw materials was placed at the service of the Empire and, by 1918, it had supplied stores and equipment to the value of £80,000,000.' (*Encyclopaedia Britannica*).

CHAPTER FOUR

The Indians Between the Two Wars

The First World War ended on 11 November 1918, and demobilisation started immediately. Munition factories and other works producing war materials came to a sudden halt. Millions of people became redundant in Britain. The demand for the services of Indians returning from the war also came to an abrupt end. After their discharge, most of them drifted back to their old haunts in the lascar colonies, which they had left at the beginning of the war. The few small colonies in Scotland were thus revived. (This was also confirmed by the late Mr Noor Muhammed Tanda who lived in Scotland from 1917 to 1919. The author was very fortunate to have interviewed this gentleman in 1969, before he died in 1975, as he was the only man then alive who had been in Scotland as early as 1917. Mr Tanda stated that when he came to Glasgow in 1917, he did not find any of his countrymen in that city and had to stay in a boarding house in the Broomielaw. However, when he was going back to India in 1919, there were a number of Indian seamen living in the Anderston district of Glasgow.)

More and more Indians and other black workers were losing their jobs because the indigenous workers and their trade unions had again started protesting against and opposing the employment of black workers. The National Sailors and Firemen's Union and the National Union of Ship Stewards, Cooks, Butchers and Bakers were openly and actively blocking the employment of black seamen and demanding their dismissal.

This sudden and unexpected hostility and rejection confounded and frustrated the black workers. But there was more to come. In an atmosphere of high unemployment, the white workers were becoming aggressive and offensive towards their black competitors in a rapidly shrinking labour market. Tension was mounting in the harbours and docklands. The inevitable happened in Glasgow on 23 January 1919. 'A serious disturbance extending for almost an hour and at moments of riotous description occurred ... among seamen at Broomielaw, Glasgow. The affray began in the yard of the Mercantile Marine offices, which following upon a heated dispute was the scene of furious fighting between white and coloured sailors and firemen. In the course of the struggle a number of revolver shots were fired and knives and sticks were freely used ... A large and hostile crowd of British seamen and white sailors of other nationalities followed the coloured men to their lodging house ... to which they ran for refuge ... It is understood the disturbance originated because of an alleged preference being given to British seamen in signing on the crew of a ship at Glasgow harbour.' (The *Glasgow Herald,* 24 January 1919).

The most damning aspect of this affair was that it was white against black. The white Scottish seamen had no quarrel with the Swedes, Spanish, Norwegians or any other non-British white sailors, who were also competing for jobs with them. It was the black British seamen, who had just helped win the war for Britain, who were despised and being harassed and denied the right to earn a living. It was unashamed and blatant racialism and not self-preservation.

The Unions' continued opposition and protests met with further success and 'in spring 1919, 130 black British seamen were on the beach in Glasgow' (Fryer, *Staying Power,* pp 298–9). And that was only Glasgow, just one port. If all the ports in the United Kingdom were taken into account, then there must have been thousands of black British seamen who were thrown on the beaches to make room for the white seamen. No wonder there were race riots not only in Glasgow that year, but also in nearly all the major port cities of the United Kingdom.

Ironically, it was not only the white workers and employers who were being so selfish and mean in denying work and a livelihood to the black workers. The British Government of the day had stooped even lower, as they conspired to deny these simple and unknowing creatures their out-of-work donations, their rightful dues after their dismissals or redundancies. 'The Employment Department sent secret instructions to Labour Exchange managers throughout the country stating: "The majority of these are eligible for out-of-work donation, but they apparently do not realise this, and it is not considered desirable to take any further steps to acquaint them of the position"' (Fryer, *Staying Power,* p 299). What a contrast and what a sudden change in attitudes! Less than a year ago the black British sailors, soldiers and labourers were being adored as heroes and saviours of the Empire for fighting the war for Britain; they were being publicly thanked and their services gratefully acknowledged by the King and the country. And so soon after that exhilarating experience, they were now being thrown on the scrap heap and denied, by the very same country, even what they had earned and was theirs by right and according to the law of the land.

The unwanted and unemployed Indians were thus having a hard time in Scotland around 1920. Most of them, driven by despair and deprivation, left Scotland for India or for England. Others lingered on here, scraping a living somehow and hoping for the best. Some, failing to find employment in port cities, left their lascar colonies and moved inland or to industrial belts in pursuit of work. A few, therefore, succeeded in obtaining jobs in various collieries and steelworks in Lanarkshire. Soon after though, protests and agitations started against their employment. Questions were asked in the House of Commons concerning the employment of lascar labour 'when thousands of Scottish workers were lying idle'. The Coltness Iron Company, owning Kingshill Colliery, admitted employing four lascars. The Company was at pains to emphasise that 'all four were British subjects, natives of Bombay; all had been on war service and possess medals; they were employed as casual labourers on surface; they were paid the same wages and worked the same hours; and they were not cheap labour' (the *Glasgow Herald,* 5 March 1920). The employers were, none the less, 'obliged' to sack their black workers. Nobody was interested in their admirable services to this nation in its hour of need. Now they were of no use and not wanted in this country. 'The trade council in the area made representations to the Ministry of Labour to have the lascars repatriated' (the *Glasgow Herald,* 12 February 1921). There was no expensive repatriation to India. The poor lascars were just made to repair to their colony in Glasgow.

Until about 1920 no obvious efforts were made by the lascars or ex-servants to settle in Scotland. They remained itinerant workers moving from one town to the other, but normally living in the lascar colonies and eventually returning to their country. This pattern started to change in the early twenties. The newcomers who began to arrive from India in that period were not seamen or servants who had either jumped ships or had been discharged by their masters. They were migrants or adventurers who had found life difficult in India, their own country, and had left it to do better for themselves and their families. In most cases they were the relations or friends of the lascars and others already in Scotland.

They left their country because the Indian subcontinent at that stage was also going through very hard times. The post-war recession had set in with a vengeance. There was no work and no jobs for a large proportion of the population. Hundreds of thousands of disbanded soldiers, who fought in the war, had made the employment situation even worse. Nearly 90% of the population of India lived in villages and depended upon the land for their livelihood. There was too much pressure on the land. The land holdings in most cases were very small and uneconomical. There were no other job opportunities for the uneducated and unskilled peasants and labourers who for generations had lived on the land. Nothing was being done by the Raj to set up relief works, factories and industries to ease the acute unemployment situation.

It is argued that it was the undeclared policy of the British Raj that the industrialisation of India was not to be encouraged. India was a huge captive and highly lucrative market for British manufacturers. A major part of British industry was geared to produce consumer goods for the Indian market. Industrialisation of India would have disturbed this very profitable arrangement. Hence the industrial development of India was conveniently overlooked. On the other hand the agricultural aspect of the economy was promoted, and in the late nineteenth and early twentieth centuries huge irrigation projects were undertaken in northern parts of the subcontinent, bringing vast tracts of virgin land under cultivation. Thousands of smallholders and landless peasants were settled on these lands in the new canal colonies. This suited the rulers as the increased agricultural products supplied cheap foodstuffs and plenty of raw materials to Britain. Also, new colonies and new towns provided more revenue and more jobs for British administrators and camp followers.

By 1920 all the new land brought under cultivation had been taken up and there were still millions of landless peasants left in India with no source of income. The unemployed, stricken with deprivation and desperation, started to migrate in search of a better living. Some moved to other parts of the subcontinent and some to other parts of the Empire. With the introduction of immigration controls in most of the dominions and colonies it was no longer easy to move to those countries. They were, however, at liberty to come to Britain without any hindrance. As British subjects, they had the privilege to enter and live in this country as they pleased. Finding all other outlets out of bounds for them, they took advantage of this privilege and started to come to Britain.

As has been mentioned in previous pages, there were small lascar colonies in the docklands of nearly all the major port cities in Scotland throughout the nineteenth century and during the first quarter of the twentieth century. But there is no evidence of any settled Asian communities, outwith the lascar colonies, in any of the cities before the mid 1920s. It is in the city of Glasgow (Valuation Roll for the year 1925/26) that for the first time we find four houses, in adjacent streets, tenanted by Indians. It means that they had acquired these properties in 1924. This was the beginning of the process of settlement of the people from the Indian subcontinent in Scotland. Their numbers at this stage were probably about 40 in the whole of the country. Glasgow had most of them, perhaps over 30 — around 20 living in the four houses of their own, and 10 to 15 still in lodgings or boarding houses in the now declining lascar colony. Their numbers began to grow steadily after 1924, and more and more Indian names started to appear in the valuation rolls of the city of Glasgow. Soon after, small groups of Indians settled in other Scottish cities, and so the community started to spread and grow in Scotland.

It was these pioneers, who came in the 1920s, who initially set the pattern and paved the way for the emigration and eventual settlement of the present nearly 50,000 strong Asian community in Scotland. Who were these adventurous people? Which part of the vast subcontinent did they come from? How and why did they come to Scotland? These are all crucial questions which beg answers. Fortunately, a few of those early arrivals are still living and they have provided answers to these and many more questions. Without their most welcome and highly valuable cooperation, it would have been impossible to record a reasonably accurate account of the presence of the Indian community in Scotland, especially between the two world wars. From the information elicited from these venerables, an interesting and poignant picture emerges.

It appears that most of these early arrivals were poor peasant farmers who had come to earn money in order to lead a comfortable life back home. They had no intention of settling in Scotland. They were migratory entrepreneurs who had left their country in the hope of bettering their and their family's future. Poverty and rampant unemployment in their own country had forced them to leave their kith and kin and try their luck in faraway Scotland. Nearly all of them were young men between 18 and 30, and mostly married. They left their families back home in the care of their elders. Under the joint family system in their own country they had no worries about the welfare of their spouses or their children.

The long separation from their families was their only concern which they hoped would be rewarded duly by their earnings abroad.

Another interesting aspect of these early travellers is that over 90% of them belonged to one particular area in the Punjab, Northern India. They came from the rural localities of the Nakodar sub-division of Jallandhar district and the Jagraon sub-division of Ludhiana district. These two sub-divisions are separated by the river Sutlej, one of the five rivers of Punjab. This particular zone lies on both banks of the river. Sub-division Nakodar is on the north bank, and sub-division Jagraon lies on the south bank. This area belongs to the oldest inhabited region of India. It was, therefore, densely populated and intensively cultivated. The land holdings had become very small and uneconomical due to the traditional inheritance division of the property of the deceased among his successors. The river Sutlej also often adds to the troubles of the people living on and near its banks. Whenever there is an unusual inundation of water in the river, it washes away huge tracts of soft land, from both sides, rendering numerous people homeless and landless. There was, therefore, always a very high rate of unemployment in this area, and constant pressure on the workless and poor to move out and look for greener pastures.

At the beginning of the twentieth century, some of the farmers from this area were given virgin lands in the new canal colonies in other parts of Punjab. Such fortunate ones left their ancestral homes to develop their new lands and start a new life. Others carried on with the tradition, started by their ancestors in the nineteenth century, of going out to East Africa, the West Indies, Australasia, Malaya, Canada, and other accessible parts of the British Empire as indentured labourers, traders, or camp followers. This tradition, however, finally came to an end when the recruitment of indentured labour was stopped in 1916.

This area also had a history of supplying seamen (lascars) to the British merchant navy. Many of the lascars in Scotland in the early 1920s were from this area. Some of these had lost jobs after the war and others had jumped ship to join the former, who in most cases were their relatives or contacts. The runaway lascars were seldom apprehended or made to return to their ships. Neither could they be deported once they had stayed in this country for more than 24 hours, since being British subjects they had the right to enter and live in this country. When this became widely known in India, especially after the First World War, many poor people who wanted to come to Britain but could not afford the passage, or could not procure the proper documents in India, made use of this device. They would enlist as seamen on British ships, at Bombay or Calcutta, and jump ship at any convenient British port to join their friends or contacts in this country. This device facilitated their passport formalities and also brought them here without any expense.

All the Indians who were in Scotland around 1920 eked out their living by taking up all sorts of unskilled and odd jobs. Some sold trinkets in the city streets and some unfortunate ones begged to survive. One of these by the name of Nathoo Mohammed was living in Glasgow. It appears that this pioneer, eventually and perhaps quite accidentally, became the anchor and the mentor of the small Indian community in Scotland in the 1920s. Destiny picked him first, to become a catalyst in attracting migrants from a specific part of India, and then to act as a host and guide to those newcomers in Scotland. His life sketch in the following pages gives a true insight into the build-up of the Indo-Pakistani community in Scotland.

NATHOO MOHAMMED

According to the entry in his passport (number 24975 issued/ renewed at Lahore on 27 April 1927), Nathoo Mohammed was born in the year 1892, at a village called Kot Badal Khan in sub-division Nakodar, district Jallandhar, Punjab. He belonged to a Muslim family of petty farmers. His forefathers had lived in that little village for centuries and tilled their land for a living. Nathoo, the first-born of his parents, grew up in the same profession. He did not receive any schooling. Perhaps

105

his parents could not afford to send Nathoo to school, as it cost a considerable sum of money to buy books, clothes and other accessories, or it may have been that his father needed the assistance of his eldest son on his small farm, as was customary. It is also possible that there was no school at that time in his village, which is situated about five or six miles south east of Nakodar, the nearest town of any importance. The river Sutlej flows about five or six miles south of Kot Badal Khan.

Nathoo had four brothers. Their father would have been very proud of his five sons, but at the same time would have worried about their future. His smallholding might have provided him with a living, but it would have been totally inadequate to sustain his sons and their families when they grew up and got married. He must, therefore, have been contemplating sending one or more of his sons abroad, as was the tradition of that region, to improve their future. He would have discussed his thoughts with young Nathoo and prepared him mentally, over the years, for his sojourn abroad.

In 1917, when Nathoo was about 25 years old and married with two or three children, he went to Bombay and signed on as a lascar on a British merchant ship. After serving as a seaman for perhaps a year or two, he was either paid off or he jumped ship, arriving in Glasgow most probably in 1919. Mr N. M. Tanda related that, when he left for London in 1919, a few Indian seamen were living in Brown Street in the Anderston district of Glasgow, and he knew them as they belonged to villages near his own village of Tanda Oora. Unfortunately, Mr Tanda did not mention any names. None the less, Kot Badal Khan, Nathoo's village, is situated only about one mile east of Tanda Oora. Also, Mr Ata Mohammed Ashraf who came to Glasgow in 1926, and is a close relative of Nathoo, states that Nathoo came to Glasgow six or seven years before him. Furthermore, as Nathoo acquired a flat at 6 Brown Street in 1924, the first Indian to tenant a flat in this district, it is very likely that he had already been present in the lascar colony, in this locality, for a few years.

Having established 1919 as the year of the probable arrival of Nathoo in Glasgow, the next question is what brought him there? What motivated him to venture to far-off Glasgow, where there was no settled Indian community, and where the chances of finding employment were far less than in London or any other English port city? As a rule, and like any other migrant moving to a new place in an alien society, he would only have gone there if he had a contact, somebody he knew and could depend upon. Unfortunately, it has not been possible to find or establish with certainty any such contact for Nathoo in Glasgow or any other Scottish city. Perhaps Nathoo was one of the 130 black British seamen who were thrown on the beach in the spring of 1919 and had no choice but to stay in Glasgow. Another possible explanation could be that, during his service as a sailor, his ship called at Glasgow a few times, and during his short stays ashore he developed friendly relations with some people, or somebody, in the lascar colony. Then, when he was made redundant, or left his ship of his own accord, he came to his friends in Glasgow. Yet another and more plausible explanation is that a friend or an acquaintance of his was already living in or near Glasgow and Nathoo planned to come to Glasgow. And there was, at least, one such person in Glasgow before the arrival of Nathoo. His name was Sundhi Din, and he belonged to a village called Balanda, which lies about seven miles west of Kot Badal Khan, the village of Nathoo Mohammed. Sundhi Din came to Scotland sometime before the First World War, as a valet to a retiring Scottish army officer, in whose service he had been, in India, for many years. A few years later his employer died and Sundhi was left on his own. He settled in Glasgow and worked first as a hawker and then as a pedlar for many years.

(The writer met Sundhi in 1959, in the former's ancestral village of Maan, in Pakistan, when he was there on a family visit. Sundhi and his family, being Muslims, had migrated to Pakistan from Balanda, which became part of India after the partition of the subcontinent in 1947. Sundhi was very old then, but he came to see me and asked where I had settled in Britain. When I answered Glasgow, his weathered face lit up and he told me how he had gone to Scotland and had lived in Glasgow for many years. Regretfully, at that time I had no idea that one day I would be trying to record the history of Asian migration to Scotland, and that the information which Sundhi possessed would be of immense value. I therefore listened to what he said with great interest, but did not ask any probing questions. Sundhi died soon after, and so I had no further opportunity to question him. I did, however, discover in the Valuation Roll of the city of Glasgow that he was the tenant of a house at 56 Water Street, Port Dundas, between the years 1925 to 1930. This information corroborated what Sundhi had told me and confirmed his presence in Glasgow until the 1930s.)

Sundhi Din and Nathoo Mohammed had much in common, for they were both *Arraein* Muslims, i.e. of the same faith and caste, as well as coming from the same area. This area had been inhabited for many centuries, and people there had long-established relationships and friendships with each other. It is unlikely, though, that Nathoo had met Sundhi before the latter came to Scotland, as Nathoo would have been quite young then. But it is probable that Nathoo's father knew Sundhi and his family and, therefore, Nathoo knew of Sundhi. Nathoo or his father might have written to Sundhi, asking him if Nathoo could come to him. It is also likely that there were other Indians with Nathoo when he came to Glasgow, people who were with him on board ship, or who joined him knowing that Nathoo had a contact and as customary they would also be looked after.

Sundhi was living in lodgings then, and working as a hawker in the thoroughfares of Glasgow. Nathoo was initiated in the same trade. But Nathoo, it appears, did not do very well in this job, perhaps due to his inability to express himself in the English language, or due to competition among hawkers in the city streets. Competition must have been intense in those days of high unemployment and severe deprivation, not only from indigenous white hawkers but also from the shops in the city. A novice dark-skinned Indian hawker, therefore, had very limited chances of making a success in the Glasgow streets. Nathoo, after a year or two, became so frustrated at his continuous failure in this trade that he abandoned hawking and started to look for a job. He did not realise, perhaps, how hard it would be for him to find employment. Nevertheless he kept roaming the streets, doing odd jobs, and enquiring at shops, warehouses and factories for a steady job.

One day he called at a warehouse owned by a Jewish gentleman in Crown Street, Glasgow, and asked him for a job. The warehouseman gave the familiar reply 'sorry, no vacancy', but then, overcome perhaps by that spirit of camaraderie which attracts two strangers in a strange land, or perhaps just a feeling of pity for the poor wretch, he called Nathoo back. He probably sympathised with him, and from his own and his community's experience told him that jobs for foreigners, especially dark strangers, were very hard to come by. He advised him to work for himself, to create his own job by going out with a bag full of children's, ladies' and gentlemen's wear, and selling those in the housing schemes of the city or, even better, in the outlying villages in rural areas where there were no shops and no hawkers to compete with. He told him to go to the potential customer instead of waiting for the customer to come to him, and if any could not afford to buy cash, then to offer them credit as the Jewish pedlars had been doing since their arrival in this country 40 years ago.

Maybe the warehouseman had a vested interest in giving this advice to Nathoo, because he wanted to add to his customers. At this stage the first generation Jews, who had taken refuge in this country in the last two decades of the nineteenth century, and who were mostly engaged in peddling, were retiring or dying out. The second generation Jews, thanks to the labours of their fathers, were opening shops and warehouses, or going into professions. Therefore, the peddling industry was on the decline, and adversely affecting the business of those who were its suppliers.

Peddling in those days, with a heavy case in one's hand or on one's shoulders, was a very tough job. The unpredictability and inclemency of the Scottish weather made it even more difficult. The drudgery of long tiring walks, the frustration of no sales, a heavy load and hunger, all added up to make a man lose heart and give up. But it seems that Nathoo accepted the advice and weathered all these adversities, and by the early 1920s was able to earn a good wage from his new vocation. When his other compatriots saw Nathoo doing well in his new profession, they gave up their respective jobs, if they had any, and one by one all became pedlars. From then on very few Indians took on jobs as unskilled labourers and no one was forced to beg to survive. Every newcomer was inducted in selling out of a case, from door to door. Many more were encouraged to come to Scotland from various small villages in the sub-divisions of Nakodar and Jagraon. Nathoo had set a trend. He had shown a way of earning a reasonable wage in an honest and dignified way. This enhanced Nathoo's confidence and courage, and when the number of Indian pedlars increased he started to supply them with the goods of their trade, even extending credit to his countrymen. This also suited the Indian pedlars, as it saved them time and labour spent in looking for their supplies in various warehouses. The credit facilities offered by Nathoo were also of the utmost benefit to newcomers who normally did not have any capital to start with.

Nathoo was now doing very well. He was selling wholesale to his countrymen in the mornings and late at night from his house, and doing his travelling rounds during the rest of the day. He was doing so well that he called over, from India, his brothers and a few other relatives. He also took a charming white girl named Louise as his common-law wife. Late in 1924 when his brothers came over, he rented another flat in Clyde Street, Port Dundas, moved there with his wife and gave the flat in Brown Street to his brothers. His wife helped him a great deal in the wholesale side of his business. Nathoo, as we know, was illiterate. Louise therefore kept the accounts and dealt with the paperwork. Nathoo Mohammed's business acumen and Louise's education produced the combination for success. But this combination also produced some unfavourable reaction from the racists and bigots in the neighbourhood, and the business success of the couple attracted jealousy and ill-will from the criminal element in the district. Tongues were wagging against the union of a black man and a white girl, and rumours were rife in the area that their house was a gold mine. Tragedy struck soon after.

On the fateful night of Saturday, 16 May 1925, at about 10.00 p.m., three men came to Nathoo's door at 5 Clyde Street. They demanded to see some jumpers and scarves which Nathoo sold. Sensing that all was not well, Nathoo refused to show them any articles or to have any dealings with them. The callers, who had been drinking, became abusive and aggressive. Two of them produced daggers and threatened to kill Nathoo. Nathoo became so frightened that he ran out of the house. The three young men stayed behind, abusing and molesting Louise. Louise eventually managed to make them leave her house. The accomplices of the three thugs, who were standing in the street, saw Nathoo running to a house at 56 Water Street, just round the corner, where Sundhi Din lived with four or five of his countrymen. Nathoo had sought safety and protection with his friends but the trouble followed him to his place of refuge. The troublesome trio, followed by a mob, went up to the close, climbed the flight of stairs and knocked at the door of Sundhi's house. Shahab Din, who had just come in from his peddling rounds, answered the door. The scoundrels called him names, pushed and shoved him and tried to get inside the house. Shahab Din, realising the danger, managed to slam the door shut on the unwelcome guests.

It appears that at this point the three ringleaders were joined by their score or so comrades at the stair head. The unruly mob knocked down the door, poured into the house and pounced upon the frightened and panic-stricken inmates. The house was only a room and kitchen. The six Indians had no chance against the fury of nearly two dozen invaders. They retreated to the bedroom and tried to close that door behind them. But they did not succeed and their assailants burst in. The two daggers which were first unsheathed at 5 Clyde Street came into action. One of the Indians let out a terrific shriek.

111

It was Noor Mohammed; he had been stabbed. The others were being attacked with sticks, stones, utensils, fists and legs. The hysterical victims pinned against the walls kept on shouting for help, and defending themselves as best they could. The violence lasted for several minutes, but no help arrived. When the ruffians saw Noor Mohammed writhing in agony on the floor with blood gushing out of his wounds, they calmed down and started to spill out of the wrecked and bloodstained house.

Two others, Sundhi Din and Mohammed Bakhsh, were also wounded, but not seriously. Nathoo, Shahab Din and Qutub Din, fortunately, escaped with cuts and bruises. A lot of goods were also stolen by the assailants. Most of the neighbours during this dreadful incident had bolted their doors and hid in their houses, afraid of getting involved. Someone, however, had the courage to run out and inform the police, who arrived soon after the villains had left the scene of the crime. An ambulance was summoned and Noor Mohammed was hurriedly transported to the Royal Infirmary. On examination it was found that the dagger had penetrated deep into the chest of the unfortunate man and his arteries were severed. The doctors could not do much for him. Noor Mohammed died soon after. He had come to Scotland from India only nine months earlier. He was 27 years old, most probably married with a young family. He had come to seek his fortune. Instead he found his grave in Riddrie cemetery in Glasgow where he was buried on 19 May 1925. The *Daily Record* of 20 May 1925 reported that Noor Mohammed was buried according to Muslim rites and about 50 Indians, both Mohammedans and Christians, were included in the funeral procession.

The police acted with speed and eight men and one woman were arrested during the same night and early morning. According to the *Sunday Mail* of 6 September 1925, the accused were the ringleaders of one of the most dangerous gangs which ever operated in Glasgow. They all resided in the Port Dundas area and had gathered around them a number of young irresponsible hooligans who, for many months past, had terrorised the people in the district. Each of them had convictions for housebreaking and each had served sentences meted out to them in Glasgow Sheriff Court, but the burglaries were the least of their activities. Dozens of decent-living men and women had been victims of their violence. The gangsters, therefore, were known for what they were to the police. Only three of the mob were eventually charged with murdering Noor Mohammed and other lesser charges relating to the incident. The trial was concluded on 3 September 1925 in the High Court of Justiciary in Glasgow.

One of the accused, John Kean, was found guilty of murder and he was sentenced to death by Lord Ormidale. This man was hanged on 24 September in Duke Street prison. The second accused was sentenced to seven years penal servitude and the third was sent to prison for nine months. There were some interesting aspects of the judge's summing-up and the jury's verdict which underlined the racist nature of this case. The *Glasgow Herald* of 4 September 1925 reported that his Lordship said 'that the case was an anxious and difficult one. Although it had been an Indian who had been done to death, he was sure that the jury would give the same consideration to the case as they would have done if the victim of the murderous assault had been a native of Scotland or England. So far as Noor Mohammed was concerned, not a word had been suggested that he was anything other than a law-abiding resident in this country.' The jury did bring a verdict of guilty against John Kean but with a strong recommendation for mercy.

There were also moves in certain quarters for a petition to be launched in support of mercy and leniency for Kean. But British justice prevailed and the criminals paid for their gruesome crimes according to the laws of the land and the norms of the day. During the trial, evidence from Nathoo and his compatriots was taken in Hindustani through interpreters, as none of the witnesses except Louise could speak English intelligibly. Thus, any unfairness or injustice to the case through misunderstanding or lack of information due to the language impediment was scrupulously avoided by the court. Mr Mathew Martin, Chief Constable of Perthshire, who had served in India and knew Hindustani well, was employed as interpreter.

After the execution of the murderer, the small group of Indians settled down again. They reverted to their quiet and secluded way of life, minding their own business and avoiding trouble. The traumatic experience of the last few months, however, had upset Nathoo. He was well aware of the fact that the gangsters had come to get him and he was very lucky to have survived. Also, it was now perhaps seven or eight years since he had left his family and his country and he might have been feeling homesick. So he decided to go home, to get away from the unpleasant memories of the assault and the murder, the trial and other tribulations. Seeing his parents, his family and friends, and having a holiday in his native land, he might have thought would do him good.

After sorting out his affairs and relinquishing the tenancy of the flat in Clyde Street, he was ready to depart. He transferred the tenancy of his house in Brown Street to the name of his younger brother, Khair Mohammed, and boarded a ship bound for Bombay early in 1926. Yes, he boarded the ship as a fare-paying passenger on his return journey, as he was rather well off now, and could afford to pay the fare.

En route to India, when his ship was making a scheduled stop at a certain port in East Africa, he met another Indian by the name of Hari Singh. This Sikh gentleman was a wanderer. He belonged to a village called Galotian, in the district of Sialkot, Punjab. While Nathoo's ship was in port, the two lonely Indians got on well with each other and became good friends. Nathoo told Hari Singh that if ever the latter wanted to come to Scotland he would be made welcome at his house in Glasgow. Nathoo then departed for Bombay and Hari Singh continued with his wanderings.

A year or so later Hari Singh took up Nathoo's offer and found his way to Glasgow. Hari Singh, it appears, liked Scotland, and he settled down in Glasgow. He usually went back home after every two or three years to see his family and have a holiday, and would then return after a few months, always bringing with him one or two members of his family or friends, thus building up in Scotland a Sikh community of his particular clan.

(The meeting between Nathoo Mohammed and Hari Singh is an assumption based on very strong circumstantial evidence. Mr T. S. Chamak, the grandson of Hari Singh (who died in the late 1940s), confirms that his grandfather was the first man from their family to come to Scotland and settle in Glasgow around 1926–7; and that he heard from his grandfather, Hari Singh, the tale of his wanderings and of his meeting a man, at an east African port, who had come from Glasgow and was going to his village in Jallandhar district, Punjab. Mr Chamak, himself, does not remember the name of that man, but knows that he was a Muslim *Arraien*, who had come to Glasgow as a seaman. Mr Chamak also emphasises that he heard from his grandfather, and his own father, that this man invited him (Hari Singh) to Glasgow.

Now at that time there were only about 40 to 50 Indians in Glasgow, and there was not much traffic between the rural villages of Jallandhar and Glasgow. There is evidence both verbal and documentary to the effect that Nathoo did leave Glasgow to go to his village in the district of Jallandhar, India, by sea in 1926; and that Nathoo was a Muslim and an *Arraien* by caste. Furthermore, there is no evidence that any of the other Indians left Glasgow to go home at any time in the year 1926.)

Returning to Nathoo, it can safely be assumed that from Bombay he travelled by train to Nakodar, the railway station nearest his village. His family and friends would have come to the railway station to receive him and to take him to Kot Badal Khan. They would have travelled the distance from and to their village in bullock carts, which were used by the farming community for the local transportation of their produce and their families. The whole village would have come out to meet or see Nathoo as the train of carts approached the village. Nathoo would have felt very proud at the reception he got, and very happy to be in his village among his kith and kin. It would have been an exciting and unforgettable day for him, with people coming to meet him and hear about his life in Scotland, till late at night.

The next few days would have been nearly as busy for Nathoo as the day of his arrival. According to custom, relations and family friends from the surrounding villages and from across the river would come to see him and to offer their congratulations to his parents (if they were still alive) and other members of the family for the safe and successful return of their son. Nathoo would be relaxing and enjoying the attention and affection of so many people. He would have stayed put in his village until every relative and friend had made their customary call on him and his parents. All these friends and relations would, before leaving, extend their invitations to Nathoo to visit them before he left again. Nathoo was obliged by tradition to pay a visit to all of them, living far or near, accept their hospitality, and stay with them for at least a day or two.

So, after resting for a few weeks in his village, he would have started on his numerous visitations. Transportation in rural areas in those days was limited to bullock carts or horsetraps. Moving from one place to another, therefore, was highly time-consuming and rather irksome, especially for somebody who had lived in a European country for the last seven or eight years. But it had to be done and Nathoo Mohammed did it. He went round and saw his relatives and friends spread over the sub-divisions of Nakodar and Jagraon, on both sides of the river Sutlej. Mr Fateh Mohammed Sharif recalled vividly the occasion when he met Nathoo Mohammed for the first time in 1926 at Mr Sharif's house. The two families were closely related and Nathoo had come to visit them at their village, Madarpura, in the Jagraon sub-division, across the river Satlej at a distance of eight or nine miles from Kot Badal Khan. Mr F. M. Sharif came to the UK in 1929 and joined his uncle, Ata Mohammed Ashraf in Belfast. He moved to London in 1933. From there he was bombed out during the War and came to Glasgow. Later on he became deeply involved in community and voluntary work and subsequently emerged as a highly respected and very popular member of the Asian community in Scotland. He was awarded the MBE in 1984 in recognition of his selfless services. He died in 1988.

During these visits and in all his conversations when he

was in India, his friends and relations would have been very anxious to know about his life and work in Scotland, particularly about the opportunities for themselves and others if they went there. Nathoo would have related the story of his success with relish to impress his listeners, and the obvious prosperity of his family would have borne him out. This would have kindled greater enthusiasm in many a heart to go to Scotland. Nathoo would have thus received many requests and even appeals from the hard-pressed peasantry and other working-class people of the area to allow them, their son or a brother to join him in Glasgow and for him to assist them there. He would have, naturally, and as the tradition demanded, acceded to their requests and promised to help and guide all those who came to him. How far he kept his promises, and how many newcomers he did help will be discussed in the next section.

Once he had finished his visitations, Nathoo would have settled down again in his village, enjoying his well-deserved rest. It is not known whether he had planned to stay as long in India as he did, or if certain family circumstances compelled him to stay longer than he intended to. What is apparent is that he did not come back to Glasgow until the latter half of 1927, having stayed away for over one year. His passport, which he had acquired when he became a lascar in Bombay in 1917, expired in April 1927. He therefore had to get a new passport before he could travel back to Scotland. On 24 April 1927, he obtained his new passport (number 24975) from Lahore. After that was done he probably started to make arrangements for his return journey. His arrival in Glasgow, sometime in the second half of 1927, is confirmed by the fact that the tenancy of the house in Brown Street was changed back to his name in the Valuation Roll for the year 1928–9.

Before he went to India, Nathoo was obtaining his merchandise from London. These arrangements were not very satisfactory as he had to depend upon the integrity and choice of the suppliers to send him the right kind and quality of garments. Also, being 400 miles away from London, he could not find out in time whether he was getting the goods at the right price or not. He therefore sent one of his brothers, named

Fateh Mohammed, to London. Fateh Mohammed settled in London and became a market trader there. On his days off he visited various wholesale establishments and selected goods for his own business and also for Nathoo, which he sent by post or rail to Glasgow. This move proved very profitable for Nathoo and his brothers. Nathoo's success, and also the steady increase in the number of Indian pedlars, inspired others, who incidentally had been looked after by Nathoo, to go into the wholesale business. A proper warehouse was opened in 1932, and another two in 1934, by Indian entrepreneurs to cater for their countrymen. These warehousemen were literate and they also knew a little English. They therefore established their businesses in an organised way in commercial premises in the main thoroughfares. Nathoo's limited wholesale business which he still operated from his house was affected adversely by this. Louise had also left him a few years back. Perhaps she could not bear the taunts and tension of living with a black man any more. Nathoo, none the less, carried on his business from his house for another few years until he was forced out of it due to lack of supplies soon after the start of World War II. During all this time he had not neglected his travelling, which was still a steady source of income for him.

Nathoo had developed asthma over the years in the damp and cold climate of Scotland and now when he was getting on in years his condition was giving him a lot of trouble. During the war, when every able-bodied man was required to join the armed forces or work in the factories to help the war effort, Nathoo was excused because of his asthma. In the winter of 1941–2, his condition grew worse and he was admitted to hospital. The disease, however, proved fatal and Nathoo died on 11 August 1942, at the age of 50. He is buried in the Northern Necropolis, Maryhill Cemetery, Glasgow.

THE PEDLARS

Most of Nathoo's compatriates in Scotland in the early 1920s were lascars or ex-servants. There were, of course, quite a number of Indian students in various Scottish universities, but here we are not concerned with them. Our concern here is with those who came to work and to seek their fortune in this land.

The number of such people in Scotland at that time was very low compared with England or even Wales; and nearly all of them were in Glasgow. Their numbers, however, started to increase steadily from the middle of the third decade. When Nathoo did well in travelling or peddling and realised the potential in that trade for hard-working young men, he sent first for his two younger brothers from India, who arrived in 1924. Also, when word spread among the Indian communities in England that their countrymen were doing well in peddling, some of them who had connections came to Scotland. But most of the newcomers came straight from India, and were mainly Nathoo's relations and friends, all from the Nakodar and Jagraon areas. Mr Mohammed Ali says that his father came to Nathoo in 1924. His family belonged to the village of Haripur, which is only a mile and half from Kot Badal Khan. The *Sunday Mail* of 17 May 1925, reporting the murder of Noor Mohammed, mentioned that 'the dead man and his fellow countrymen only came to Glasgow about nine months ago', indicating that the deceased and two or three of his companions, obviously Shahab Din, Qutub Din and Mohammed Bakhsh, came in about the middle of 1924. This confirms the arrival of at least half a dozen newcomers to Glasgow in 1924. Mr Mohammed Ali does not know whether his father came alone, or with another two or three as was the norm. It would be more likely that he came with a small group, making it probable that between six and twelve new faces joined the community in that year.

1925 was a traumatic year for the small Indian community in Glasgow. The brutal attack on one of their houses and the dreadful murder of Noor Mohammed must have been a terrible experience for those quiet and timid people. Nevertheless, more newcomers kept joining them. Covering the funeral of the murdered man, the *Daily Record* of 20 May 1925 reported that 'about 50 Indians ... were included in the funeral procession'. This figure of 50 Indians in Glasgow, in May 1925, is probably about right. Some mourners, though, might have come from

119

outside Glasgow for the funeral, but then some from Glasgow may not have been able to attend, thus balancing the numbers. In the photograph of the funeral procession printed in various newspapers, many white people, both male and female, can be spotted in the congregation. These were, perhaps, the kind neighbours and friends who attended the funeral. In spite of all the suffering and sorrow during this year, at least three more flats were added to the stock of houses tenanted by the Indians in Glasgow.

Mr Ata Mohammed Ashraf and his cousin Ghulam Mohammed Sharif, of Madarpura village, came in 1926 to join Nathoo who was their close relative. Mr Thakur Singh of Haripur village also came to Nathoo in the same year. He was, probably, the first Sikh Jat to come to Scotland. Another gentleman by the name of Ali Mohammed, of the village of Chak Mughlani, arrived with possibly three or four others before the close of the year 1926. According to Mr Ashraf, when he came 'there were about 40 to 45 Indians in Glasgow, all living in the Anderston and Port Dundas districts. They were mostly illiterate Muslim peasant farmers from villages in the Nakodar and Jagraon areas. There were also two or three Pathans, from the North West Frontier Province, two or three lascars from Mirpur in Kashmir, and two or three from Bengal. Many of these people were ex-seamen who had jumped ship,. . . two or three were ex-soldiers who were in this country during the war and had come back here after getting demobbed in India. All of them were engaged in selling door-to-door out of bags'.

By the end of 1926 there must have been over 60 members of this growing community, as every year since at least 1924 between six and twelve new arrivals have been traced. Mr Khair Mohammed came in 1927. He came to join his brother Boota 'who had come here three to four years earlier'. They were from Sadrpur village, situated on the southern bank of the river Sutlej in the sub-division of Jagraon. There were five in the group in which Khair Mohammed came, and they all came to Glasgow. Another four traceable newcomers in 1927 were Qadir Bakhsh and Noor Mohammed of Salimpur, Narain Singh of Pabam, and Mansa Ram of Talwan. There is evidence

Under this Stone Lyes Interred
the Body of
WILLIAM HAMILTON Surgeon,
who departed this life the 4th Decem. 1717.
his Memory ought to be dear to this Nation, for the Credit he gain'd y. English
in Curing FERRUKSEER, the present
KING of INDOSTAN of a Ma-
lignant Distemper by which he
made his own Name famous at the
Court of that Great Monarch;
and without doubt will perpetu-
ate his Memory, as well in Great Britt.
as all other Nations in Europe.

William Hamilton's funerary inscription.

The Mughal Emperor, Shah Alam, granting sovereign rights in
Bengal to Robert Clive, August 1765.

A dinner party in the 1840s. The guests all have their own servants.

An elaborate hookah.

Alexander Gardner, proud of his Scottish heritage, wearing his tartan uniform made by native tailors.

William Palmer with his Indian wife, the Bibi Faiz Baksh, his children and maids, Calcutta, 1786.

The British revenge after the uprising of 1857.

His Highness Mahrajah Duleep Singh in his youth.

Queen Victoria with Munshi Abdul Karim, Indian Secretary to HM the Queen at Balmoral.

A nautch girl. An Indian dancing girl entertaining British officers.

Two smiling Indian nannies (from Madras) seen pushing the prams of their wards, Ian Davidson and his cousin Mary, in Great Western Road, Glasgow.

The staff and committee of the Muslim School, run by the Muslim Mission, Glasgow, in 1962.

Nathoo Mohammed.

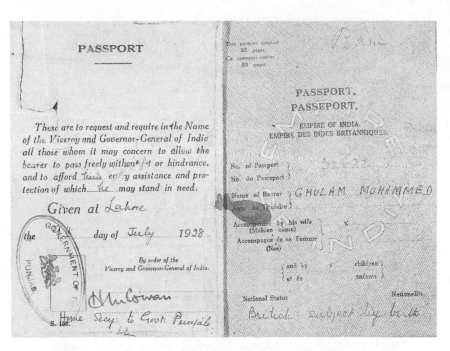

The inside cover and page 1 of the passport of Ghulam
Mohammed, who came to Scotland in 1928.

that 15 persons came in 1928, and it is most probable that there were quite a few more. Thus their numbers by the end of 1928 were perhaps about 100, and they had tenanted at least ten houses by then.

It must be said that it is impossible to trace every newcomer who came from India in those years. It is, therefore, very likely that there were more than those who have been traced and listed here. Thus the figures given in this study should not be taken as definitive, but as reasonably accurate estimates.

This unusual phenomenon of uneducated simple people, from remote villages in a relatively small and obscure area of Punjab, coming to Scotland to make their fortunes is indeed perplexing. The key to this enigma, of course, is Mr Nathoo Mohammed. As we know, he was doing rather well since he started peddling. He had called over two of his own brothers and also a few other relations and friends. With three of them here things were even better. Their letters and particularly their remittances back home carried the news of their good fortune in Scotland. Their families would have also talked about or shown off their new-found affluence to their relations, friends, and others living in their own and other villages. This revelation then acted as a stimulus for all young men living in those sleepy small villages and induced many of them to head for Scotland. Soon the small community of ex-lascars in Scotland was swamped by the new breed of young Indian pedlars.

The steep rise in the number of newcomers from 1927 onward can be attributed to Nathoo's visit to India, and to the multiplication of the contacts then available in Scotland. During his stay in India, Nathoo inspired and encouraged many, and his promises of help and hospitality would have prompted even the most reluctant to come over. Also, all those who were now here, and had been encouraged and helped by Nathoo, were in turn encouraging and helping their own relations and friends to come to Scotland. Thus the process of chain migration started by Nathoo in the early twenties was in full swing by the late twenties. Within another couple of years there were young men in Scotland from Tanda Oora, Mahim,

Balanda, Pabam, Talwan, Kartarpur, Haripur, Mehadpur, Malri, Nur Mahal, Adarman, Budowal, Lodhiwal, Burj Gujran, Malsian, Kiri, Kot, Salimpura, Sadrpura, Madarpura, Kishanpura, Sidwan, Tehara, Bhainie, and many more little and insignificant villages spread over a small congested area within a radius of about 10 miles around Kot Badal Khan, in the heart of Punjab.

The increase in their numbers soon created serious problems for the peddling fraternity. Each of them, so far, had his own territory, certain villages where he worked exclusively. When there were not so many, each of them knew the other's patch and avoided it as a gesture of goodwill and comradeship. But when their numbers grew the 'violation' of 'marked' areas became common. The newcomers, sometimes inadvertently, and sometimes out of necessity, started to trade in the territories 'belonging' to others. Thus the amicable and mutually beneficial, but entirely voluntary arrangement, of non-interference in each other's territories was upset. This resulted in ill feelings and also loss of business for all concerned, as the supply became greater than the demand. Furthermore, too many traders offering to sell goods on credit encouraged the not so well-off clients to take on more than they could afford to pay. This produced bad debts, which the poor pedlars could ill afford. This unsatisfactory situation resulted in some of the more desperate but adventurous ones starting to move out of Glasgow in the late twenties. The first group of three or four to 'migrate' from Glasgow, went to Edinburgh, perhaps in 1927. The same year another party left for Dundee. In 1928 a few appeared in Aberdeen. This was the beginning of the dispersal of the Indian pedlars all over Scotland. In a few years time, they were to become a familiar sight in the streets and squares of villages and towns all over Scotland, even in the remote islands.

SETTLEMENT IN EDINBURGH

Edinburgh, being the capital city of Scotland, had various official and colonial connections with India. Many Indian dignitaries and officials came there in those days on social or business trips. A lot of Indian students attended Edinburgh University and about 200 of them were normally resident in that city every year. It is most likely that these students had contacts with the Indian community in Glasgow. The Edinburgh Indian students, as has been mentioned already, were very well organised. Perhaps some of those students helped the first group of uneducated pedlars to settle in their city. Or perhaps one of the pedlars had old lascar connections which he used to facilitate their arrival and settlement in Edinburgh. In any case a few Indian pedlars had reached Edinburgh by 1927.

Mr Girdhari Lal Khatri (born in 1907) came to Edinburgh in September 1929. He was from the village of Mehadpur, situated six miles south of Nakodar and about four or five miles west of Kot Badal Khan. He says that when he arrived there were only five or six Indians, apart from students, in Edinburgh and they were all engaged in peddling, as 'unemployment was the order of the day then'. Three of this small group belonged to Tanda Oora village, a couple of miles east of Mehadpur. They were all lodging with Scottish families. Mr Khatri joined them in lodgings as well as in vocation, and started earning a living by selling readymade garments in housing schemes and villages surrounding the city. Mr Khatri married a local lady in 1933.

The Edinburgh community did not expand over the years. Mr Sher Mohammed of Tehara village, in the sub-division of Jagroan, came to Scotland in 1935. His relatives, who had moved to Edinburgh from Glasgow in 1927 or 1928, sponsored him to come over. According to him, there were only between eight and ten Indians resident in Edinburgh in 1935, and they were all travellers. All of them were then living in Jamaica Street, about half in a house owned by one of them and the other half in a lodging house, maintained by a Scottish lady, a couple of doors away. Thus this small group maintained their cohesion in the big city. There were also three or four Indian pedlars living in lodgings at Broxburn, and two or three at Inverkeithing, both near Edinburgh. These two groups had also come from Glasgow. Mr Sher Mohammed states that he did not know English at all. He was therefore given intensive tuition in necessary English words and phrases by his friends before he was put on the road with a bag.

Mr Wali Ahmed Khan arrived in Edinburgh in 1937 to join Mr Bal Krishan, a friend of his father's. He also confirms that there were only between eight and ten Indians living in that city when he came. Mr Khan had a good schooling and was a reasonably educated gentleman. He knew the English language and had served an an officer in the Shanghai (China) Police force before he came to Scotland. But he also could not find employment anywhere in Scotland, and had to resort to peddling to survive. According to Mr Khan, the total number of Indians resident in Edinburgh at the start of the Second World War was about ten, and this figure is confirmed by Mr Khatri and Mr Sher Mohammed. This means that, in the twelve-year period since the arrival of the first batch of Indian pedlars from Glasgow in 1927, their numbers had gone up by only six or seven. Although Edinburgh was attracting most of the students coming from India, obviously it proved the least attractive place for the Indian workers or labourers. The few pedlars in the city had to travel to the outlying mining communities and poorer working-class villages to find trade. Nobody from the environs of the city proper would entertain them. The reserved and snobbish attitude of the citizens of Edinburgh towards these dark strangers was somewhat intimidating and discouraging as has been made clear by the interviewees from that city. This major impediment probably militated against the growth of an Indian community in Edinburgh between the two world wars.

As the distance was not that great and there were frequent transport facilities between the two cities, the Edinburgh group kept in constant touch with the Glasgow community. From Edinburgh they usually travelled to Glasgow every weekend. This gave them the opportunity of seeing their friends regularly, listening to all the latest news from home, brought by the steady stream of newcomers, and also of buying their merchandise from Glasgow wholesalers.

Mr Bal Krishan had gone home to India towards the end of 1937 to visit his family. He came back with his wife in 1939, just before the outbreak of the Second World War. This was perhaps the first family unit among the resident Indians, and Mrs Bal Krishan was probably the first Indian female to join that community in Scotland. A couple of Indians joined the armed forces during the war and the rest found employment in war-related works. The Edinburgh community remained static until well after the war. It was not until the dust had settled down after the independence and the partition of India that Edinburgh saw any addition to its resident Indian community. The traffic of students which had halted during the war years started again in 1945. A restaurant to cater for the tastes of Indian students, and also for those Scots who had acquired a taste for exotic Indian food during the period of their service in that country, was opened by Mr Wali Ahmed Khan, in Lothian Street, in 1946. This in all probability was the first Indian restaurant in Scotland.

SETTLEMENT IN DUNDEE

As has been mentioned, three or four Indian pedlars left Glasgow for Dundee in about 1927. It must have been a very reluctant and tentative move on their part as Dundee is about 80 miles from Glasgow. Those who were going to Dundee would have known that they would not be able to remain in regular contact with the main community in Glasgow, and that they would become isolated. The situation, however, was such that they had to leave Glasgow and try their luck in a new territory. The question then arises, how and why did they decide to go to Dundee? Had they a contact there or did they just take a chance? There is a strong possibility that they had a contact, otherwise it would have been rather difficult for those illiterate, simple, and diffident strangers to get settled in a new and strange city. Dundee was a seaport frequented by Indian seamen and with wide and well-established connections with India, especially the Province of Bengal. So it is possible that this contact was a seaman, or someone else from India, and he looked after this first group.

There was, we know, a general practitioner, an Indian doctor called J. D. Saggar, who had been practising in Dundee since 1925. Dr Saggar was from the same area of Punjab as most of the Indian pedlars. Therefore, it is very likely that his presence in Dundee was known to some in Glasgow, and those who departed for Dundee may have gone to him for help. Sadly, those who came to Dundee in 1927, and Dr Saggar himself, are all gone now. It is, therefore, not possible to establish with certainty exactly when and how or to whom those pioneers went. One gentleman, who came to Dundee in 1931, is fortunately still alive. He is 85-year-old Mr Mohammed Boota, who talked very highly of Dr Saggar and reminisced that the good doctor always helped and took care of his countrymen. This statement, in the absence of any evidence to the contrary, gives support to the argument that the contact of the first group to Dundee was Dr Saggar.

According to Mr Boota, who incidentally is now affectionately known as Uncle Boota in the Dundee Indo-Pakistani fraternity, there were about ten of his countrymen in Dundee when he joined them. They travelled on bicycles with their merchandise in the rural areas around Dundee, as the transport facilities there were not as regular nor as good as around Glasgow or Edinburgh. Mr Boota had no education at all. He was thus unable to speak or understand English in his early years, and used signs and gestures with his hands and face to communicate with Scottish people or to do business with his customers. Some of the Indians started to go as far as Aberdeen, Peterhead, Banff, and Elgin from Dundee, using trains and buses to call at such far-off places. The Dundonian pedlars obtained their supplies from London as well as from Glasgow. Sometimes they travelled to Glasgow at the weekends and at other times ordered their supplies which were sent to them by post or rail. Mr Boota also recalls that there were a lot of comings and goings to and from Dundee in the 1930s. People would come from Glasgow, stay a few months in Dundee, establish their rounds in an area or a town in the north east of Scotland and then move there. Thus Dundee, because of its situation perhaps, acted as a springboard for the dispersal of Indian pedlars to the north of Scotland. Not very many of the Indians settled in Dundee. In 1939, there were between 15 and 20 of them, living in groups in four or five houses in the Hill Town area of the city.

DR J. D. SAGGAR

The most interesting Indian, however, in Dundee in those days was Dr Jainti Dass Saggar. He was one of those Indian students who decided not to go back to his own country. Born in 1898 in a small village called Daherra in the Ludhiana district of Punjab, young J. D. Saggar came to Dundee as a student in the year 1919. He graduated in 1923 as a Bachelor of Medicine and Bachelor of Surgery from the University College, St Andrews. He also obtained diplomas in public health and in ophthalmic medicine and surgery. In 1925 he started his practice in Dundee. At that time he was perhaps the only Indian resident in Dundee.

In a few years he gained the confidence and respect not only of his patients but also of the other citizens, by his professional skill, his courteous manners and his genial personality. He became an active member of the Labour Party and involved himself in community work to help the poor and the under-privileged. Being a bachelor, he soon won the hand of a native girl, Jane Quinn, daughter of a bailie and town councillor of the city of Dundee. To marry a white girl in those colonial days would definitely have caused a stir, if not a storm, but to marry the daughter of one of the city fathers, the doctor must have had impeccable credentials and a most impressive personality and character. In 1936 he was elected a town councillor, topping the poll in his ward. He thus became the first black or Asian local authority councillor in Scotland.

He served as a Dundee town councillor for 18 years. During his political career he won a great measure of popularity from colleagues of all political opinions, and a lasting respect for the sincerity with which he championed so many causes. To be elected as a councillor in 1936, from a ward where there was not a single black vote, is indeed a remarkable achievement. To sustain that achievement for 18 years, however, is even more remarkable for an Indian gentleman who came from nowhere and became a popular and a successful politician of his adopted city. He was greatly admired in the Labour and trade union movements. As a councillor he became the secretary of the Dundee Town Council Labour Group. It was probably due to his efforts and his influence in the local Labour Party that Mr Krishna Menon was adopted as Parliamentary candidate for Dundee in 1939. Mr Menon was a councillor then for St Pancras in London. Soon after, though, his candidature was suspended because of certain differences which arose between Mr Menon and the Labour Party.

Health and education were two of the services in which councillor Dr Saggar had a deep interest. He was convenor of the Corporation's Public Health Committee for a long time. On the education side, he was always seeking to provide opportunities that would give the ordinary child a chance to have the best in education. In the 1954 municipal elections, his wife Jane was also elected as a councillor and they became the first man and wife team on the Dundee Council. This team did not last for long, however, as only a couple of months later Dr Saggar died at the early age of 56. Paying tribute to him on his death, the then Lord Provost of Dundee, the Rt Hon. William Hughes said: 'He was a man full of compassion for everyone in need ... he came to Dundee from halfway across the world but no son of Dundee had greater love for its people or worked harder in their interest. Dundee is much the poorer by his passing.'

Dr Saggar had invited his two younger brothers to join him, and a nephew also came later. One of the brothers, Dhani Ram, also qualified as a doctor and joined the practice in 1931. He became a popular and respected citizen in his own right through his involvement in so many voluntary welfare organisations and other acts of public service. He died in 1974 after a full and successful career. The tradition of General Practice is now being carried on by Dr Karam Saggar, the nephew of the deceased Dr Saggar. In recognition of the services of the Saggar family to the people of the city,

Dundee Corporation named one of their streets 'Saggar Street' in the 1970s. A library was also opened in 1974 in memory of the Saggar brothers.

ABERDEEN REACHED

A small party of Indian pedlars had also reached Aberdeen by about 1928. It is not clear whether they had come straight from Glasgow or had moved up from Dundee. Obviously from Dundee it would have been easier for them to establish connections with Aberdeen and to prepare the ground before appearing there in the absence of any definite contact. We are told by Mr Boota, who lived in Dundee throughout the 1930s, that the city was used as a stepping stone by most of those who penetrated into the north and north east of Scotland in that period. It is, therefore, quite possible that those pathfinders, having at first come from Glasgow to Dundee, a little later moved on to Aberdeen.

The possibility of a contact in Aberdeen, however, cannot be ruled out, as evidence has come to light that an Indian gentleman lived in that city from 1903 to 1951. The circumstances surrounding his arrival in Aberdeen are very romantic as well as somewhat tragic. Diwan Tulsi Dass was born in 1882 at Lahore into a high-caste Hindu family. His father Diwan Gurditt Mall was a well-off and well-known advocate of Lahore. Young Tulsi Dass was sent to London by his father in 1900 to study medicine at King's College. During his studies he met and struck up a friendship with an attractive young girl named Grace Maxwell Muller, daughter of Dr Charles Maxwell Muller, a surgeon of King's College. Soon the friendship between the two young people developed into a serious romance and they decided to get married. Unfortunately for the couple, the parents on both sides, for obvious reasons, disapproved of their romantic involvement and opposed their permanent union. Grace was under 21 years of age and thus unable to marry under English law without the consent of her parents, which they refused to give. The young lovers, impatient to take their sacred vows and be together, therefore decided to elope to Gretna Green in Scotland, where English law did not apply. However, at the railway station ticket office in London, in their haste and excitement, they forgot the name Gretna Green and bought tickets for Aberdeen, the only major place name in Scotland they could recall at that particular moment. They therefore duly arrived in Aberdeen in June 1903.

The runaway couple did not know anybody in Aberdeen and had no contacts whatsoever in that part of the country, but somehow they found accommodation and settled down. On 19 July 1903, they got married at the Registry Office and thus love triumphed over race, class and creed barriers. Sadly, their respective families disowned them so that, having found each other, Mr and Mrs Dass lost their parents. It is certain that Mr Dass never went back to India after his marriage and none of his family ever came to visit him in Scotland. Mrs Dass, however, was eventually forgiven, at least by her mother, who did let her daughter visit her occasionally in London.

Mr Dass must have found a good job or may have gone into a business of his own soon after the marriage, as only a few years later he became quite a successful businessman, owning a billiards saloon and also a general store in Rosemount, Aberdeen. During the First World War, Mr Dass enlisted and joined the armed forces. On his return from the army after the war, he went into the taxi business and also became a partner in a garage business. A few years later he took up teaching Hindustani at Aberdeen University. So, by the late 1920s, he had achieved a reasonably prominent position in the city and society he was living in. It is therefore possible that he was known to some Indian seamen or servants who had been in Aberdeen during the second or third decades of the present century, or who had heard of him from other sources. In that case, the Indian pedlars who went to Aberdeen in the late 1920s might have sought the help and cooperation of Mr Dass.

Mr Dass died in Aberdeen in 1951 at the age of 69. However, one of his daughters, Mrs Susan Selby who is now 82 years old, remembers an Indian 'salesman' (pedlar) by the name of Mr Rahmatullah, who used to call on her father and play chess with him. Unfortunately, because of her advanced age and rather poor health, she is not able now to recollect any approximate dates or even the relevant period. She does, however, remember the circumstances in which her father met Mr Rahmatullah. According to Mrs Selby, her father was called out one night to a hospital in Aberdeen to interpret for some Indian patients who were suffering from gas poisoning. It so happened that a newcomer from India had joined a group of Indian pedlars working in the vicinity of Aberdeen. They were living in lodgings which had gas lamps in the bedrooms. For some reason or other, the newcomer had to go to bed last and was therefore told to put out the light before he turned in. Now this illiterate or semi-literate young man from a backward small village in India had never used or even seen gas lamps. The only lamps he had ever used or seen in his native land were the simple earthen oil lamps which one blew out to put off the light. He therefore blew out the gas lamp and went to sleep. As the gas had not been turned off, it soon filled their bedroom. Their landlady, or somebody else in the house perhaps, smelled the gas, investigated and called the ambulance. The hospital staff and the police, finding themselves unable to communicate properly with the gassed Indians, called upon Mr Dass for his assistance in interpreting. Unfortunately, one of the Indians died but the others survived. Mr Rahmatullah was either a survivor or another member of that little group. (I am grateful to Mrs S. Selby and Dr Gurudeo S. Saluja of Aberdeen for this information. Without Dr Saluja's cooperation it would not have been possible for me to speak to Mrs Selby. Mr Muhammed Ali confirms the gas incident, which he says happened before his arrival in 1938. Indeed it is Mr Ali who gave the information that one of the Indians involved in the gas accident died.)

There is, however, no evidence of any long-term settlement of Indian pedlars in Aberdeen during the period between the two world wars. The groups which operated in and around Aberdeen and the north in those days were like roving pedlars. They stayed at a place for a few months, or even a year or so, and then moved on to another town or another area. Glasgow remained their base, which they usually returned to, from wherever they were, after every four or five weeks, to see their friends and relations and to obtain their supplies.

FURTHER DISPERSAL AND DEVELOPMENT OF THE COMMUNITY

In the meantime many more newcomers from India were joining their relatives and friends in Scotland. By the end of the third decade, the total number of Indians operating as door-to-door salesmen in Scotland must have been about 175, approximately 125 in Glasgow and the rest scattered in various other places. In the 1930/31 Valuation Roll for the city of Glasgow, there are at least 21 houses registered as being tenanted and occupied by Indians. The rapid growth in their numbers corresponds with the higher demand for and acquisition of more houses. At the same time the number of houses occupied by them gives us a reliable clue to the size of the community.

Another interesting feature of their settlement, particularly in Glasgow, is that they were congregating in old and congested areas of the city. In 1928, out of the ten houses they occupied in Glasgow, eight were in the Port Dundas district of the city and six out of those eight were in one street, i.e. Roslin Place. In 1930 the total number of houses occupied by them in the same area had gone up to about 15, and ten were in Roslin Place. The reason for their attraction to the Port Dundas area, and particularly to Roslin Place, was that the properties there were dilapidated and derelict. The houses were in a terrible state of disrepair. The rent, therefore, was very low and in some cases nil, and the houses were 'available' even to the Indians. Naturally, the thrifty Indian pedlars, like all poor immigrants, flocked to these terrible slums in the narrow and dingy streets of Port Dundas. They were also occupying a few houses in the Anderston district of Glasgow. These were slums too, but not as bad as the Port Dundas hovels. In addition, according to the records of the year 1930/31, they had acquired a couple of houses in the Gorbals area which lies on the south side of the River Clyde and which was notorious for its slums and deprivation. In the next few years the bulk of the Indian community in Glasgow came over to the Gorbals when the Port Dundas tenements were demolished in the mid and late thirties.

In 1930, a very important event occurred in the political history of Scotland. An Indian politician residing in the United Kingdom participated in a Parliamentary by-election held in the Glasgow Shettleston constituency in June of that year. The by-election was caused by the death of the Rt Hon. J. Wheatley M.P. (Labour) in early 1930. The Communist Party put up Mr Shahpurji Saklatvala as their candidate. Mr Saklatvala did not do very well in this contest in Glasgow. He received only 1459 votes, a mere 5.8% of the total votes cast, but he became the first Asian or black candidate to contest an election for a public office in Scotland. He did far better in London where he was twice elected as Member of Parliament from Battersea North constituency, first in 1922 and again in 1924. Although he was a member of the Communist Party, his candidature was endorsed by the Labour Party in 1922. On winning that seat he became the first Asian Labour/Communist M.P. and the third Asian to enter the British House of Commons.

Saklatvala was the son of a rich businessman of Bombay. He was born in 1874 and received a good education. He came to Britain in 1905, to join the family business of J. N. Tata which had its offices in Manchester. Becoming interested in politics, he joined the Liberal Party. Soon he became disenchanted with the Liberals and left them to join the Labour Party. A little later he abandoned the Labour Party for the Communist Party. All his life he fought for the independence of India and the freedom of all from colonialism. He devoted his life to the cause of socialism and fought for the rights and welfare of the British working classes.

1931 saw the start of the economic recession in this country. The working classes and the poorer people were the worst affected. Soon they had no work and no incomes. The hungry thirties had set in with a vengeance. The Indian pedlars and other traders felt the effects of mass unemployment and the resulting poverty and deprivation. The trade of the pedlars was dependent upon credit clientele from the poorer working classes. Those were people with low incomes who, being unable to buy with cash from the shops, bought on instalments from the Indian pedlars. Under the prevailing circumstances many of these people had no incomes. They were therefore neither in a position to take on any more debt, nor able to pay the weekly instalments for goods they had taken already on credit. The hard-working simple travellers were shocked by these ominous developments. The trade which, a short time ago, was providing them with enough income to keep themselves here and maintain their families in India, became so bad that they could hardly earn enough to survive alone. The whole Indian community became frustrated and afraid of the future, but newcomers kept arriving as news of the misfortunes here had perhaps not yet reached them in the Punjab. By the middle of 1932, when the slump had become very severe, some of the Indians in Scotland became so discouraged and disappointed that they lost their nerve and returned to India. It was after the return home of those dejected people that the flow of new arrivals abated a little.

Those operating in industrial areas like Glasgow, where unemployment had become very acute, moved out to the farming and fishing communities. Instead of giving up and packing their bags, they decided to look for new territories and greener pastures. Nearly all the small bands which left the cities at this stage headed for the north and north east of Scotland. The rural areas and the fishing towns of this region were probably not as badly affected by the recession as the industrial belts; also, perhaps the lack of shopping facilities in those far-flung hamlets, farmsteads and villages made the inhabitants appreciate and patronise the service provided by these strangers. Whatever the reason, the Indian traders managed to do better in those new areas than the places they had left. This encouraged more of their compatriots to move out of the cities and join them. The congestion of too many traders in the industrial areas and the severe competition among them was thus relieved to a great extent, and those remaining behind were also then able to do a little better. This situation, in which the community was forced to disperse on a much larger scale than it had been doing steadily since 1927, proved quite beneficial all round. Now everybody was at least making both ends meet and some were even doing better.

The economic situation started to improve during the latter half of the year 1933. The Indian community, though now split into small units and spread all over central and north eastern Scotland, was also feeling a little happier and regaining its confidence. The aura of this revived confidence and regained sense of security did not take long to reach the banks of the Sutlej and other parts of the Punjab. The newcomers started to arrive again in larger numbers than before. Some of those who had gone back in the last couple of years also returned. The Mirpur connection also became active at this stage, and from then on there were a few but steady number of arrivals from that part. The relations and friends of Hari Singh were further adding to the number of arrivals. The North West Frontier and the Bengal connections strangely remained inactive, and not many came to join those who were in Scotland from these two regions of India. The bulk of the new faces again were from the two sub-divisions of Nakodar and Jagraon.

Another development at this stage was the appearance of an occasional individual from a part of the Punjab which had been colonised under a new irrigation project at the beginning of the twentieth century. As has been mentioned earlier, some farmers from Nakodar and Jagroan areas were given virgin lands in the new canal colonies. These colonists, naturally, maintained their links with relatives and friends in their old villages. Their new abodes were at a distance of only about 150 miles from their original homes. Communications, therefore, were easy and frequent and so the colonists were also aware of the exploits of those of their relations who were in Scotland. The first generation colonists were now old men with grown-up sons and even grandsons. They themselves were perhaps quite content to develop and farm their new lands in their new surroundings, but they prompted their sons and grandsons to join their relations in Scotland, to maintain and enhance, if possible, the relative prosperity of their growing families.

The two particular new villages from where this process started are in a district recently renamed Faisalabad, but originally called Lyallpur, after Sir James Lyall, Lieutenant Governor of the Punjab from 1887 to 1892. These villages lie at a distance of about one and a half miles from each other; one is called Chak No. 477 G.B. alias Kot, and the other Chak No. 482 G.B. alias Jagraon. The colonists who settled at Chak No. 477 G.B. came from a village called Kot Mohammed Khan, situated on the south bank of the river Sutlej, in the sub-division of Jagraon, and those who occupied Chak No. 482 G.B. emigrated from the town of Jagraon and its surrounding villages in that sub-division. When this district was developed as a canal colony in 1904, the British administrators of the time named or numbered these new villages as 477 G.B. and 482 G.B. (G.B. stands for Goghera Branch, the name of the irrigation distributory.) The settlers, however, gave the names of their ancestral villages to their new abodes, and hence the double names which are now in common use. In the 1930s only a few came from these villages, and one of these was Mr Sher Muhammed (see Chapter 5). But after the independence and partition of India, migrants from this area, as we shall see, dominated the scene in Scotland.

Until 1932, the Indian traders bought their merchandise from Nathoo Mohammed and other local warehouses. Dealing with warehouses managed by non-Indians was rather inconvenient for them due to their language limitations. Nathoo, as we know, was trading in a small way from his house, and was not in a position to supply everything to everyone. The number of Indian travellers in Scotland at that time was such that they required a proper substantial warehouse from where they could buy all the goods needed for their trade. To attract the Indian fraternity, this warehouse had to be prepared to extend credit, as Nathoo was doing, and the staff had also to be able to converse with the Indian clients in their own language, as most of them were unable to understand and speak English very well. Realising the need and potential for such a business, a young Indian entrepreneur by the name of Mohammed Kaka (of the village of Kiri) opened his drapery and textiles wholesale premises at 96 Brunswick Street, Glasgow, in 1932. In the same year, a grocer's shop to cater for the tastes of the Indian community was opened by Mr Sher Qadir and his Scottish wife Mary.

The next year saw the opening of another warehouse by Mr G. M. Sharif and Mr A. M. Ashraf in Oxford Street, and a general store by another trader in Glasgow. By the end of 1935, therefore, there were at least three wholesale warehouses and three grocery/general stores owned by Indian businessmen. The tradition of Indo-Pakistanis going into the textile/drapery and grocery businesses thus started in the mid thirties. The Valuation Roll for the year 1935/36 shows at least six business premises and 34 dwelling houses occupied by members of the Indian community in Glasgow. Fourteen of their houses and three business premises were in the Gorbals district, signifying that the process of their concentration in that area had started in earnest. This also indicates that their numbers in Glasgow in the mid thirties were nearly 175, and if we add 125 to that, the approximate number of those outwith Glasgow, then the total in Scotland in 1935 would be about 300. Around this time they had penetrated as far as Wick, Thurso and the Outer Hebrides.

It is strange though that there is no evidence of these traders operating anywhere in the south of Scotland during the period between the two world wars. They reached as far as Stroma and Stornoway in the north, yet they did not travel south to towns as near as Melrose or Moffat. One possible reason for their absence from this region could be that sizable market towns were evenly spread over this area, and farmers and the general rural population had easy access to these towns with good shopping facilities. Hence, they did not encourage or patronise the Indian pedlar. Another factor could have been the attitude of the lowlanders and borderers towards the Indians. Perhaps they were not as friendly and as considerate as the highlanders and islanders, and this discouraged the timid and sensitive Indians from establishing their business contacts in that area.

Life was a lot easier now for those who were living in Glasgow. They had easy access to their merchandise which they could obtain any time they desired. The traditional ingredients for their food and all the spices were readily available from the shops owned by their countrymen. These shops, and especially the warehouses, also served as meeting places for those lonely men, where they met their friends and heard all the gossip. They had very little, if any, communication with the local people beyond their trade dealings. They did not go to public bars or clubs as most of them did not drink, and not many of them could afford to drink anyway. They did not finish their rounds till late in the evenings, and so did not reach home till late at night. Their lack of confidence and their deficiency in the English language prevented them from going to the dance halls and the cinemas. Their lives, therefore, revolved round their work.

The routine of their normal day was simple and unvaried. After breakfasting, they went to the warehouses to replenish their stocks and to meet their countrymen. Before noon they would come back to their homes, have lunch, pack their bags and go out on their rounds to their particular area or village for that day. They used buses to get to their destinations. Most of their business was done in the late afternoons or evenings when the workers had come home and all the members of a family were in the house. This kept them out for long hours and they often caught the last bus home. On getting home tired and hungry, they made their supper at that late hour and ate together when everybody had come in. Their only recreation was sitting together at night or on Sundays and chatting to each other about their work, their past, their future plans and mostly about their families back home. They were quite content with such a dull pattern of life. Other forms of entertainment and recreation required money and time, and they could afford neither. They had many commitments and other responsibilities, such as maintaining their families back home, saving regularly for their fares to return home and for the capital needs of the family. To avoid boredom and nostalgia, and to live as economically as possible they lived in groups and acquired houses near each other.

The arrival of a newcomer from India was always an important and exciting occasion for the whole community. On such occasions everyone would try to go to meet and welcome the new arrival. He would be invited, along with those he came to join, for a meal by most groups in their houses. Such dinner parties provided better opportunities for the hosts to hear from the guest all the news about their people back home, and for the guest to get to know everybody. A few days after the arrival of the new man, his training would start. He would be taught the necessary English words and phrases, the names and descriptions of the various garments he would be selling and he would be familiarised with the currency. He would also be made aware of the geography of the area he would be operating in. Every member of the community, and especially his relatives or friends from the same village, would encourage and assist him morally as well as financially to prepare him for the work. When ready, the novice would be taken out by one of his friends, told to remain with him all day and observe him during his rounds. In a couple of days the beginner would be told to 'knock the doors' (canvass for sales) on one side of a street, while his friend would start on the other side, to encourage him and to keep an eye on him. Within a few days the novice would develop enough confidence to go out alone and face the day on his own.

Those who were going back to India, either for good or on a visit, after spending a term in Scotland, were also accorded special treatment. They were also dined and feasted by their compatriots before their departure, and given messages and presents to be delivered to the latters' families. They were ceremoniously seen off at the railway station by most of their colleagues and given a sentimental farewell.

It appears that the community in those days was very close-knit. They had a lot of regard and concern for each other. There were no differences of caste, creed or religion. Muslims, Sikhs, Hindus, and those who were called untouchables in India, lived here together in the same houses. Most surprisingly, however, in many cases they not only shared the same kitchen, but also ate from the same pot. This could never have happened in India. It came about because in every house the cooking at night was usually done by one member of the group on a rota basis. This man always came home earlier than the others on the night when it was his turn to prepare the meal for all those living in that house. So, whatever his caste or creed, he was the cook for that night, and the others were glad to partake of the food he had prepared when they came home late at night, tired and hungry after a hard and usually a cold and wet day's toil. This sudden disappearance of centuries-old caste and creed barriers was perhaps also due to the insecurity felt by the members of the small Indian community in this alien atmosphere. Long absences from home and a strange environment compelled them to ignore their age-old taboos and seek solace and security in the companionship of their own kind. The relations between different religious communities in the Punjab at that time also appeared to be remarkably harmonious and amicable. In the case histories compiled during the research for this study, it has been revealed many times that Sikhs and Hindus came to and were looked after by Muslims in Scotland and vice versa. The following statement by Mr Kartar Singh Seran (a Sikh gentleman) proves this point and further elucidates the state of the Indian community in this country, particularly in Glasgow, in the thirties.

'I came to Glasgow in 1932 with Mr Ali Mohammed alias Painter (a Muslim), who belonged to our village Madarpura, in the Jagraon sub-division of Ludhiana district. He had come to Scotland, probably in 1927, and went back on a visit towards the end of 1931. Ali Mohammed and my father were close friends. My father was planning to go abroad himself, but Ali Mohammed advised him to send me instead, and took it upon himself to look after me in Scotland. So I accompanied Ali Mohammed when he returned from India.

There were between 60 and 70 men from India in Glasgow then, all engaged in peddling. They were living in groups of four to eight, depending upon the size of their particular house, in the Cowcaddens/Port Dundas, Anderston and Gorbals areas. Most of them, though, were in Roslin Place and Maitland Street, Port Dundas. These were dilapidated properties, in a state of utter disrepair, with nominal or no rents. Ali Muhammed and I stayed in Seaward Street, on the south side, in the house of Mr Ghulam Mohammed. Muslims, Sikhs and Hindus all lived together. We had a common kitchen; food was cooked in turn by one member of the group for all, and all ate together at one table from one pot. There was a lot of regard, affection and concern for each other in those good old days. A newcomer was fed, clothed and looked after by the members of the community without any regard to his caste or creed until he was able to stand on his own feet.

I acquired the flat I am still living in in 1936 (in 1956 I bought this flat). My brother Hazara Singh joined me in 1949. Early in 1950 my brother and I spotted Mohammed Shafi in a warehouse in Glasgow. He had arrived only a day or two earlier. Mohammed Shafi belonged to our village, and being a Muslim he had migrated to Pakistan after the partition in 1947. Hazara Singh and Mohammed Shafi had grown up together and used to be very close friends. We therefore insisted that he come and stay with us, for old times' sake, which he kindly did until he got his own flat a year or so later.'

Life was rather hard and comparatively uncomfortable for those who had left the cities and were working in rural areas in the north of Scotland or on the islands. They normally went out in small groups and lodged with local families in a village or town in the area of their operations. Due to lack of transport facilities in the rural areas, some used bicycles while others just tramped from one village to the other or from one farm to the next. They obtained their merchandise by post or rail, and occasionally one or two of them travelled to Glasgow and carried it back for the whole group. They bought their foodstuff from the local grain stores and prepared meals themselves in their lodgings. Contact with their own countrymen was very infrequent and communication with their families in India was only through the exchange of an occasional letter. They led very deprived, isolated and harsh

141

lives. Their isolation was so bad that they were seldom aware of their religious festivals and rarely performed any religious rites or observed their obligations.

Mr Khair Mohammed was one of those who left Glasgow in 1929. First he went to Aberdeen where he had friends. From there he moved to Dundee in 1930. Dundee proved no more profitable than Aberdeen. So with two or three others he moved to Tain, where they stayed for three years. Then they operated from Dingwall for a couple of years. In 1936 Mr Khair Mohammed crossed over to Stornoway, on the Isle of Lewis, which a relative of his had reached a year before, in 1935. According to Khair Mohammed this gentleman was the first Indian ever to reach that place.

Mr Khair Mohammed narrated that, if ever they could not get back to their lodgings after finishing their business in the evenings, it was often very difficult to find accommodation for the night. On such occasions they would ask a farmer's permission to spend the night in his barn where they slept on the hay. Alternatively, they would go to the local police station and ask for their assistance in finding accommodation. The police were always very helpful and obliged by either finding them lodgings or accommodating them in the 'cells'. He added that at times local people were reluctant to give them lodgings because some of them 'were scared of us dark strangers'. The children and women were particularly afraid of the 'bogeyman'.

To illustrate this xenophobia he related the following incident. 'One day while working near Tain I came to a large mansion. I knocked on the door a couple of times before I heard a faint "come in". On opening the door I found myself in a spacious hall with many doors leading off it. I knocked timidly on two or three doors before I again heard someone saying "come in". I opened that door, looked into the room and saw an old lady sitting on a chair by the fireside. When she looked up and saw my dark apparition she gave a frightful shriek and collapsed unconscious on the floor. Confronted with this unexpected scene I panicked and ran out of the house. I got such a fright that I ran back all the way to our lodgings and hid myself in our room, feeling sure that the police would soon come for me. When my colleagues returned at night I told them what had happened and they also became scared. Fortunately, no police arrived to arrest me. The fate of the old lady was never enquired into either, as all of us avoided that locality for a long time after.' Mr Mohammed, however, emphasised that in normal circumstances the attitude of the police and the public towards the Indian pedlars was generally sympathetic and helpful.

This phenomenon is also confirmed by Mr Mohammed Ali who came in 1938 to join his father. He stated 'My father was living at Elgin with another four of our countrymen. I was the sixth to join that group. We stayed there till the end of 1939 when we came back to Glasgow after the start of the war. The attitude of the Scottish people towards us, especially in the rural areas, was very good. The behaviour of the police was excellent. If any of us got lost, and many of us often did, and we asked a policeman for directions, the burly policeman on many occasions would carry our heavy case (in spite of our protestations) and take us to our destination.'

The latter half of the fourth decade of the twentieth century saw a very heavy increase in the traffic from India. The base of the Indian community in Scotland was Glasgow, so nearly everybody came there first. From there some went on to their friends in other places but most remained in Glasgow. The community, it appears, had put behind it the difficulties of the early thirties and the marks of the recession had disappeared by now. Confidence had been restored fully and they were doing well again. A couple of men of foresight had even brought over their young sons to be educated in Scotland. The first Indian boy to come over was 11-year-old M. Azam, who came in 1936 and was admitted to Buchan Street Primary School, probably in the same year. The second young scholar was M. Ibrahim Ashraf, who came in 1937 at the age of 14. He enrolled at Allan Glen's, and after his matriculation went to Edinburgh University where he did his Ph.D in agriculture. When asked about his reception and treatment at his school, he said that he did not experience any colour prejudice, intolerance, abuse or name-calling from any quarter. He added that people did notice one who was obviously different, but more as a curiosity than on account of his race or colour. Incidentally, Dr Ashraf was awarded the M.B.E. in 1965 for his services to the United Kingdom. He is perhaps the first member of the Indo-Pakistani community settled in Scotland to be so honoured.

According to the comments of those who came in the 1920s and 30s, the general attitude of the Scots towards the Indians in and around cities like Glasgow, Edinburgh and Dundee was also tolerant and inoffensive. The then ubiquitous Indian pedlar was called Johnnie by the people of Scotland and referred to as 'Johnnie the darkie'. In his presence he was called by his name, if it were easily pronounceable, otherwise he was addressed as John, or more commonly Johnnie. In his absence, however, the appellation 'the darkie' was added after Johnnie, perhaps for want of a surname. The pedlars did not mind being nicknamed 'Johnnie' and tolerated the offensive-sounding appellation 'darkie', believing that it was used for identification rather than derogatory purposes. None of those spoken to have said anything against the behaviour of the Scots. Most of them have emphasised that they did not experience any racial prejudice, abuse or discrimination. The Scottish people, they maintain, were very helpful and friendly towards them.

Most of these men, as has been mentioned before, were illiterate and were at first unable to speak and understand English. Those who had any schooling were also unfamiliar with English, as they learnt only Urdu or other vernaculars in their village schools. Through time, though, they enhanced their vocabulary by listening and learning, and some eventually became quite proficient in the English language.

Another difficulty most of them faced was the recording of the accounts. They all sold on credit and accounts had to be kept for all the customers. It was no trouble for those who knew any of the Indian languages, as they kept their accounts in that language. But those who could not write at all were left to devise their own particular ways. Some requested their customers to maintain their accounts themselves, others asked their clients to record their own entries in their particular accounts kept in the book of the traveller. Yet others trusted their memory, or followed their own ingenious ways of keeping their accounts in order and remembering who lived where and who owed how much. One old gentleman always drew a crude picture of the house or a feature of the house of the family he dealt with to identify them. Another drew small circles for every pound, a small perpendicular line for every shilling and a little horizontal line for every penny owed to him on a separate page of his notebook for every account. It seems that whatever they lacked in education they made up for with ingenuity.

For some, even getting on the right bus was a problem, as they could not read the number or the destination displayed on the front of the vehicle. They therefore waited at the bus stop and shouted their destination to the conductor or driver on the arrival of the bus. If anyone on the bus shouted back 'yes Johnnie' they hopped on, otherwise they waited for the next bus and again went through the same exercise. Life for those pioneers was really hard and even frustrating and humiliating sometimes, but they endured it all with fortitude and resilience. They did not make any fortunes during their toils in this land. What they earned was a rather small return for their entrepreneurship and the hard labour they put into their profession. However, compared with what they could possibly have earned in their own country this was a lot. In their own country they would most probably have been unemployed and living in abject poverty. In this country they were, on an average, making about one pound and ten (old) shillings (£1.50) a week. They lived frugally on approximately one third of this and saved, more or less, one pound per week. That was about five pounds a month, equivalent to 70 rupees in India. A monthly income of 70 rupees in India in those days was a great boon, as the average income of a labourer there was then about 10 to 15 rupees, or just about one pound per month. They were, therefore, quite happy and content to be in Scotland.

The Indian community in Scotland, and particularly in Glasgow, had attained the size and reached that stage, in the late 1930s, when every secluded and encapsulated group requires some kind of organisation and discipline in it, to safeguard its interests. A couple of ex-students had also joined the peddling brotherhood by then. These young men abandoned their studies for one reason or the other and, after failing to find suitable employment, took up peddling to survive. One of these educated pedlars was a Mr S. M. Joshi. According to Mr Bishen Singh Bans, 'He rendered a lot of help to his compatriots. As most of them were illiterate, Mr Joshi wrote and read their letters. He helped them in applying for and obtaining their trade licences. He interpreted for them and advised them how to stay on the right side of the law. He was, indeed, a godfather and a guide to his countrymen as long as he lived.'

Mr Bans himself came to London as a student, but due to unexpected changes in his circumstances he could not continue with his studies. He came to Glasgow in 1936 and says 'In 1937 we formed the "Hindustani Majlis", the Indian Association, to look after the welfare of Indians living in Scotland. This Association also took care of the burial or cremation arrangements of its members who died here. We contributed three (old) pence each to make up these expenses for our dead comrades.' This Association was, then, perhaps the first Indian organisation to be formed by the Indian community, as distinct from the Indian students, in this country. Mr Bans also stated that 'All the Indians in Scotland then were either Muslims or Sikhs, except two, Mr Joshi and another.' This is corroborated by Mr Santa Singh, who came over from the village of Mahim in 1938. He says 'There were about 200 Indians in Glasgow when I came. Most of them were Muslim *Arraiens* from the Nakodar and Jagraon areas. There were about 20 Sikh Jats, a few so-called untouchables, some Bhatra Sikhs (Hari Singh's clan) and only one or two Hindus.' Both Mr Bans and Mr Santa Singh are of the opinion that the first Sikh Jat to come to Scotland was Mr Thakur Singh of Haripur village and his contact here was Mr Mohammed Nathoo.

146

The absence of Hindus from the Indian immigrants was not surprising. In India, especially in its northern parts and particularly before World War II, all trade and commerce was in the hands of the Hindus. They were the village shopowners and the city factory proprietors. They were the village moneylenders and big banking magnates. Being the educated class, they were the village schoolteachers on the lower cadre, and powerful and influential civil servants on the higher end. They were the elite of Indian society, rather well-off and with no reason to migrate. Also, caste and religious considerations inhibited the Hindus from going abroad, as it was not considered possible for them to maintain their caste and religious obligations during a journey abroad and in a foreign land. The Muslims and Sikhs, on the other hand, were mostly farmers, peasants, labourers and soldiers. They were generally uneducated and poor, and willing to move with no such caste or religious fetters to restrain them.

Before the start of World War II in 1939, the Indian community had, perhaps without realising it, planted its roots in Scotland. They had organised themselves socially and culturally by founding their Indian Association. They had their own warehouses from where they could get their merchandise and financial support if they needed it. They had their own grocery stores to buy the required foodstuffs and condiments from; they had their own houses or they were living in the houses of their own countrymen, where they were able to dress, cook, behave and move about according to their own traditions and culture. They were a happy and growing community of young and middle-aged men, all self-employed, hard-working, law-abiding citizens, toiling in a strange land to better their and their children's lot. They came not to stay permanently and settle in Scotland, but to make their 'fortune' and go back to their near and dear ones left behind in their small villages. They had, nevertheless, created their own little India in the heart of Scotland.

The only thing they could not obtain, at that time, was the hallal meat, as no Muslim butcher had yet opened a shop. Some of the Muslims, therefore, bought their meat from the

Jewish kosher shops. Others abstained from eating meat, or had an arrangement with farmers or city poulterers where they bought live hens or chickens and killed those themselves according to the Muslim rite.

CHAPTER FIVE
World War II and After

LIFE DURING THE WAR YEARS

Britain's entry into World War II upset the tranquillity and trade of the Indian travellers. Being far away from their homes and their families, they were fearful and in some instances panic-stricken. A few who were lucky enough to get passage on ships bound for India went back. Others had no choice but to stay put. The introduction of rationing soon after the declaration of war put an end to their businesses as they could no longer procure the goods they dealt in. So all those who had been operating in the Highlands, the islands and the north east of Scotland came back to Glasgow. Most of those who were in Dundee and Edinburgh remained there, but everyone else from all over the country converged on their base, the city of Glasgow. During the call-up for service in the armed forces, not very many of the Indians in Scotland were accepted. Perhaps they were not thought fit for active service due to their lack of English language. Anyhow, they were enrolled to work in the munition and ordnance factories at Hillington and Bishopton, etc. By mid 1940, the community had adjusted to its new style of life, working for regular hours on the factory floor. Lack of letters and news from home worried them, but the fact that India was far away from the theatre of war was consoling.

As almost all of the Indian people in Scotland had congregated in Glasgow, their numbers in that city had risen dramatically. In the Valuation Roll for the year 1940/41, at least 74 houses are listed as occupied or tenanted by them. This figure indicates that above 400 of them were living in Glasgow in 1940, and perhaps another 50 or so were in other places, making a total of about 450 in Scotland. Most of them in Glasgow were now residing in the Gorbals; fifty of their houses were located in that particular area. This congestion in one place and a more settled life made them aware of the dereliction of their religious obligations. The need for the observance of their respective religions in turn motivated them to set up religious organisations and establish religious premises.

The Muslims, being the largest group among the Indians in Glasgow, were the first to form an organisation called 'Jamiat Ittehadul Muslimin', or the Muslim Mission, in 1940. The main objectives of this organisation were to look after the religious needs of the Muslim community in Scotland. The Mission hired premises in Gorbals Street and converted these into a temporary mosque. A couple of years later, a billiards hall with six adjoining flats in Oxford Street was bought and the mosque was transferred there. These premises served the Muslim community until the mid 1970s when, due to the redevelopment of this area, the building had to be demolished. The Sikh community followed suit and formed their 'Guru Singh Sabha', the Sikh Association, in 1941, with similar objectives to the Muslim Mission. They bought a flat at 79 South Portland Street a couple of years later and converted it into a temple.

The peddling trade did not cease altogether during the war years. There were people who had been able to 'dodge' both the draft and the factories, and they carried on the trade if and when they could get a little merchandise. Coupons had been introduced during the rationing and these helped them to acquire some goods. Some of those who were working also continued to trade in a limited way, during their spare time or holidays, to make some extra money.

The exigencies of the war brought the Indians into close contact with the local people. So far, they had avoided mixing with the Scottish people and had no social connections with them. They had business dealings with them but, due to language barriers, cultural and religious differences and their natural inhibitions, they had not tried to develop these into social links. The war conditions, however, forced them into working, meeting and mixing with the Scots in factories, in the unavoidable queues and in the air-raid shelters, etc. The Indians, like everybody else, resented this uncomfortable state of affairs in the beginning, but eventually got used to and benefited from this situation. They made friends with the natives, they learnt to speak better English due to their prolonged contact with the Scots, and both the hosts and the guests got to know each other better. A few romances also blossomed, culminating in happy marriages between a few young Indians and Scottish girls.

The massive support and active participation of the people of the Indian subcontinent in the war effort, and the involvement and performance of the Indian community in Scotland in the production of armaments and other war materials, enhanced their standing among the native people. The preferential treatment accorded, in those days, to the armament and ordnance factory workers, on public transport and in many other aspects of life, helped the Indians to shed, to some extent, their feelings of inferiority and submissiveness. Mr Mohammed Hussain, who came to Scotland in 1939 from the village of Kartarpur, near Nakodar, had only worked for a couple of months as a pedlar when he was made to work in the Royal Ordnance Factory at Bishopton. He related with pride that, on showing his pass to the bus conductor, he was always allowed to board the bus before any white passengers. He has still got that cherished pass and has obviously taken good care of it, as it is, even now after 50 years, in very good condition. Mr Bans, who worked in the ordnance factories at Bishopton and Hillington, became a foreman and had both Indians and Scots working under him. All this helped the Indian community to gain confidence and to take part in the mainstream of Scottish life. Thus the war conditions brought about the beginning, though in a small way, of the integration of the Indian immigrants into Scottish society.

In 1943, during the Bengal famine, the Scottish Indian community felt confident enough to organise a famine relief campaign to help their stricken brethren. The then Lord Provost of Glasgow, the Rt Hon. John Biggar, was approached and persuaded to accept the patronage of the campaign. A flag day was held on 20 October 1943, and the people of Glasgow were requested to donate generously. According to Mr Bans the response was excellent, and over £3000 was raised from the streets of Glasgow for the relief of the victims. The community also held meetings and sought support for the independence of India during the war years. People like Jimmy Maxton, Willie Gallacher, and other sympathisers were invited to address such meetings. Some of the Indians even started to participate in May-day parades and other anti-colonial rallies.

The Indian community remained static numerically up to the end of the war, as the journey from and to India was fraught with dangers during the hostilities. When the war ended the ordnance factories also came to a halt and the workers became redundant. The Indians did not waste any time in looking or waiting for other jobs. They picked up from where they had left off in 1939, and returned to their peddling right away. Many, however, first went home to see their families from whom they had been separated for so long.

The Indian Community After the War

The change of Government in Britain after the Second World War heralded auspicious news for the Indian subcontinent. The Labour Party headed by Mr Attlee was in favour of granting independence to India. There was, therefore, much rejoicing and a feeling of great expectation both in India and among the Indians living in Britain.

The comings and goings between Scotland and India resumed soon after the end of the war. Many who had gone back to India at the beginning of or during the war were returning to Scotland, along with many newcomers who had been prevented from coming in the course of the war. At this stage the reconstruction of the post-war economy was in progress in Britain and there were plenty of jobs available. There was, however, a serious shortage of labour in the country due to heavy war casualties and considerable emigration from the United Kingdom soon after the war. The demand for labour outstripped the supply, and employers were thus obliged to recruit foreign workers.

The Indians in Scotland, however, did not show any interest in seeking employment in industrial works or factories, etc. They had reverted to peddling after the war, and the new-comers were also being persuaded and guided to do the same. Perhaps there were not as many jobs here as in England, or perhaps the Indians in Scotland did not qualify for the jobs available. Their preference for peddling could also have been because of their cultural inhibition to work for others when opportunities existed to work for themselves. There is a common saying in the Punjab, '*Udham khaitri, madham bupaar, nakhid chaakri,*' meaning that farming requires initiative and is the best profession, business requires patience and comes next, but service is servitude, and for the servile. So, tradition-ally, the Punjabis (and most of the Indians in Scotland then, as now, were peasants or farmers from the Punjab) normally shun service if they possibly can. Whatever the reason, the vast majority of Indians stuck to travelling for themselves. Those who had been operating in rural areas before the war went back to their old territories, and the community dispersed again all over central and north eastern Scotland.

THE INDEPENDENCE AND PARTITION OF INDIA

The pre-independence and the post-independence disturb-ances and upheavals in the subcontinent during the years 1947 and 1948 again reduced the number of newcomers to Scotland. The speculative political atmosphere and the widespread communal riots made every Indian feel insecure and uncertain of the future. Not many, therefore, ventured to leave their homes and families at such a critical time and under such an unpredictable state of affairs.

It might help the reader to understand the situation better if a brief account of the happenings, particularly the factors which led to the partition of India and the after-effects of the partition, was given at this stage. The Indian subcontinent is a huge territory. This vast land has been the birthplace and cradle of many religions and civilisations. The Hindu religion, however, has been the faith of a great majority of the people since the Aryan migration to this country, some four thousand years ago. Muslims came to India in the eighth century A.D. and ruled the country for one thousand years.

Muslim rule was replaced by British rule in the nineteenth century. When British rule was coming to an end, in the middle of the twentieth century, serious differences arose between Hindus and Muslims concerning the constitution of a democratic independent India. In 1947 India had about 400 million inhabitants, about 280 million professing the Hindu faith and about 100 million belonging to the Muslim religion. Sikhs, Christians, Jains, etc., were smaller minorities. Muslims, although 100 million in number, were still a minority in a country of 400 million. They were therefore concerned about their future in a democratic India, where they would have to live among three times as many Hindus who were widely different from them in religion, culture and traditions. The Muslim leaders discussed their apprehensions with their Hindu compatriots and urged them to grant the Muslims certain mutually acceptable constitutional safeguards to ensure a secure and honourable future for them in a free India, before the transfer of power and the departure of the British.

The discussions between the leaders of the two communities failed to resolve the situation. The Indian Muslims, therefore, resolved to demand a separate state made up of the north western and eastern provinces of India which contained a higher proportion of Muslim inhabitants. This desperate demand met with vehement opposition from the British Government as well as every other Indian leader to begin with. However, when they realised the earnestness and the determination of the Muslim masses, they relented and accepted the division of India into two separate states. Thus, on 14 August 1947, the new state of Pakistan appeared on the map of the world. On 15 August, the day after the emergence of Pakistan, India attained independence from British rule.

The Indians living in Scotland (the majority of whom being Muslims had unwittingly become Pakistanis), though far away from their homeland, also rejoiced at this auspicious occasion. The Muslims celebrated fittingly the creation of Pakistan, and the Sikhs and Hindus the freedom of India. But their joy and jubilations were short-lived. During the campaigns for the independence of India and the creation of Pakistan, relations between the Muslims on one hand and the Hindus and Sikhs on the other had been embittered, and communal riots had become a common phenomenon in many parts of the subcontinent. When it became certain that the country was to be divided before independence, communal bitterness and hostility escalated and erupted in widespread turbulence and violence. In certain parts of the subcontinent there was a complete breakdown of law and order. Mass murders, arson and looting were committed with impunity. There was no security of life or property for Muslims in India, and for Hindus and Sikhs in the new state of Pakistan.

The provinces of Punjab and Bengal were the worst affected, as these vast regions, where Hindus and Muslims had lived together in harmony for centuries, were divided between India and Pakistan. The parts which went to form Pakistan contained millions of Hindus and Sikhs who felt unsafe in the new country where they had become a minority. Similarly, Muslims in certain parts of India, where they had lived for generations, were also feeling insecure and afraid of the future. Thus, to find peace and security, the minorities on both sides of the borders began to migrate. The Hindus and Sikhs in Pakistan, particularly from the Pakistani Punjab, left for India and the Muslims from the Indian Punjab and some other regions abandoned their homes and sought refuge in Pakistan. Nearly 15 million people were uprooted and turned into refugees during those unparalleled mass migrations, and tens of thousands were massacred during their flights from one country to the other.

As has been mentioned in previous pages, nearly all the Indians in Scotland in those days were from the Jallandhar and Ludhiana districts of the Punjab and most of them were Muslims. Unfortunately for these Muslims, this area remained part of the Indian Punjab after the partition, and all their families were thus suddenly and unexpectedly put into a dangerous plight. In the confusion and chaos which accompanied the partition of the subcontinent, the post and telegraph system had also broken down in the Punjab. Those in Scotland, therefore, lost touch with their families in India and were naturally very concerned about the safety of their kith and kin. Living in Scotland, they themselves were safe, but lack of news from home and the uncertainty surrounding the fate of their families was a matter of grave concern for them. They suffered this mental torture until they heard from somebody or some sources that their families or those who had survived had reached Pakistan. The few Hindus or Sikhs here, who were from the areas which were conceded to Pakistan, went through similar agony and distress until their respective families had found their way to India.

By early 1948 conditions had improved in the subcontinent as the bulk of the migrants or refugees from both sides had made for the safety of their new countries. But the plight of the refugees was not over yet, as having left their homes, their vocations and their assets in the country of their exodus, many of them were still without a house to settle in and without a profession to provide them with a regular income in their country of refuge. It took many years for the millions who had migrated from one side to the other to settle down in their new environments and resume their normal lives. However, those who were lucky enough to settle down early and had connections in Scotland were anxious to come to this country. They began their endeavours to that end without wasting any time. Not very many though, succeeded in reaching Scotland in the years 1947 to 1949 because of severely restricted travel facilities.

There was a great scarcity of passages available for Indians on ships from India to Britain during this period. This was because of the exodus of British families and army and civil service personnel from India. Just before, and for a considerable time after the independence of India, returning British people were given priority on ships en route to Britain. Most of the Indian passengers had to wait for long periods before they could secure a passage. This frustrating situation further curtailed the number of those who wanted to come to this part of the Empire from the subcontinent. Mr Sardar Muhammed is a classic case. He stated that he and his family migrated to Pakistan in 1947 from their ancestral village, Madarpura, in India. Early in 1948, when he had settled his family in their new abode, he began his efforts to reach Scotland to join his father. It took him two years to secure his travel documents and buy his passage from Karachi, so that he did not arrive in Scotland until 1950.

Furthermore, restrictions were imposed upon certain categories of travellers to the United Kingdom by the Governments of both India and Pakistan. However, out of those few who somehow managed to reach Scotland in that period, most were Muslims from the two villages of 'Kot' and 'Jagroan' (mentioned in previous pages) in the canal colony of Lyllpur, Pakistan, and the rest were Sikhs and Hindus from the old Jagraon and Nakodar areas in India. These people were not disturbed during the partition of the country, as they were dwellers of areas which became parts of Pakistan and India respectively. They therefore had nothing to hinder them from coming over, if they could, to Scotland in the turbulent years of 1947 and 48.

EXPANSION OF THE INDO PAKISTANI COMMUNITY

The travel situation had eased by early 1949, as nearly all the British members of the establishment of the Raj and their families had left the subcontinent by then and returned to Britain. There were still restrictions, though in Pakistan and in India, on the issuing of travel documents for the United Kingdom, particularly to uneducated or non-sponsored persons with no satisfactory means of financial support abroad. This was in order to prevent people leaving the country who might become destitute abroad and resort to begging, or even hawking or peddling. Hawking or peddling in Britain by their nationals was considered a disreputable profession by the politicians and bureaucrats of the now independent and proud nations of India and Pakistan. As a matter of fact, the Pakistan Government required travellers going abroad to sign a declaration stating that they would not indulge in hawking or peddling during their stay abroad, and most probably the Indian Government had a similar requirement in force.

However, those who were determined or desperate to come out found ways round those restrictions. One of the ways round them was for the person wishing to come over to request his contact in Scotland to obtain admission for him in any technical training college or language teaching institution. As such institutions had very few entrance requirements, admission was easy. When this was done, the admission certificate was sent to the person concerned in India or Pakistan, along with a notarised sponsorship letter from the contact stating that he would be responsible for the board and lodging and all other expenses of the prospective student during his studies in Scotland. Such documents helped to circumvent the prevailing restrictions as, when presented to the authorities in the subcontinent, the applicants were treated as students and granted travel documents without any fuss. Once in Scotland the 'student' never went near the college which had facilitated his arrival in this country, nor did the college or institution bother to question the sponsor whether their 'student' had arrived or not. Meanwhile, the newcomer's training in his new vocation, peddling, had begun and was completed in the shortest possible term to prepare him for the work he had come to do.

This does not mean that there were no genuine students coming to Scotland from the subcontinent at that stage. On the contrary, the number of students attending Scottish universities and other institutions, from both India and Pakistan, had risen after 1947 and kept rising in the 1950s. It was, in fact, the rising number of students and the liberal travel facilities available to them which had given this idea to those who used this ploy to beat the restrictions imposed on other travellers.

From the early 1950s the flow of migrants to Britain from the Indian subcontinent began to rise sharply. High unemployment in both India and Pakistan was a major factor, forcing many people to migrate. However, the most important factor which increased the number of Pakistanis, and, to a lesser degree, Indians, coming to Scotland was the widening of the contacts due to population movements in the subcontinent in 1947, and their subsequent dispersal over wider areas. The Muslim communities from the Nakodar and Jagraon areas, which had long established connections with Scotland, migrated to Pakistan and dispersed in all directions, settling in properties left by Hindus and Sikhs in numerous villages and towns. This dispersal of those previously compact and cohesive communities brought them in contact with new people and new friends who, in most cases, had no traditions of migration and no contacts abroad. On the other side, in India, the abandoned houses of Muslims who had migrated to Pakistan were occupied by Hindu and Sikh refugees from Pakistan. Thus they started their new lives among people and communities (the remaining Hindus and Sikhs of the villages) who had long-established traditions of migration and working overseas. In both countries, therefore, the contacts widened and the process of chain migration expanded.

To cite an example, Mr Yaqub Ali (about whom we shall hear more in a subsequent chapter) migrated with his parents and other members of the family from the village of Sadrpura in Jagraon sub-division and settled at a town called Pakpattan in Pakistan. His elder brother, Sardar Ali, came to join a cousin in Scotland, probably in 1949. Mr Yaqub Ali arrived in 1952 to join his brother. Then a number of new friends and contacts of the Ali brothers from Pakpattan followed them to Scotland. Thus the contacts kept multiplying and the pool of sponsors in Scotland kept getting larger with every new arrival from the subcontinent. With an increasing number of Indians and Pakistanis here, there was a corresponding rise in the flow of remittances to the dependent families in the subcontinent. This further motivated many more people to come to Scotland.

Another factor which contributed to the increase of the Asian community at this stage was the introduction of families and dependants. Until 1950, only a few wives from India and

Pakistan had come to join their husbands in Scotland. First came Mrs Bal Krishan to Edinburgh in 1939, followed by Mrs Chanda Singh to Glasgow in the same year. Mrs K. S. Rakhra arrived in Glasgow in 1947, followed by Mrs M. Ismail in 1948, and only a few more from India and Pakistan until 1950. From the early 1950s, however, more and more wives and children were brought over to establish family units in Scotland. This marked a new trend in the Indo-Pakistani community. Up to this point the tradition was to leave the family back home, work here for a few years, make a little 'fortune' and return home either for a visit or for good. With the formation of family units here, the community began to implant its roots more deeply in Scotland. This was the first positive step (perhaps inadvertent at the time) towards their eventual settlement in this country. The early 1950s thus introduced the elements of rapid growth and permanent settlement among the migrant pedlars from the subcontinent.

In 1950, the total population of Asians in Scotland was about 600. Their numbers more than doubled in the next five years and stood at about 1300 in 1955. More families had arrived by then, and a sprinkling of brown children had made their appearance in various schools in Glasgow, Edinburgh and Dundee. It is interesting to note that, in spite of the fact that about 70% of the Indo-Pakistanis in Scotland were Muslims, the earliest families to come to Scotland were all (from India) of Hindu and Sikh faiths. The first Muslim family to come to Scotland was perhaps that of Mr M. Ismail in 1948. Mrs Sakina Ismail, who still lives in Glasgow, related that the all-male Muslim community of Glasgow did not approve of her coming over. She was, though, soon joined by another Muslim wife, Mrs Niamat Ali, in the same year. No other Muslim families came over until about 1952. The delay or hesitation on the part of the Muslim families was for cultural and religious reasons. Eventually such reasons and traditions were compromised for the sake of family unity and a normal settled life. However, as the Hindu and Sikh families from India had started coming over earlier, they had nearly completed the process of family reunion before the introduction of the Commonwealth Immigrants Act in 1962. Muslim families, having started late and also being reluctant to come in many cases, did not achieve total family unions until about 1980.

The 1950s saw another change in the pattern of life of the Asian community. The industrial boom of this period had brought relative prosperity to the pedlars. The seasoned and mature pedlars were doing very well. However, many of the newcomers, who had no history of peddling in their families, found it hard to persevere and carry on in that trade. Many of them were reasonably educated young men and, in some cases, they came from well-to-do families. They were initiated into peddling on their arrival by their friends or relatives as they themselves were in that trade. But the unmerciful Scottish weather, the frustration of no trade due to lack of experience and tough competition from an increasing number of other Asian pedlars and, above all, the humiliation of being followed and pestered all day by the local children in the streets and alleys of villages and housing schemes was too much for the novices. The local children on many an occasion used to follow a pedlar, especially a new face, chanting: 'there is a darkie, johnnie the darkie, hello mister darkie, here comes a darkie, darkie blarkie . . .' and so on. All this was unbearable for many young men and they gave up peddling as a result.

Many of the newcomers, therefore, began to look for alternative occupations. The industrial expansion and the resulting prosperity had by then elevated many native Scottish workers to a higher social order with better paid jobs and social working hours. There were, therefore, jobs available with unsocial hours, or which were menial, unpleasant or labour-intensive. From these jobs rejected by the locals, the Asians in turn discarded the menial and went for the rest, e.g. driving or conducting in the transport departments of the city corporations and unskilled or semi-skilled work in bakeries, the building industry, chemical works and jute mills, etc. Thus, from 1955 onwards, more and more newcomers began to take paid employment, and fewer and fewer took up peddling. Peddling or self-employment, none the less, remained the occupation of the majority of the Asians in Scotland until at least 1959. The records show that between 1951 and 1960 most of the pedlars' licences issued by the Glasgow City Corporation were to Asians.

The prevalent economic prosperity in Britain, in the 1950s, had attracted proportionately and numerically far more immigrants to England than to Scotland. Cities like Birmingham and Bradford each had more Asians than the whole of Scotland. The labour-hungry factories and mills in those areas were being manned by immigrant labour due to shortages in the local labour force. However, the industrial boom had begun to decline by the middle of 1957 and the recession started to bite hard early in 1957. In the ensuing mill closures and redundancies, the immigrant workers were the first to be laid off. Thus a great number of the Asians working in the textile mills of Yorkshire, and in the foundries and factories of the Midlands, lost their jobs.

In Scotland the situation was different. Here, the Asians had mostly taken up jobs which were rejected by the native workforce, so none of the Asian employees in Scotland lost his post. As a matter of fact, the transport services of all the major Scottish cities were still looking for staff. So when, in 1957, the redundant Asians of Yorkshire heard of this strange but very welcome situation, they rushed to Glasgow and Edinburgh in their scores to fill up those vacancies. This was the first instance, to be followed by many more in the future, of internal migration of Asians from England to Scotland. This process of internal migration and the ever-increasing arrival of relatives, friends and families from the subcontinent took the total number of Asians in Scotland to about 4000 by the end of year 1960. Glasgow had about 3000, Edinburgh around 200, Dundee abut 100, with a few hundred scattered over the Highlands, islands and north east of Scotland.

THE RUSH TO BEAT THE BAN

A campaign to restrict the entry of immigrants to Britain from the Indian subcontinent and the Caribbean had been gathering force in England since the mid fifties. At the beginning of 1961, it became quite apparent that the Conservative Government of the day was actively considering the introduction of such restrictions. The impending ban on entry to Great Britain started a stampede in those countries. From April 1961, therefore, more and more newcomers from Pakistan, India and the West Indies began to arrive in the United Kingdom to beat the ban, and their numbers kept growing every day until the last day before the restrictions became effective on 1 June 1962. Scotland also received part of the 'beat-the-ban' rush but only a fraction of its fair share. The reasons for this lack of interest in Scotland were, perhaps, its considerable distance from the main immigrant 'reception centres' in England, and also the lack of employment opportunities in this part of the United Kingdom.

The 1962 Commonwealth Immigrants Act put an end to the long-standing right of British subjects and Commonwealth citizens to enter the mother country without any restrictions. This was the first and most significant step towards the complete cessation of Asian and Afro-Caribbean settlement in this country. After the introduction of this Act, only the dependents of those already here and work-permit holders were allowed into the United Kingdom. From now on, fearing further controls even on dependents, family units began to be established in earnest in this country. As long as there was freedom of movement, the majority of the Pakistanis and many Indians had kept their options open, working here and keeping their families in the subcontinent, perhaps more inclined to eventually going back home. But with families here and children born and bred in this country, their ties with 'back home' began to weaken and their roots began to deepen in Scotland.

The living and working patterns of the Asians had begun to change during the mid fifties. This change had become quite obvious in the late fifties and had accelerated in the early sixties. Most of the newcomers were by then already seeking steady employment, and some of the older and hardened pedlars were also moving away from peddling and looking for other more dependable and less arduous vocations. The following table listing the number of pedlars' licences issued by Glasgow Corporation every year to the Indians and Pakistanis from 1951 to 1965 confirms this trend:

Year	Licences	Year	Licences	Year	Licences
1951	263	1956	287	1961	171
1952	306	1957	283	1962	186
1953	307	1958	371	1963	166
1954	351	1959	283	1964	136
1955	304	1960	199	1965	108

It is obvious that the downward trend starts from the year 1955. As regards the high figure of 1958 and the steady figures of 1957 and 1959, these were due to the effects of recession in those years. As jobs became scarce, those who had come from England and did not qualify for employment with Glasgow Corporation's transport department, along with the newcomers from the subcontinent who had failed to find a job, took out peddling licences to try their luck in that field. Soon, however, they became disenchanted with peddling and found other and easier ways of earning a wage as unemployment began to ease with the advent of the economic boom of 1959/60. Thus, from 1960, the number of Asian pedlars in Scotland started to decline very sharply and by the late 1960s very few of them were left in that trade. (No records of pedlars' licences are available from August 1965 onwards. 62 licences were issued to Asian pedlars from January to July 1965. This averages nine licences per month and this figure has been extended to cover the whole year.)

The great majority of those who did not go into peddling found work in the transport services of the major Scottish cities. In the late 1950s and in the 1960s, for instance, Indian and Pakistani bus drivers and conductors made up more than half of the work force of Glasgow Corporation's transport department. It was during this period that the department was able to produce a large surplus over expenditure more often than usual because these drivers and conductors were normally never absent, were good timekeepers and always hungry for overtime. The dependence of the efficient running of the transport service in Glasgow on the Indian and Pakistani staff in those days can be ascertained from the fact that, on the day when India and Pakistan went to war with each other in 1965, there was chaos in the city. All the Indian and Pakistani drivers and conductors were in a state of shock and were either glued to their television sets or tuned in to radios to find out what was happening back home. Thus the public transport service came to almost a standstill for most of the day.

RAPID GROWTH AND DIVERSIFICATION OF VOCATIONS

By the mid sixties, the newcomers had swamped the long established and once dominant peddling fraternity. The old pedlars now made up perhaps less than 15% of the total Asian community. About 70% of the Asians were in employment and the rest had become shopkeepers — grocers, newsagents, restaurateurs and retail and wholesale drapers. Nevertheless the trend set by the pioneering pedlars of being one's own boss or the tradition of self-employment was still as strong as ever. The old hands who had saved enough from peddling bought shops, in order to accommodate their sons or brothers who had joined them recently and who were unwilling to go into peddling or were unable to find other employment. Those who had come in the 1950s and later were working hard, taking up as much overtime as they could get (in some cases by giving 'gifts' and presents to the members of the staff in charge of timekeeping and shifts) because they were aspiring to be their own bosses one day. Most of them had no social lives: they either worked or slept. They did not gamble and very few drank. They led austere and frugal lives and saved devotionally, to better their own and their families' future. Almost every Asian's priorities were the same and firmly set in a proper order, i.e. to work hard, to save fast, to buy a house, to call the family over and to purchase a shop. Hence their entrepreneurial spirit was dormant, not dead.

However, for those who had already acquired their businesses and were practising their entrepreneurial skills as grocers, newsagents etc., there were difficult times in those early days. The few Asian shopkeepers who were catering for their own community were doing well. But others who relied on the custom of the members of general public, the indigenous Scots, were not finding many patrons, at least during normal shopping hours. In the early stages, and more or less until the late 1960s and early 1970s, there was considerable reluctance or perhaps apprehension among Scots towards Asian-owned shops. Local people often walked out of shops on seeing an Asian face behind the counter. The Asians, to counter this resistance and to survive, kept their shops open till late at night, in many cases up to midnight, employed local staff, and also lowered the prices of their merchandise.

Late opening did bring in the reluctant customers as other shops were then closed, but it also encouraged criminals to attack those shops in the dark of night and rob the defenceless Asian shopkeepers. Similarly, whereas the lower prices attracted some price-conscious customers during the day, they also brought about censure and hostility towards the Asian shopkeeper from other traders in the locality. On many occasions the local traders' associations approached the manufacturers and/or suppliers of goods and persuaded them to discontinue their supplies to the Asian shop until the Asian shopkeeper brought his prices into line with neighbouring shops. Nevertheless, in due course, the restrained but mutually beneficial contacts between the struggling Asian shopkeepers and their reluctant customers began to develop into better communications and good relations, and slowly the barriers of resistance and hesitation began to disappear.

During the early sixties Scotland received another wave of internal Asian migrants from the Midlands and Yorkshire. The jute mills of Dundee were experiencing a shortage of labour at this juncture when that industry was doing rather well. The indigenous workers were not interested in the vacancies as work in the jute mills was unpleasant, required hard labour and unorthodox hours. Most members of the Asian community of about 100 in Dundee were already employed by the jute industry. Through them the call went out to their relatives and friends in the Midlands and Yorkshire that jobs were available in Dundee. The response was so good that within a year or so about 500 Asians answered the call to take up those jobs and keep the Dundee jute mills humming efficiently and profitably.

In addition, many hundreds of doctors and nurses came to Scotland in the 1960s from the new Commonwealth countries and alleviated the acute under-staffing in the Health Service. In the 1960s and early 1970s the Health Service in this country would certainly have collapsed without the presence and services of those doctors and nurses, who for a considerable period of time constituted more than 50% of the total medical staff.

Also, in the 1960s Scotland received a number of Asian migrants and refugees from the newly independent East African countries of Kenya, Malawi and Uganda. (A large number of Asians were later expelled from Uganda and they arrived in the early 1970s.) The forefathers of these people had been brought over from India in the nineteenth century by the British to help them in the colonisation and administration of their East African territories. In consideration of their peculiar circumstances and their services to the Crown, they were granted the status of British subjects and given British passports. When those colonies became independent in the 1960s, the British handed over power to the local politicians and left. The Asians who were born and bred in those countries, and who were used to a social status above the indigenous population because of their comparative affluence and their important role in the colonies (which were resented by the locals), now found themselves in a hostile atmosphere of post-independence euphoria and Africanisation. Many, therefore, left voluntarily but some were later forced to go, leaving most of their worldly possessions behind.

Most of these newcomers were either professionals or possessed wide entrepreneurial skills and experience. After settling down in this country, they somehow managed to enter into various businesses and created employment instead of seeking employment for themselves. For instance, the Okhai family, stripped of their wealth, left Malawi and settled in Dundee in 1966. None of them claimed any social security or other benefits on their arrival in this country. To start anew and make an honest living, without any capital, Ibrahim the elder brother started a one-man painting and decorating operation. This led the family into the property business a few years later. In 1981, the Okhais made headlines in the national press when they paid £2.2 million for Scotland's well-known but languishing James Keiller's Confectionery and Preserves Factory. Soon the Okhais regenerated this famous factory and ensured the continued employment of about 350 workers. A little later they bought over Stangate Soft Drinks Ltd, with a work force of about 275, and also Chesbourne Wholesale Stationers Ltd, employing about 70. Thus this one family, which arrived in Scotland as penniless refugees, has so far provided work and brought prosperity to about 700 Scottish families directly, and many hundreds more indirectly. Their astounding success is due mainly to their hard work, their determination and their entrepreneurial skills.

By 1970 the Asian community had grown to probably about 16,000, including children born in Scotland. This fourfold growth in the preceding ten years was due mainly to the beat-the-ban rush of 1961/2, and following family reunion, the high birthrate among Asian families (most were young and in their productive years), the internal migration from England, the arrival of the East African Asians and the medical personnel from the New Commonwealth. There was, in addition, the arrival in the 1960s of another Asian community, Chinese migrants from the British territory of Hong Kong.

THE CHINESE AND VIETNAMESE

The story of the Chinese migrants in Scotland is similar in many respects to the tale of the immigrants from the Indian subcontinent. Britain forged, or perhaps more accurately forced, trading links with China in the seventeenth century at about the same time as with India. In the eighteenth century

Chinese robes, furniture and ornaments, etc., became very popular among the British aristocracy. To meet this demand, British ships took opium to China and brought back the desired goods to Britain. Also in the eighteenth century, the East India Company began to recruit Chinese seamen on their ships. In the nineteenth century Chinese sailors became an integral part of the lascar colonies in all major British ports. So, like Indian seamen, it was perhaps Chinese seamen who first came to Scotland. In 1842, Britain attacked China and occupied Hong Kong, thus extending colonial links with the Chinese people. More and more Chinese sailors were being recruited by British shipowners after the introduction of steamships. This gave rise to resentment among British sailors and there were protests and agitation against the employment of cheap Chinese crews, 'the yellow peril', in many British ports at the close of the nineteenth and at the beginning of the twentieth century. Nevertheless, during the First World War, tens of thousands of Chinese sailors were enlisted to help win the war for Britain. At the conclusion of the war, however, all these men were dismissed.

There is evidence of the presence of Chinese, along with Indian lascars, in the dockland and Port Dundas areas of the city of Glasgow before and after the First World War. However, in Scotland, the Chinese community did not grow out of the presence of Chinese seamen as in the case of the Indo-Pakistani community. There is no evidence of any settled Chinese community in this country before 1960. The first Chinese migrants (mostly single men) came to Scotland in the late 1950s and early 1960s and opened Chinese restaurants. All of them were internal immigrants dispersing from overcrowded Chinese centres like London and Liverpool. England had had settled Chinese communities in many cities since about the middle of the nineteenth century. All the traditional 'reception centres' of Chinese immigrants, therefore, were in England. After the establishment of the People's Republic of China in 1949, the influx of migrants from Hong Kong increased considerably and the traditional reception centres became saturated. Hence, the dispersal for economic survival and their arrival in Scotland. Thus, by the early 1960s, a few Chinese restaurants were already trying to attract the Scots to their 'sweet and sour' cuisine. And it did not take long for the Chinese chefs to establish their credentials in the field of gastronomy and to win over regular patrons in Scotland. This patronage encouraged more Chinese to venture up to Scotland and by 1970 about 2000 of them had joined the fast-growing Asian community in Scotland.

The Asian community had not only grown numerically in the past ten years but also in its social stature, in its confidence and in its financial and business standing. For example, the writer was appointed as the first Asian magistrate in Glasgow in 1968. And he was elected a councillor to the City of Glasgow Corporation in the local elections held in 1970 from a predominantly white ward. The Asians had begun to participate in the political and social life of their new country. This participation was being appreciated by the Scottish people and was bringing rewards to the Asian community in the form of their acceptance, their recognition and in the opening of communications and the creation of understanding between the hosts and the migrants. Up to about 1965, the Asians had lived in their self-imposed isolation. But the presence here of their families, and their children, their business expansion and their aspirations for their future in this country were all now motivating them to leave behind their seclusion, seek integration and involve themselves in the general mainstream of life. In the late sixties they had also begun to leave their original places of settlement in run-down inner city areas and move into the better residential localities of their respective cities.

Their moving into new areas, however, had its own problems. Some owners of properties and certain estate agents refused to sell to Asians. A number of mortgage companies and building societies declined to entertain Asian clients. Also, there was occasional opposition from within the neighbourhoods which often resulted in the abuse and harassment of Asian families. Racist graffiti, dirt through letter boxes, damage to property, etc., were some of the tricks used by the bigots and racists to unnerve and make the Asian families leave. Nevertheless, in time, the patience and perseverance of the Asians and the goodwill and support extended by some Scottish neighbours triumphed, more often than not, over the intolerance and insanity of others. Eventually most of the Asian families found peace and tranquillity in their new homes.

The 1970s witnessed further expansion, wider dispersal, greater integration and the gradual consolidation of the Asian community in Scotland. The expansion was due firstly to the continued arrival of wives and dependent children, mainly from Pakistan and Hong Kong, to join their husbands and parents. This process continued until 1980, by which time almost all if not all families had been reunited. Internal migration was again another factor which added to the numbers of Asians in Scotland. However, this movement was totally different in its quality, quantity and velocity from the previous ones. As has been mentioned already, the Asians in Scotland had picked up the spirit of entrepreneurship from the pioneering pedlars, further developed it and applied it successfully. Many of them had already become successful businessmen owning shops and restaurants by the early 1970s, and many more were laying the foundations of their enterprises. There were seemingly better chances of success for Asian businesses in Scotland than in England, as an increasing number of Asian-owned businesses were prospering in this part of the country. The Asians in the United Kingdom have always been a mobile, interconnected and well-informed community. When news of the successes of the Scottish Asian entrepreneurs spread to England around 1970, many of their aspiring compatriots there sold their homes and headed north with all their savings to acquire or start a business.

To illustrate this process, we can look at the case of 22-year-old Mr M. Sharif who came to England from Pakistan during the beat-the-ban rush in 1961. He had contacts in Southall, so that is where he went and worked until 1963. He then moved to Huddersfield and found work in a factory, staying there until 1976. By then he had bought a modest house, brought over his family and saved a few hundred pounds. He had friends in Glasgow (who had also come from the Midlands a few year earlier) who were in business and doing well. They encouraged him to come to Scotland and assisted him in buying a small grocery store in Cumbernauld, near Glasgow. From that small shop Mr Sharif moved into bigger shops. In 1986, he bought a big wholesale drapery and clothing store in Glasgow which now has a turnover of millions of pounds and employs over a dozen staff.

At first this phase of re-migration from England was slow though steady. However it gathered pace towards the mid 1970s and continued at that speed until the mid 1980s. In this period of about 10 years a considerable number of Pakistanis, Indians, Bangladeshis and Chinese moved from various parts of England and established successful businesses in Scotland. There was, though, another Asian community on its way to Scotland.

In the mid 1970s the United Kingdom, along with many other countries, agreed to accept war refugees from Vietnam. About 1000 of these destitute people arrived in Scotland. As these newcomers came under an agreed plan and according to a timetable, they were settled under an organised and 'well devised' scheme. Many statutory and voluntary organisations assisted in their rehabilitation. The Vietnamese community was split up into smaller sections, to achieve dispersal, and settled in a number of towns all over Scotland. Many of the refugees, however, did not feel secure and happy living in 'designed' small communities and soon became restless. Many, therefore, when they had gained a little confidence and had developed contacts with their relatives and friends living in England, left Scotland to seek the insulation of their own communities and culture. However, some of them remained in Scotland and are settling down well in their new country.

HERE TO STAY

The community had progressed very well in social, cultural and political fields in the decade from 1970 to 1980. An

Asian migrant i.e., the author, participated in the February 1974 Parliamentary elections as a Labour Party candidate and another contested the 1979 General Election on behalf of the Conservative Party. Although both candidates were unsuccessful, their participation raised political awareness among Asians and enhanced their confidence and their self-respect. Stronger links were forged with all major political parties and an increasing number of Asians became active in politics. A number of Asian candidates took part in municipal elections throughout this decade in various cities. The author, as the sitting Glasgow councillor defended his seat successfully three times in the 1970s and served as a bailie of the city and as Chairman of the Police Committee. Another half a dozen or so Asians were appointed Justices of the Peace in this decade. All this political activity and civic and social advancement boosted the morale of the community and helped to develop in them a sense of belonging to this country.

Around the mid 1970s, awareness of racism and discrimination rose sharply as the second generation Asians came of age and found out that they were not being treated equally. There had always been some racism and prejudice in Scotland and the pedlars and other first-generation Asians had often experienced it. But, having been born and brought up under the British Raj, with all its awe and reverence, in India, they were accustomed to the authority and supposed superiority of the British. They, therefore, expected and accepted resignedly certain disadvantages and humiliations in the homeland of their 'masters'. But their children, who were born and/or brought up in Scotland, had not gone through such humbling experiences. They had grown up in this society and gone to school and played with the local children as equals. They therefore had similar aspirations and expected the same privileges as enjoyed by their white peers.

Many a young Asian, like the second and third generation Jewish and Italian youngsters, did not want to join his father's business or work in his shop. He wanted to work orthodox hours for a steady wage. But when things did not turn out as expected, and they had to suffer the humiliation and frustration of unemployment and lack of equal opportunities based on racism and discrimination, they rebelled against the system and society. And, in contrast to their elders, they hit out, they complained bitterly and they accused openly and boldly those in authority of discrimination and racism. Thus the evil menace which had been tolerated and kept hidden and hushed by the parents was exposed and challenged by their children. Hence new organisations were formed during this period, and the existing Asian associations were strengthened and encouraged to fight for the rights of their members and to combat prejudice and racism in Scottish society.

The decade from 1970 to 1980 also saw a considerable increase in religious awareness and related activities. The Asian community at this stage had at last accepted the fact that they were here to stay. They accordingly changed their outlook and their thinking in relation to their future in this country. New mosques, temples and religious schools were set up in every locality and every town with a viable Asian community, to ensure the spiritual welfare of the present and future generations. Work started on Scotland's first purpose-built mosque in Glasgow in 1979. This beautiful mosque was completed and 'officially opened' in 1984 by the Imam of Islam's holiest shrine, the Kaabah in Mecca. This is probably the biggest mosque in Europe and can accommodate about 2000 worshippers.

By 1980, the Asian community in Scotland stood at about 32,000. This carefully estimated figure includes Pakistanis, Indians, Chinese, Bangladeshis and Vietnamese and their children. There were also many other ethnic minority groups in Scotland at this stage from other parts of the Commonwealth and many other countries, e.g. the West Indies, Africa and the Middle East. Most of these people, for one reason or another, had also come to Scotland from England in the past ten or fifteen years, as there were very few people from these countries in Scotland in the early sixties, other than students. Moreover, a small number of Chilean refugees arrived in this country in this decade to escape from oppression and persecution in their own homeland. The approximate total population of all ethnic minority groups in Scotland in 1981, according to the well-founded estimates of the Scottish Office Central Research Unit, was 38,400, comprising 31,900 Asians (24,900 Indo-Pakistanis, 5900 Chinese, 1100 Vietnamese) and 6500 others (1500 Africans, 1000 West Indians, 4000 others). (It is interesting to see that the estimated number of Asians is very close to my own estimate.)

The Asian community had doubled in the past decade. This significant increase was again due to a considerable number of families arriving from Pakistan, Bangladesh and Hong Kong, as well as the movement of over 500 entrepreneurial Asian families from England to various parts of Scotland during the period from 1970 to 1980. This was perhaps the last 'abnormal' growth in a decade of the Asian community in Scotland. With immigration controls now watertight, and the reunion of families (except some Chinese) completed by 1980, the era of immigration from the New Commonwealth had come almost to an end. The only newcomers from the Indian subcontinent from 1980 onwards were occasional brides, fiancées and fiancés. As regards the fiancés, they were only allowed to enter Britain if they could (miraculously) convince the British immigration officers based in Pakistan, India and Bangladesh, that they were going to Britain for a genuine marriage and not for a 'marriage of convenience'. There was, nevertheless, still a steady seepage of Asian families from England who were buying shops and stores in Scotland. By the late 1980s, this internal migration had also dried up considerably, and thus almost all the external factors which had been influencing the rapid growth of the Asian community in the past were eliminated before the approach of the 1990s.

However, there have been new developments during 1990 concerning the status of certain British subjects in Hong Kong. About 50,000 Chinese families of this British colony have been granted British passports, giving them the choice to leave Hong Kong and enter the United Kingdom, if they so desire, before or after the Chinese takeover of those territories in 1997. How many of these families will exercise their choice only time will tell, but there is a chance that perhaps a majority of these people may eventually come to Britain and Scotland will receive its share. If that happens, then we might see another external addition to the Asian community in Scotland in the last decade of this century.

In the decade from 1980 to 1990, the Asian community made rapid advances in the fields of commerce and business. During this period Asian-owned businesses increased in number and expanded their trade and operations. By 1990, approximately 65% of Asian families owned a business of one sort or the other. Asian-operated stores, shops, restaurants and take-aways could now be found in the remotest parts of Scotland. Enterprising Asians had reached nearly every town and village in the length and breadth of Scotland. They were not afraid, anymore, of moving their families away from the comforts and security of their own kind and their own community. They had, in fact, become bold enough to move into strange and far-flung indigenous communities and seek comfort and security from them along with their custom.

Expansion and consolidation was an important aspect of the Asians' commerce and trade in the 1980s. Small businesses grew big, and big became bigger and better. Grocery, clothing, drapery, hardware, and fancy good trades were now dominated by Asians in Scotland, not only in retail but also wholesale. Castle, probably the biggest wholesale cash and carry in Europe, is owned by a Pakistani family operating from Glasgow, as is the group of huge warehouses owned by the Sher family. United Wholesale Ltd is yet another up-and-coming extensive family concern. All these businesses have created hundreds of jobs, and those who started early and have done well are aiming even higher in the 1990s.

The success achieved by certain Asians has been fantastic. Mr Sher Mohammed, who founded the Sher family empire, came to Scotland in 1938 from the village of Kot/Chak no. 477 G.B. in the canal colony district of Lyllpur. He had no schooling and could not speak a word of the English language on his arrival in Glasgow. His two younger brothers joined him in 1948. They all worked as pedlars, living together and pooling their savings. In 1953, Sher and his two brothers opened a small wholesale drapery and clothing warehouse to cater for the fast-growing Indo-Pakistani peddling community. The fourth brother joined them in 1953. Sher Muhammed and Muhammed Ali, the new arrival, who was an educated young man, ran the warehouse while the other two, Hashmat Ali and Rahmat Ali, carried on peddling. In a few years, the indigenous retail traders, noticing the competitive prices, variety of merchandise and the quality of service at 'Sher Brothers', also began to patronise them. Thus the business started to grow. In 1968, Sher Brothers made their fourth move to even bigger premises in order to contain the volume of their expanding business. In 1976 they opened 'Bonny Pack', another wholesale store, one of the biggest in Scotland, dealing in toys and fancy goods. In 1986 'House of Sher', a Do-it-Yourself store was opened by Sher Brothers in huge premises in the heart of the city of Glasgow. In 1990, yet another big wholesale cash-and-carry was opened dealing in groceries, cigarettes and confectionery. All these stores have millions of pounds of turnover each and employ scores of staff. Mr Sher died a few years ago, and the other three brothers have now retired. The business is now being run by their children and their children's children under the leadership of Rafiq Sher and is growing every day.

The success and rapid rise of Mr Yaqub Ali, boss of Castle Cash and Carry and A. A. Brothers is even more impressive. As has been mentioned earlier, Mr Ali came to Glasgow in 1952 at the age of 19. He had attended a vernacular primary school in India until only the age of nine. Thus he had no knowledge of English at all. Like everyone else, he also began peddling in and around Glasgow but, unlike everyone else, he went to Skerry's College to learn English at evening classes for a couple of nights a week. In 1956 Mr Ali and his elder brother, like the Sher brothers, opened a drapery wholesale warehouse. When in the early 1960s the number of Asian pedlars began to decrease rapidly, the Ali brothers had to abandon their small warehouse. Mr Ali in the meantime was still carrying on his peddling business, and so the closure of the warehouse did not make him jobless.

In 1965, Yaqub with his youngest brother Taj, who had been working as a conductor on the Glasgow buses, founded the firm of A. A. Brothers and bought a licensed grocer's business in Motherwell, Lanarkshire. He gave up peddling and devoted all his time to his new venture. He soon realised the potential for cutting prices in the liquor trade, and in 1966 introduced considerable reductions in the prices of beers, wines and spirits in his shop. This was perhaps the first time in Scotland that a trader had reduced the prices of those well-loved commodities by so much. In spite of the opposition from his competitors, and a degree of suspicion and lack of cooperation from the distillers, he did a roaring trade during the festive season of 1966. In 1967, A. A. Brothers opened a branch in Glasgow and introduced prices which were much lower than anywhere else in the country. The turnover of that one shop shot up to £50,000 per week in no time, as queues of customers kept getting bigger and longer. The press, radio and television gave a further boost to the business by writing articles on 'a Pakistani who had to show us Scots how to sell whisky', broadcasting live interviews with delighted customers who were saving a lot of money by buying from A. A. Brothers, and showing queues hundreds of yards long of patiently waiting customers outside the shop. This venture proved such a huge success that Yaqub Ali opened a few more branches in and around Glasgow.

In 1973, Mr Ali entered the wholesale grocery wine and spirit trade and established a warehouse at Hamilton. Again his technique of cutting prices to the barest minimum and profiting from the huge turnover was successful. Soon he had to expand to meet the demands of his clientele. To expand in a big way he acquired a 24-acre site in Glasgow and built Europe's biggest wholesale cash-and-carry warehouse and named it Castle. Castle Cash and Carry was officially opened by H.R.H. Princess Anne in 1983. Yaqub Ali was awarded the O.B.E. in 1984 for his distinguished services to trade and industry. Thus someone who came to Scotland from Pakistan in 1952 as an illiterate young man of 19 with only a couple of pounds in his pocket, was already a millionaire in 1984, and a proud recipient of the Order of the British Empire. In 1991, according to the *Scottish Business Insider*, A. A. Brothers had a turnover of £98.66 million and assets worth £10.41 million. The company employed 448 staff and was listed as number 109 in the *Insider's* table of the top 200 Scottish companies. In July 1991, Mr Ali won the Scottish Free Enterprise Award of the 'Aims of Industry' for his contribution to free enterprise in Scotland. The chances are that, with his past record and speed of success, Mr Ali may yet climb further heights.

However, the story of the Asians in Scotland is not one of sweet success only: there are and there have been many failures and ample frustrations. The Asians have mostly worked hard, putting in very long hours and accepting lower returns. Even then, some have not been successful at all and others are struggling to make both ends meet. Many are caught up in the trap of self-employment, knowing that they would not be able to find any other employment to feed their families if they abandoned their not very profitable businesses. They also lack the resources and the initiative to make a fresh start or to diversify. They are thus resigned to carry on their languishing businesses and live in relative poverty in order to save themselves from the indignity of unemployment or receiving social security benefits. Often they also feel obliged to keep up their pretences, as those who are not in business are not thought very highly of in the Asian community, unless of course they are highly skilled professionals. Similarly, there are many who have never been able to own a business of their own, nor have they been able to secure permanent well-paid jobs. So where there is success there is failure, and where there is affluence there is poverty: this is as true of the Asian community as of any other. But their rate of success is and has been far higher than their rate of failure.

Diversification and innovation have been another hallmark of the Asian community during the last decade. Many of the Asian adventurers have been bypassing the traditional trades of grocery, drapery and catering and entering into new avenues and wider fields. Clothing manufacture, the motor trade, petrol stations, the furniture trade, estate agencies, insurance brokerage, property development, video film leasing, etc., are new ventures which the Asians are undertaking in increasing numbers. If one looks at their track record, then there is every reason to believe that they will also do well in their new enterprises. 'Azad Videos' and 'Global Videos', names which can already be seen in many Scottish towns and cities, are owned by Pakistani entrepreneurs.

As regards the Asian population of Scotland in 1992, again only an approximate estimate can be made without any accurate records. There were, as has been mentioned, a couple of external factors which added to the natural growth of the Asian community in the decade from 1980 to 1990. The accumulated effect of these factors cannot be more than an approximate inflation of 5000 to the natural growth, in a decade, of a comparatively young community. The estimation of the approximate size of the Asian community in 1992, however, also depends upon the reliability of the figures we arrived at for 1981. If those figures are a reasonably accurate estimation (and in all probability that is so), then there would be about 45,000 Scots of Asian (Pakistani, Indian, Chinese, Bangladeshi, Nepalese, Vietnamese and Malaysian, etc.) origin in Scotland in the beginning of the year 1992, and they would constitute about 80% to 85% of all the ethnic minorities. The total population of all the ethnic minority groups, i.e. the Asians, Africans, West Indians, and other non-Europeans, who are now living in Scotland would be approximately around 55,000 people.

The 'other non-Europeans' referred to above include small groups of Arabs (from various Middle Eastern and North African countries), Turks, Iranians, Chileans, etc. Most of these immigrants, except the Chileans, have also come up from England during the past decade. As their numbers are rather small and their outward appearances somewhat similar to the Asians, they have not been noticed or recognised, as yet, as separate ethnic groups, by the public, press of politicians. Neither have any of these groups themselves made any serious efforts, so far, to assert their respective presence or demand recognition.

The bulk, perhaps about 35,000, of the ethnic minorities are settled in Strathclyde Region, predominantly in Glasgow and its suburbs, followed by Lothian with about 7000, Tayside with approximately 3500, Grampian with nearly 2500, Fife with about 1500, Central Region with around 1500, the Outer Hebrides with about 300, leaving the rest of Scotland with about 3000. As regards the population of each specific group, it appears that the Pakistani group is the largest and constitutes between 45% and 50% of the total population of all the ethnic groups in Scotland. Indians make up about 20% to 25% of the total, and the Chinese between 15% and 20%. The Afro-Caribbean community makes up about 7% to 8%, and all others about 8% to 10% of the total figure. All figures quoted here are, of course, approximate estimates based on information available from various sources, i.e. the electoral registers, the regional education departments, the Community Relations Councils, and the Scottish Office, etc. The true figures, with other details of the population of Asians and all other ethnic groups in Scotland, will be available after the conclusion of the 1991 census which includes questions about the ethnicity of the citizens and other relevant information.

CHAPTER SIX

Cultures and Customs of the Newcomers

The ethnic minorities in Scotland are a composite group with long established, strong cultural traditions and diverse faiths. Those from Pakistan, Bangladesh, Malaysia, Turkey, Iran, Arab and North African countries are almost all Muslims. Indians are mainly Sikhs and Hindus with some Muslims. Afro-Caribbeans are mostly Christians with small numbers of Hindus and Muslims. Most of the Chinese have complex religious beliefs based on Buddhist and Taoist faiths and their centuries-old customs and traditions. A small number of the Chinese are Christians. All of these groups feel proud of their respective cultural heritage and are determined to preserve it, as far as possible, in their adopted country.

This is the first period in the history of Scotland when sizable groups of so many different faiths and cultures have settled here. It would therefore be of benefit to the readers if a brief exposition of the beliefs and customs of each of these groups was given in order to create an awareness and understanding of the background, the traditions and the outlook of these new members of Scottish society. This would help towards a better understanding of their attitudes to life, their difficulties and their aspirations in their new environment. Over half of the total population of the ethnic minorities belong to the Islamic faith. We shall, therefore, first explore Islam to discover the culture and the way of life of the Muslims.

ISLAM

The Arabic word Islam means voluntary surrender and sub-mission. It also means peace. The Islamic way of life is peaceful submission to the ultimate divine code revealed to the prophet Muhammed 14 centuries ago. Islam claims to be the continuation and indeed the culmination, in its comprehensive and universal form, of all the previous divine religions preached by various prophets, to their respective people, throughout the history of mankind.

The prophet of Islam, Muhammed, was born at Makkah (spelt Mecca in English) in Arabia in A.D. 571. His father died a couple of months before his birth and his mother died when he was only six. He belonged to a noble family descended from the Patriarch Abraham through his son Ishmael. He did not receive any education and spent his childhood tending the goats and camels of his uncle who brought him up. When he grew up he became a trader in partnership with a rich lady of Makkah, whom he later married. Up to the age of 40 he was not known as a preacher, an orator or a statesman. He was, however, well known in the corrupt and cruel society he was living in as an honest, virtuous, kind and charming gentleman. He was given the titles of 'trustworthy' and 'truthful' by his fellow citizens for his integrity and his excellent character. He was concerned about the abject laxity of the people he was living among and used to withdraw to a cave near Makkah for contemplation and meditation. It was during one of these sessions in the cave, in the fortieth year of his life, that the Archangel Gabriel appeared to him, told him of his mission and conveyed to him his first revelation from God.

For the next 23 years of his life the prophet carried on his mission with all his commitment, using all the meagre resources at his disposal. He suffered severe opposition and persecution, and finally had to flee from his place of birth, but within that span of 23 years he succeeded in fulfilling the mission the Almighty had entrusted him with. Before his death in A.D. 633 the whole of the Arabian peninsula had received and accepted the message and he had done the ground work for the divine message to reach the whole world. Within two decades of his death the Islamic ideology preached by him had produced a casteless and a classless cosmopolitan civilisation which held sway in this world for one thousand years.

The divine message or the guidance which was revealed gradually to the prophet, through the Archangel Gabriel, on pertinent occasions during his missionary life of 23 years, was meticulously recorded and also committed to memory by many of his companions. The *Quran*, the Muslim holy book, is the true and complete record of all those divine revelations. The *Quran* for Muslims is the word of God and is to be adhered to and obeyed in letter and in spirit. Over and above giving spiritual and temporal guidance, the *Quran* lays great emphasis on learning, knowledge, reflection, reason and research. To stimulate the quest for knowledge perhaps, the *Quran* on occasions refers to certain scientific data and specific ideas that have been discovered only in modern times, e.g. 'Do not the unbelievers see that the Heavens and the Earth were joined together, then We clove them asunder', 'God is the one Who created the night, the day, the Sun and the Moon. Each one is travelling in an orbit with its own motion', 'And We made from water every living thing', '(We) sent water down from the sky and thereby We brought forth pairs of plants (of both sexes) each separate from the other', etc.

The Islamic Article of Faith reads 'I believe in Allah the God almighty, His Angels, His revealed Books, His Prophets and the Day of Judgement, I believe that good and evil is determined by God, and I believe in life after death'.

Islamic faith is based on the Unity or the Oneness of God. Muslims, therefore, prefer to use the Arabic word Allah for God. The word Allah means One true God and it has no plural or gender, thus avoiding any possible allusion to or confusion with any of the man-made gods. Allah is the Creator and Sustainer of the Universe: 'He is God, the One and Only; God, the Eternal, Absolute; He begetteth not, Nor is he begotten; And there is none like unto Him.' (*Al-Quran*). A Muslim believes that prophets and messengers of God have come to every nation and every people all over this planet throughout the ages to guide or reform people and they are all to be accepted and respected. The *Quran* confirms various scriptures of earlier prophets and messengers: 'Say, we believe in that which was revealed to Abraham and Ishmael and Isaac and Jacob and the tribes and that which was given to Moses and Jesus and to other Prophets, from their Lord' (*Al-Quran*). However, the *Quran*, being the comprehensive, universal and final divine revelation, supersedes all the earlier messages and scriptures.

The Muslims further believe that a day will certainly come when this world will end and every living thing in it will die. God will then establish a new order and resurrect all the dead — right from the beginning of the world to its end — to be judged. On that day every person will be rewarded by God according to his or her deeds during life on earth. Earthly life is a prelude to eternal life after death and only those who live this life according to the divine code of conduct will deserve the everlasting bliss and delights of heavenly life.

The Practice of Islam

Islam is not just a religion but a way of life which comprehends and governs every aspect of the life of a believer. Practising Muslims, therefore, are obliged to follow wholly and totally the guidance and standards set by their faith throughout their earthly lives. The fundamental obligations of a Muslim, better known as the five pillars of Islam, are as follows:

1. The creed — To pronounce knowingly and voluntarily 'there is none worthy of worship except Allah and that Muhammed is His messenger'.
2. Obligatory prayers — A practising Muslim is obliged to pray five times a day, at dawn or before sunrise, at mid-day, in late afternoon, at sunset and before retiring. The prayer is preceded by ablution (wudu), i.e. washing of hands up to the elbows, face and feet in the prescribed manner. There is more merit in praying collectively in a mosque or at any other place but Muslims can pray

individually wherever they happen to be at the prescribed time except the *Jumá* i.e. Friday prayer which can only be performed in congregation. Regular prayers are the practical demonstration of faith.

3. Fasting in the month of Ramadhan — From dawn to sunset every day of the month of Ramadhan a Muslim is obliged to abstain from eating, drinking, smoking, and also from malice, evil deeds or desires and any other antisocial or unethical activities. Fasting is an annual exercise designed to refresh and raise a person's moral and spiritual standards above selfishness, greed, laxity, anger and other vices. Children, old, infirm or sick people, wayfarers or travellers, breastfeeding or menstruating women, etc., are all exempt from fasting. Similarly, many such categories have full or part dispensation from daily prayers.

4. Zakah (the welfare contribution) — It is obligatory for all Muslims to pay annually 2½% of their net savings, and of the value of their jewellery and precious metals. There is a different rate for one's animals and agricultural produce. In practice it is an annual demand on a person's net estate. It is neither a charity donation nor a tax because charity is optional and taxes can be used for Government projects. But Zakah can be spent only on fixed acts like helping the poor and needy, the sick and disabled, the oppressed and lonely, to free those in bondage or under the burden of debt, and for other similar welfare purposes. This obligation is designed (a) to ensure an equitable distribution of wealth in society and to prevent the accumulation of wealth in a few hands, and (b) to ensure the welfare of the needy in society.

5. Hajj (the pilgrimage to Makkah) — This is an annual event obligatory once in a lifetime for those Muslims who have the means to undertake the journey to Makkah in Saudi Arabia. It involves a visit to the House of God, the Kaabah, and a few other places near Makkah. The Kaabah, according to Islamic belief, was first built by Adam for the worship of Allah the One true God and then rebuilt by Abraham and his son Ishmael, since when it has been

in continuous use. Every year hundreds of thousands of Muslims, from every corner of the world, gather there to perform the ritual of Hajj. Every male pilgrim is required to dress only in two white shrouds of cloth, one to cover the body from the waist downwards and the other to cover the upper part of the body. Thus all marks of wealth and rank are discarded and all distinctions of race and colour are forgotten as princes and proletarians, rich and poor, black and white, all dressed alike, rub shoulders with each other, pray together and stay together during these ceremonies spread over six or seven days. This unique multitude of people of all races, ranks and colours symbolises and indeed demonstrates most impressively the brotherhood, the unity and the equality of mankind on this Earth as proclaimed by Islam.

Social and Dietary Regulations

Under the Islamic code gambling, games of chance and usury are strictly forbidden, and all trades and professions related to these are disapproved. Sexual immorality, slander, oppression, injustice and breach of trust are cardinal sins. Aggression and arrogance are condemned; harmony and humility are recommended. Tranquillity and obedience to authority are enjoined; disorder and defiance of law are prohibited. Excess and extremism in any form are barred; temperance, piety and moderation are decreed. Love and respect for parents, elders and neighbours, and affection and kindness to children are decreed for every Muslim. Contrary to Western custom, Muslims are required to cover their heads and put on their hats as a mark of respect.

Males and females, unless related, are not allowed to mix freely after the age of about 12. In social and religious gatherings, therefore, males and females are segregated. Music and dancing are forbidden. Men and women are obliged to dress properly and modestly. Women are required to cover their whole body from head to ankles and not to wear tight or otherwise revealing garments. Muslims, males and females, are not allowed to expose themselves, even in front of members of their own sex. It is recommended that Muslim males support beards and trim or shave their moustache.

Soon after birth a Muslim baby is washed and Adhan (the call to prayer) recited in its ears. On the seventh day the child is named and its head shaved. A certain sum of money is donated to charitable causes or given to the needy, and a feast held for relatives, friends and the poor as acts of thanksgiving. Baby boys are circumcised on the seventh day or later. At death the body of a Muslim is required to be buried as soon as possible. To prepare for burial the dead body is washed, perfumed and shrouded, the male in three and the female in five sheets of cloth in order to cover every part of the body. Then the funeral prayers are said and the body interred in a grave. Islam forbids cremation.

Islam puts great emphasis on cleanliness of the body and of the mind. To keep one's body clean there are standard regulations for optional and obligatory bathing and washing which ought to be done in clean running water. Muslims thus prefer to take a shower under running water rather than a bath in a tub full of stagnant water. Muslims cannot perform their daily prayers unless their bodies and clothes are clean and free of dirt or pollution of any sort.

Islam allows the consumption of all clean and wholesome foods. As regards meat, it must be hallal, i.e. of animals killed according to the prescribed method which is similar to the biblical rites. Eating the flesh of pigs, dead animals and blood is strictly forbidden. The use of alcohol and other intoxicants is prohibited completely, and all trades and vocations related to the manufacture, conveyance, sale and storage of intoxicants, for human consumption, are condemned. Hence a Muslim cannot accept from or offer an alcoholic drink to a guest or a friend. Muslims are required to eat or drink with their right hands, to refrain from conversation during meals, to drink liquids slowly and in a sitting position, and to wash their hands before and their hands and mouths after eating.

Islamic Festivals

The two 'Eids' are the most important festivals for the Muslims. Eid-ul-Adha is celebrated on the tenth day of Dhulhajj, the last month of the Islamic (lunar) calendar, to commemorate Patriarch Abraham's test and his sacrifice of a ram in place of his son. Muslims all over the world offer sacrifices of rams and other animals, in the tradition of the Patriarch, on this day, and the meat of sacrificed animals is distributed among relatives, friends and the poor. The festivities last for three days but special congregational prayers are held only on the first day. This festival also marks the end of the ceremonies of Hajj, the annual pilgrimage to Makkah. The Eid-ul-Fitr is celebrated on the first of Shawwal, the tenth month of the Islamic calendar, to mark the end of Ramadhan, the month of fasting. The congregational prayers are held in the morning, and friends and relatives are visited and given gifts later in the day. Children are also given presents and bought special clothes on this Eid, and hence they look forward to it more eagerly.

There are other notable dates in the Islamic calendar, i.e. the Prophet's birthday, the Night of Power, the Night of Ascension, and *Ashura* or the tenth of Muharram (the first month of the Islamic calendar), but these are all solemn occasions requiring devotional activities rather than festivities. However, all the Islamic festivals and solemn occasions are celebrated according to the lunar calendar and, as the lunar calendar is about ten days shorter than the solar calendar, these festivals revolve and are always about ten days earlier every year.

HINDUSIM

Hinduism is one of the oldest religions in the world. Over the centuries it has accumulated a complex and bewildering diversity of thought, doctrine, legend and ritual within its very wide bounds. It is, therefore, almost impossible to define the Hindu faith in even reasonably accurate terms. To make an effort, however, Hinduism may perhaps be described as a sort of combination of a religious fraternity and a social organisation. As a religious fraternity it represents its numerous schools of thought with their innumerable sects, each worshipping its own major as well as minor deities and venerating and propitiating semi-divine beings, consecrated objects, holy places, rivers, plants, trees and animals. As a social organisation, Hinduism is based on the caste system, with its roots embedded in the ethnic make-up of the Indian people. The Aryans comprise the higher castes, i.e. Brahmans, Kshatriyas and Vaisyas, and the non-Aryans make up the rest, i.e. Sudras and untouchables.

The orthodox Hindu philosophy, none the less, rests upon pantheism, the doctrine that everything in this universe is a manifestation or a part of One Absolute Being — Brahma (Creator) or Parmatama (Supreme Self). This is perhaps the nearest that Hinduism comes to the concept of monotheism.

The Hindu scriptures consist of Vedas, Upanishuds, Puranas, Bhagavad Gita, Mahabharata, Ramayana and many other Sashtras and Sutras written by various sages in different ages. Like the diversity in thought and doctrine, Hindu literature and liturgy are also plentiful and diverse. The object and the mode of worship varies with every sect and every caste. The object of worship could be a major deity, a minor god, goddess, saint, hero or any other thing. The most important Hindu deities are: Brahma the Creator, Vishnu the Preserver and Shiva the Destroyer with their respective consorts Sarsvati, Lakshmi and Parvati; Rama and his wife Sita, Krishna and his wife Radha, Ganesha the elephant-headed god, the monkey god Hanuman, etc. Of the goddesses the favourites are Durga or Kali, Annapurna and Sitala.

The mode of worship is usually connected with the image of the object or the god worshipped. Hindu temples are adorned with idols and images of the favourite gods of the devotees. The image into which the spirit of the particular god is believed to have been introduced by the rites of initiation is treated with great reverence and respect. Lamps and incense burn before it, it is washed and dressed, and food, flowers and other offerings are placed before it. Hymns are sung, supplications made and prayers offered before the images. In addition to the temples, and more importantly, every family has its own household shrine with the images of its particular gods which are worshipped morning and evening. A Hindu is also allowed to discharge his/her religious rites and obligations by proxy and a priest may be hired for a fee to perform the rites for a devotee.

The two pillars of the Hindu faith are, first, the concept of reincarnation, i.e. works, wandering and release. This refers to the process of the repeated birth of a soul in various bodily forms, sometimes lower and sometimes higher. The actions of the soul in one life determine its position in the next. Only when a soul has achieved perfection through its series of works, i.e. good deeds during earthly lives, does it attain salvation and eternal bliss. The second pillar is the concept of a social order, i.e. the caste system. The Brahman is at the top of the caste system: he is believed to have arisen from the head of Brahma, the spirit of the universe; the Kshatriya (the warrior) is next, from his arms; then the Vaisya (the farmer, the trader, the artisan) from his thighs; and then the Sudra (the serf) from his feet. The Ganges is the sacred river where every Hindu longs to go one day to plunge into its holy waters, to wash away sins.

Social and Dietary Traditions

Most Hindus are vegetarians but in certain sections consumption of meat, other than beef, is common. High-caste Hindus are not permitted to eat meat, but lower castes are exempt from this restriction. The slaughter of cows and the presence of beef cause great offence to adherents of the Hindu faith as they regard the cow as a sacred animal and venerate it. According to Hindu religious law, the consumption of alcohol, association with a drinker and trading in alcohol are all major sins. The eating of onions and garlic is condemned in some sections. Taking food with (or even near) and having physical contacts with non-Hindus is also proscribed to adherents of certain sects. Food must be taken by the right hand and the hands washed thereafter.

Marriage between persons of different castes is forbidden. Every caste is subdivided into numerous branches of its own called *gotras*, and marital union between persons of the same *gotra* is also forbidden. The marriage ceremony involves many intricate and laborious rituals. To complete the process the bride and the groom circle round the holy fire, which is prepared for this purpose, and the couple pour libations on it while the priest recites the mantras. After completing seven circles, the bride and the groom put garlands round each other's necks as a public manifestation of their acceptance of each other, and vermilion powder is applied to the forehead of the bride as a mark of her being duly married. There are many ceremonies related to pregnancy and childbirth. About two weeks after the birth a service is held and the child is given a name. Relatives and friends are invited to this happy occasion, a feast is held and alms given to the poor. A few weeks later the family astrologer is called to prepare the life chart (*kundly*) of the infant.

Hindu dead are cremated and the funeral pyre is lit by the eldest son. The ashes are put into the river Ganges by the male descendants. The departed soul is believed to live in 'preta loka', the world of souls, where it 'requires' sustenance before it is reborn. This is 'provided' by the descendants through Brahman priests, first for 10 to 30 days following the death, and then at the end of every year and on other propitious occasions. All the funeral rites must be performed by a son or a grandson, and so a male descendant is highly important for a Hindu.

Music and dance, being associated with religious devotions and ceremonies, are encouraged and patronised. The joint family system is adhered to. Orthodox Hindus take cleanliness as a fetish and wash their bodies or certain parts thereof several times a day. Bathing naked, exposing oneself and looking at other naked or exposed persons are all sins. Nothing is undertaken or begun without consulting the astrologer or finding out the propitious hour.

Notwithstanding what has been said above, it must be noted that most Hindus in this country, and many even in India, have now become very liberal in their beliefs and attitudes. They have relaxed, replaced and even abandoned many of their old conventions and customs. There have also arisen, over the last few hundred years, some Hindu sects in India which have departed from their traditional beliefs. Their temples are completely devoid of images or idols and they appear to believe in One Omnipotent, Omniscient and Omnipresent God. These new developments, therefore, make it even more difficult to define the Hindu faith.

Hindu Festivals

The important festivals are:

1. Shivratri, in honour of Shiva, which is held about the middle of February. A fast is held during the day and a vigil at night.
2. Holi, a kind of carnival celebrated in late February or early March, commemorating the frolics of young Krishna. During these festivities people dance and sprinkle yellow or red colour on each other.
3. Rama Navami, the birthday of Rama, which is celebrated near the end of March.
4. Janamashtami, the birthday of Krishna. This is celebrated in August or September.
5. Durga Puja and Dussehra. This is held around September or October. The image of the goddess Durga is worshipped for nine days during this festival and on the tenth day Dussehra is celebrated to mark the victory of Rama over Ravana, the demon king of Lanka.
6. Divali, the festival of lights, which is celebrated in October or November to commemorate the return of Rama after completing 14 years of his exile. The goddess Lakshmi and the god Ganesha are worshipped, and sweets and food are distributed among friends and relatives.

(As most of the Hindu festivals are celebrated according to

certain adjustments between the lunar and the solar calendars, the dates vary every year.)

[I am grateful to Mrs S. Mukherjee for her advice on Hinduism — B. M.]

SIKHISM

The word Sikh means a disciple or a learner. The Sikh religion originated in the sixteenth century, in the Punjab province of undivided India. Nanak was the founder of the Sikh faith. He was born in 1469, at a village called Talwandi (now Nankana Sahib) forty miles to the north west of Lahore in what is now Pakistan. His father, a Hindu Kshatri, was the village record keeper. Nanak's education began at about the age of five and he learnt Persian, Arabic and Sanskrit. He had an inquisitive mind and spent much of his time having discourses with learned people of different religions and meditating to find the truth. Soon he became convinced that there was only One, Absolute God, and he rejected his ancestral faith which involved numerous gods and goddesses. His father arranged for his marriage at the age of 18 to try to distract him from his spiritual indulgences, but to no avail.

At the age of 27 he left his family and started his wanderings in search of knowledge and the truth, which took him not only to the length and breadth of India but also to Ceylon, Nepal, Burma, Tibet, Iran, Iraq, Arabia and Afghanistan. During his journey to Arabia, Nanak dressed as a Muslim pilgrim, prayed as a Muslim and performed the pilgrimage at Makkah. He also visited the grave of the prophet Muhammed at Medina and then turned back to India, stopping for some time at Baghdad in the company of some Muslim saints. In 1990, the author, while in Baghdad, visited the place where Nanak stopped. It is well preserved and bears a plaque with the following inscription: 'In memory of the Guru, that is the Divine Master, Baba Nanak fakir aulia, this building has been raised anew with the help of seven saints'. It is dated 927 Hijra (A.D. 1520–21).

On his return the Guru (the Master), as he was known, settled with his family, as a farmer, at Kartarpur, a town which he had founded earlier on the right bank of the river Ravi. He had a considerable following and to feed his followers who called on him he founded the institution of langar (free kitchen), which has since become an integral part of the Sikh faith. Everybody was welcome to this kitchen irrespective of caste, creed or sex. Guru Nanak died in 1539. It is reported that at his death a controversy arose between the Hindus and the Muslims regarding his last rites. The Muslims claimed that the Guru was one of their faith and should be buried by them. The Hindus on the other hand maintained that he was a Hindu and his body should be cremated by them. However, his body is said to have disappeared mysteriously during the night and thus the matter was settled without further ado.

Before his death Nanak had appointed a successor who was called Guru Angad. Angad recorded the sayings of Guru Nanak along with his own recollections and devotional reflections in a book. This was the inception of the *Granth Sahib*, the holy book of the Sikhs. Every Guru from then on, and there were eight more, added his own contribution as well as selections from other sources, both Hindu and Muslim, to the holy book. The fifth Guru Arjan, however, enlarged the *Granth Sahib* considerably as nearly half of it is attributed to him. He also built the famous Golden Temple at Amritsar, a city which was founded by his predecessor Guru Ramdas. The foundation stone of the Golden Temple was laid by a Muslim saint, Mian Mir, on the request of the Guru.

The tenth and last Guru of the Sikhs was Gobind Rai, who took over the Guruship in 1675 at the tender age of nine years. On 13 April 1699, he changed his name to Gobind Singh (following the last Guru, all the Sikhs have taken the affix Singh, meaning 'lion', since that day), reorganised his followers in a more disciplined way and gave the name of Khalsa (pure) to the Sikh fraternity. He also instituted elaborate initiation rites for admittance into the Sikh order.

The Sikh Faith

Belief in One, Absolute, All powerful, Perfect, Self-existent,

Infinite, Incomprehensible, Creator, and all-loving God is the backbone of the Sikh religion. Sikhism rejects the worship or veneration of idols and images. It condemns the caste system and indeed encourages people, through its own institutions of common kitchen (langar) and communion (karah prashad), to break the barriers of caste and creed by eating together and mixing freely. Sikhism discourages ritualism, religious vestments, ostentatious prayers and penance. The highest form of worship according to the Sikh Gurus is 'Ajapa Jap', the meditative silence, utterance (of God's praises or attributes) of the heart and not of the tongue. Nevertheless, congregational prayers are held in gurdwaras, the Sikh temples, mornings and evenings' to recite parts of or hymns from the *Granth Sahib*. With some modifications, the Sikhs believe in reincarnation of the soul. After the death of the tenth Guru the *Granth Sahib* became the living Guru and God's representative on earth. The focal point in the Sikh temples, therefore, is always the Guru *Granth Sahib* (the holy book) placed on a high pedestal. Every Sikh entering the temple bows to it and places a cash offering in front of it as a mark of its authority and the reverence accorded to it.

To give them a distinctive appearance initiated Sikhs are obliged to wear the five Ks: 1. the Kes, i.e. unshorn hair; 2. the Kangha, i.e. hair comb; 3. the Kara, i.e. iron bangle; 4. the Kirpan, i.e. sword; 5. the Kachh, i.e. drawers reaching to the knee. Some of these items have soldiery uses as well as spiritual meanings. Sikhism discourages hermitage or renunciation of the world and encourages family life. Honest earning, honest living, sharing with and caring for others is ordained for the followers of the Sikh faith. A loving, peaceful, charitable and truthful life is demanded of a true Sikh. 'Truth is above everything: but higher still is the living of Truth' said Nanak.

Social Customs and Dietary Regulations

A male Sikh wears a turban to maintain and protect his unshorn hair which, being very long, is normally rolled up into a bun at the top (crown) of the head. The use of tobacco is strictly forbidden, and thus to offer or expect a cigarette or a cigar, etc., from a Sikh can cause offence. There appear to be no distinct injunctions for or against the consumption of meat and liquor. Consequently some Sikhs eat meat (except beef) and drink alcoholic drinks, whereas others refrain from consuming meat and abstain from intoxicants. At Sikh marriages the bride and the groom together go round the *Granth Sahib* four times, while a priest is reciting from it to accept each other into wedlock and to affirm their faith in that holy book.

The newborn child and the mother are taken to the temple as soon as convenient after the birth where a thanksgiving service is held and the child given a name. At death the body is washed, wrapped in a sheet of cloth and cremated. However, in this country some Sikh families, following the local custom, dress the body in a suit belonging to the deceased instead of wrapping it in a sheet. It should be noted that, as the ancestors of almost all the Sikhs were converted from Hinduism, they still retain many of the Hindu customs and cultural traditions, some with certain modifications and others in their original form.

Sikh Festivals

The birthdays of the ten Gurus of Sikhism and their respective death anniversaries are all celebrated fittingly by the adherents of the faith. However, the two most important festivals are the birthday of Guru Nanak, the founder of the Sikh faith, in November, and the birthday of Khalsa or the Baisakhi in mid April. It was on the day of Baisakhi, in April 1699, that the Sikh brotherhood was reorganised and given the name Khalsa by the last Guru, Gobind Singh. The festivities involve the continuous recitation of the *Granth Sahib* for 48 hours, starting from the Friday morning and ending on the Sunday morning. After the recitation congregational prayers are held which are followed by the communion (karah prashad) and common kitchen meal (langar). All celebrations are held in a Sikh temple (gurdwara) which is also used as a community centre.

[I am grateful to Mr B. S. Saggu for his advice on Sikhism
— B. M.]

RELIGIONS AND CUSTOMS OF THE CHINESE

The two leading religions of the Chinese community are
Buddhism and Taoism. Ancestral worship is also practised
by some and about 4% to 5% of the Chinese in Scotland
belong to the Christian faith.

Buddhism

Buddhism arose as an offshoot of Hinduism in the Behar
region of India in the fifth or sixth century B.C. Its founder,
Gautama Buddha, was a royal prince of the Hindu religion
who renounced his faith and the world when he was 29 years
old. After six years of wanderings and meditation he achieved
enlightenment and founded his own school of religious thought
which is called Buddhism. The main beliefs of Buddhists are:
Transmigration or reincarnation of the soul in a very extreme
form and the eventual passing out of existence of the soul
after numerous cycles of rebirth in different states and various
forms; to follow the Noble Eightfold Path (right belief, right
intentions, right speech, right action, right earnings, right
effort, right thinking and right meditation) which leads to
nirvana or the final salvation of the soul; compassion and
kindness to all creatures and condemnation of all evil deeds.
Buddhism believes in numerous heavens and hells and in the
existence of gods and deified beings in the heavens, but it
appears to have no concept of God, or a supreme deity.

Taoism

Tao means the 'way' and religious Taoism evolved over many
centuries from Philosophical Taoism which had developed in
China in the fourth and third centuries B.C. Kou Chien Chih
made Taoism an organised religion in the early fifth century
A.D. Soon it was declared a state religion in China. Taoists

believe in and worship a plethora of deities, deified mortals and ancestors. They have a god for every conceivable thing or idea. Like Buddhists they believe in numerous heavens and hells. Piety, patience, simplicity, devotion, harmony and contentment are the main characteristics of Taoism. Use of charms, geomancy and other methods of foretelling the future and fortune are common practices among Taoists. To achieve longevity and worldly or material blessings medicines, magic, mental concentration, physical exercises, diet, alchemy, baths and breath control are all used devotionally. Taoism has been influenced greatly by Buddhism from which it has absorbed many ideas.

Chinese Festivals

Buddhism and Taoism, the two main Chinese religions, have become so close by assimilating each other's ideas that now their respective deities are often worshipped together within one temple. Thus the festivals of both religions and indeed of Confucianism and other cults have become common and are celebrated by all Chinese. Many of their customs, and aspects of their culture, are therefore observed in their celebrations of traditional Chinese festivals. There are five major Chinese festivals. The most important and the most colourful of these is the New Year festival. This is celebrated during the first few days of the first moon of the Chinese Lunar New Year. Over and above the usual merrymaking and dances, visits and gifts are exchanged between relatives and friends, and children are given 'lucky' money, in red packets, during these festivities. The Ching Ming festival is celebrated in springtime and it is customary to visit the graves of ancestors on this occasion. The Dragon Boat Festival is celebrated on the fifth day of the fifth moon in early summer. On this joyous occasion dragon boat races are held and people eat cooked rice wrapped in lotus leaves. The Moon Cake Festival or the Mid Autumn Festival is celebrated on the fifteenth day of the eighth moon. Gifts of moon cakes, wine and fruit are exchanged on this day and adults as well as children go to the countryside or parks at night carrying colourful lanterns to honour and appreciate the full moon. The Chung Yeong Festival is celebrated on ninth day of the ninth moon. This is another occasion on which the graves of ancestors are visited to honour and pay respects to the departed souls.

SIMILARITIES

Having outlined the various faiths and traditions of the main ethnic groups in Scotland it ought to be emphasised that there are far more similarities in the spiritual heritage of different people than there are disparities. It is obvious that the basic teachings of every religion are based on truth and goodness. Every faith preaches mutual love and respect, piety and patience, charity and kindness, harmony and tolerance, and truth and justice. The ethos and teachings of other religions, therefore, are not any different from the ethos and teachings of Christianity. The beliefs and practices do vary within the different faiths but the ultimate spiritual and social aims of all religions are similar. Religions, like humans, differ only in shades or colours, and are almost identical in substance and character. The various faiths of people, therefore, do not change their nature or their feelings. Thus the outlook on life in general of adherents of other religions in Scotland is little different from that of their fellow Scots who are Christians.

Furthermore, diversity of customs and cultures in a society ought to be a source of enrichment of life for the community at large and not an excuse to keep the communities apart. It should be remembered that a living and thriving culture is the one which continuously welcomes and accepts new ideas, whereas a moribund culture builds high walls around it and rejects anything new. The new ideas, new customs and new cultures brought over by the new settlers have already made an appreciative impact on the way of life in Scotland. This infusion of new ideas and practices into the Scottish culture is bound to enrich life and enhance the pleasures of living for all in a multicultural Scotland.

CHAPTER SEVEN

Conclusions and the Future

Then let us pray that come it may,
As come it will for a' that,
That sense and worth, o'er a' the earth
Shall bear the gree, and a' that.

— *Robert Burns*

In the last fifty years over 50,000 people of different cultures and of non-European origins have made their home in Scotland. This number constitutes about 1% of the total population of this country. If this small number, this latest addition to Scottish society, had been white-skinned all major problems concerning them would probably have been solved by now and, like the Irish, Italians and Poles, these people would have been assimilated into Scottish society. The reality, however, is that they are of a different colour: they are easily and readily distinguishable because they are brown, black and yellow. They cannot blend physically and visually into the 99% white inhabitants of this country like their predecessors. This difference of colour, therefore, perhaps more than anything else, has been militating against their smooth and serene settlement in this country.

Furthermore, these newcomers have not only a different physical appearance but also different cultures, customs and religions. To add to the complexity of the matter, there are even great differences among various sections of these newcomers. If the susceptibilities or sensitivities of one section of this composite ethnic minority are affected, and there is a reaction to that from that particular section, the whole minority community ends up suffering from the counter-reaction of the indigenous population. The prejudice and racism which evolves from such situations is usually directed towards all sections of the minority because the agitators

201

and mischief-makers cannot and do not want to distinguish between various sections of the ethnic minorities. We have experienced this phenomenon during the Rushdie affair and the Gulf crisis. In both these situations only the Muslim minority of this country was directly involved, but the bigots and racists exploited these occasions to spread poison and harass all ethnic minorities.

The problems are many and complex. Scotland, like the rest of the United Kingdom, has had its share of racial tensions and racial trouble, but serious trouble here has been sporadic and isolated. There was resentment against and opposition to the employment of colonial labour just before the First World War. After the war, in 1919, there was a riot one afternoon in the docklands of Glasgow caused by mounting tension between white and non-white workers competing for jobs. Then there was the murder of an Indian pedlar in 1925 in Port Dundas, Glasgow. There have been a number of serious physical attacks on Asian and Afro-Caribbean people, their business premises and their houses in Scotland over the years, culminating in the murder in Edinburgh of Ahmed Sheikh, a Somalian student, in January 1989.

There have also been substantial racial discrimination and racial prejudice in Scotland. After 1950, when the numbers of the Indo-Pakistani community started to increase rapidly and those immigrants began to buy houses outwith their 'colonies', they encountered considerable antagonism from the sellers, neighbours and estate agents. In the 1960s, when the Asians began to take over corner shops and stores, they met with indifference and lack of patronage from the Scottish public. People of Asian and Afro-Caribbean origin have mainly been able to find jobs rejected by the Scots, and promotions so far, even in those sectors, have been rare. Isolated ethnic families in some housing schemes are being subjected to racial harassment. In many a school and street all over Scotland, racial taunts and torture are making miserable the lives of many youngsters. Lack of equal opportunities in employment and services is quite common even in the 1990s. Institutional racism and individual prejudice are still barring the way of many capable and brilliant black and brown young people.

In spite of all that, there is no denying that the Asian community and other black people have fared comparatively better in Scotland than their kind in England. Scotland has a good reputation, among members of the ethnic minorities in England, for tolerance and friendliness towards strangers. A great majority of the members of the ethnic minorities believe that race relations and relevant conditions are better in Scotland than in England. This belief is obviously confirmed by the flow of Asian and Afro-Caribbean people from England to Scotland. It is a fact that, in the last 30 years, Scotland has received a considerable number, perhaps between 30 to 40% of the population of its ethnic minorities, through internal migration from England. What makes Scotland so attractive to Asians and others, and why is the race relations situation considered to be comparatively better here? This is a difficult question but perhaps the following facts may help to provide an answer.

1. In Scotland the population of ethnic minorities has been so small that the racists or mischief-makers have never been able to use the numbers argument to cause alarm or apprehension amongst the Scottish public. The biggest concentration of Asians, Afro-Caribbeans and other non-European people in Scotland is in Glasgow, and even there they are about 3% of the total population of that city.

2. There has been seldom any large-scale or serious competition for jobs between the Scots and the ethnic minority workers since the mid 1920s. Until the mid 1950s, the Asians in Scotland were almost all pedlars and self-employed. In the late 1950s and 1960s most of them worked in the transport services of various Scottish cities. The transport service was shunned by the Scots as it involved shift work and unsocial hours. There was, therefore, no concern or resentment against the recruitment of large numbers of Asian bus conductors and drivers. On the

contrary, the staff-hungry authorities appreciated their services and the public admired them for their courtesy and assistance. It was, indeed, the commendable conduct of these Indian and Pakistani drivers and conductors which initially helped to allay the fears and phobias of the Scottish people and promote an atmosphere of goodwill and friendliness towards them.

All candidates for work in the transport services had to pass a written test, over and above the other standard requirements for driving and bus conducting. The written test was to establish their ability to read, write and enumerate. This educational requirement discouraged un-educated immigrants from coming to Scotland as there were no other suitable jobs available for them. This barrier raised considerably the proportion of educated Asians in Scotland. Being educated, more and more Asians have been going into businesses and self-employment, since 1960, creating jobs for the Scots instead of competing for jobs with them.

3. In the public services, competition has also been unnotice-able and negligible, particularly in the 1950s and 60s. The early pedlars mostly lived in their privately rented or bought houses. When the community started to grow in the 1950s, they rarely sought council housing and the emphasis ever since has been on home ownership. Even now less than 5% of the ethnic minority in Scotland, compared to well over 50% of the indigenous population, is housed in the public sector. Similarly, there were very few demands on social security, education and even health services up until at least the late 1960s.

4. The Asian businesses, after overcoming initial resistance, have contributed considerably over the years towards bringing about mutual understanding and creating better communications between the immigrants and the host community. Every day dealings between the ubiquitous Asian shopkeeper on the one hand, and his numerous local customers, suppliers and distributors and their indigenous employees on the other, have helped to widen the contacts

and promote better relations and racial harmony. Since the mid 1960s, the Asian entrepreneurs have been dealing with and employing a steadily growing number of local people. Consequently, social, professional and economic contacts between the immigrants and the Scottish people have been increasing at a very fast rate.

5. Resignation and complacency about racial prejudice and discrimination by the first generation Asians have also contributed towards the 'no problem here' concept. Their intentions were good and their attitudes, although presenting for a time a false picture of the scene in Scotland, nevertheless prevented the situation from being sensationalised and aggravated.

6. The ethnic minorities in Scotland have a good record of staying out of trouble. Incidences of drunkenness, immorality or serious crime are rare in the Scottish Asian and Afro-Caribbean communities. They cherish their spiritual beliefs as well as their material values. They believe in family life and family unity, and are dedicated to giving their children a good education. By their attitudes and their contributions to Scottish society, they are building up the reputation of being responsible citizens.

7. Lastly, there is a lot of truth in the belief that Scottish people in general are more tolerant and accommodating than their English cousins. Even in India during 200 years of the Raj, the Scots were usually far more forbearing and far more considerate towards their Indian subjects. This characteristic of the Scots could be due to the mixed make-up of Scottish society or to their sympathies being with the other underdogs, considering that they themselves have been underdogs to the English for a long time. Whatever the reason, the Scots in general are tolerant and more friendly towards strangers.

Having said all that, it does not mean that all is well in Scotland. Yes, race relations are comparatively better in this part of the United Kingdom than in many other parts.

True, the ethnic minorities are, in general, happier here and doing well in trade and commerce. But there is no room for self-congratulation or complacency, because discrimination and racism, individual as well as institutional, and a lack of opportunities do exist in present-day Scotland. The new generations of Asians, Afro-Caribbeans and others labelled as ethnic minorities are already in revolt, and they are not going to tolerate for long and live with the present humbling and humiliating state of affairs. They do not think of themselves as immigrants. They have not seen any other society or any other country. They are the new Scots. They want to be and they deserve to be treated like any other member of Scottish society.

It is heartening to note, though, that the local authorities and others in authority have at last accepted the reality of the situation and are in the process of introducing measures to combat discrimination and racism. The mere introduction of preventive measures, however, will not save the new Scots from the humiliation of being rejected for a job or being ignored for promotion or being denied a privilege or a right on account of their origin or colour. The measures introduced must be made to work and produce the desired results. This can only be achieved by efficient monitoring and on-going reviews in order to make any necessary amendments whenever and wherever they are required. At the same time there ought to be effective deterrents which actively discourage the malefactors and those who ignore the introduction or proper implementation of the anti-racist, anti-harassment and anti-discrimination measures.

It must also be said that almost all that is being done at present is remedial work. It may cure the disease or at least lessen the misery for a time, but it will not eradicate the disease and prevent it from recurring. To get rid of racism and its ramifications altogether is a herculean task. It requires a change of heart and change of attitudes, something which it could take a generation of dedicated policymakers and planners to achieve. But a start has to be made and there is no time like the present to do that.

To conclude, it ought to be said that the new Scots have their part to play in achieving both the short-term and long-term objectives of racial harmony. They must narrow their own differences and pool their energies and resources to fight vigorously for their and their children's proper place, and all the privileges due to them, in the society they are now part of. The most effective and the quickest way for them to do that is through politics, which will give them the power to achieve their goals. Regrettably, the new Scots of Asian and Afro-Caribbean origin have so far not achieved any significant successes in the civic and political fields. They must therefore become actively and more effectively involved in politics and all other aspects of Scottish life. Without compromising their culture and their customs, if they so desire (and it can be easily done), they must be seen to be part of the Scottish scene. They must start fighting and winning their battles from within the boundaries of their political constituencies by gaining selections and winning elections to reach the corridors of power — the local councils, the regional councils, Parliament and right up to the House of Lords. When they reach there, they will have power — power to influence legislation and to make changes. They would then be able to look after their interests better and solve their problems, if there were any still left. The hearts and minds also, perhaps, would then begin to change for the better and we would all be able to proclaim:

A man's a man for a' that, ...
For a' that, and a' that, it's comin' yet for a' that,
That man to man the warld o'er shall brithers be for a' that.

— *Robert Burns*

Bibliography

Atkinson, G. F. *Curry and Rice* (1859)
Brown, J. *The Religious Denominations of Glasgow* (1860)
Bryant, G. J. 'Scots in India in the Eighteenth Century', *The Scottish Historical Review*, April, 1985
Cain, A. M. *The Cornchest for Scotland* (1986)
The Calcutta Gazette, 4 December 1794
Calpi, T. *The Italian Migration to Scotland: Fiction and the Future*
Cleland, J. *Enumeration of the Inhabitants of the City of Glasgow*
The Daily Record, 20 May 1925
The Edinburgh Indian Association Magazine, 1883–1983
Edwardes, Michael *Raj: The Story of British India* (1969)
The Encyclopaedia Britannica
Faderman, Lillian *Scotch Verdict*
Fryer, X. X. *Staying Power*
The Glasgow Courier, 6 September 1834
The Glasgow Herald, 19 August 1897
The Glasgow Herald, 22 August 1913
The Glasgow Herald, 21 April 1914
The Glasgow Herald, 14 October 1914
The Glasgow Herald, 1 January 1916
The Glasgow Herald, 24 January 1919
The Glasgow Herald, 27 September 1919
The Glasgow Herald, 5 March 1920
The Glasgow Herald, 12 June 1920
The Glasgow Herald, 12 February 1921
The Glasgow Herald, 4 September 1925
The Glasgow Herald, 29 October 1988
The Glasgow Herald, 11 February 1989
Grey, C. *European Adventurers in North India* (1929)
Handley, J. E. *The Irish in Modern Scotland*

Hecht, J. *Continental and Colonial Servants in the Eighteenth Century*
India Office Records L/P & J/6/322 No. 99
Johnston, T. B. *A History of the Working Classes in Scotland*
Kay, Billy *Odyssey*
Kincaid, D. *British Social Life in India 1608–1937*
The Lounger, 8 October 1785
Maclaren's Guide to the Exhibition
Malabari, B. M. *The Indian Eye on English Life* (1895)
Mason, P. *The Men Who Made India* (1985)
Mayhew, H. *London Labour and London Poor* (1861)
Miles, R. *Racism and Migrant Labour*
Mirza Abu Talib Khan *The Travels of Mirza Abu Talib Khan*
Ruffer, J. G. *The Big Shots*
Salter, J. *The Asiatics in Britain* (1873)
The Scots Magazine, September 1782
The Scotsman, 25 November 1926
The Scottish Business Insider
Spiers, P. *The Nabobs* (1932)
Stevenson, R. L. *The Master of Ballantrae*
The Sunday Mail, 17 May 1925
The Sunday Mail, 6 September 1925
Visram, Rosina *Ayas, Lascars and Princes* (1986)
Yule and Burnell *Hobson Jobson*
Zubrzycki, J. *Polish Immigrants in Britain* (1956)

Index

A. A. Brothers, 177–8–9
Abdul Karim, Munshi, 88, 89
Abdullah, 84
Abercrombie, Sir Robert, 48
Aberdeen, 84, 122, 126, 129, 130–1, 142
Aberdeen University, 74, 76, 130
Act of Union, 1707, 38
Adam, John of Kinross, 55
Adarman, 122
Adhan (ie call to prayer), 188
Africa, 174
Africans, 175, 180
Afro-Caribbeans, 163, 181–2, 202, 203, 205, 206
Agra, 37
Ahmedpur, 50
Aitchison, Sir Charles, 53
Alam, Mr Mahboob, 97
Ali Mohammed of Chak Mughalani, 120
Ali Mohammed Painter, 140, 141
Ali, Mrs Naimet, 160
Ali, Sardar, 159
Ali, Taj, 178
Ali, Yacub, 159, 177–8–9
Aliens, Act of, 1905, 22
Aliens, Act of, 1919, 26
Alva, 41
America, 21, 23
Amritsar, 79, 80, 195
Anderson, John, 53
Anderston Glasgow, 106–120, 132, 141
Andrew, Sir William Patrick, 55
Angad, Guru, 195
Angles, 7
Annapurna, 190
Arabs, 180
Argyll, 6
Arjan, Guru, 195
Aryans, 6, 190
Ashraf, Ata Mohammed, 106–120, 137
Ashraf, M. Ibrahim, 143–4
Asian Pedlars, 4, 164, 177
Asians, 1, 2, 161, 162–3–5–6–7–8, 170–1, 174–5–6–9, 180, 202,
Auchlyne, Shootings of, 68
Aurangzeb, Mogul Emperor, 38
Australia, 94, 104
Austria, 32

Ayr, 22
Azad Videos, 180
Azam, M., 143
Aziz Ahmed, 89, 90

Bahadur Shah, Emperor, 78
Bahawalpur, Amir of, 50
Baillie, John Professor, 53
Baird, General Sir David of Newbyth, 48
Baisakhi, 197
Bal Krishan, 124, 125, 160
Balanda, 107, 122
Balfour of Balbirnie, 42
Balkans, 63
Ballantyne, John Robert, 53
Banff, 126
Bangladesh, 175, 182
Bangladeshis, 172–4, 180
Bans, Bishen Singh, 146, 151, 152
Bapat, Pandurang Mahader, 78
Barbados, 8
Beg, Nazir, 75
Begum Murad Baksh, 50
Behar, 39, 44, 46, 198
Belgium, 96
Bengal, 39, 44, 46, 49, 50, 75, 91, 120, 125, 135, 155
Bhagavad Gita, 190
Bhainie, 122
Bibi's (Native Mistresses), 43
Birmingham, 162
Black Prince, 67
Bogle of Daldowie, 42
Bombay, 49, 54, 75, 100, 105–6–114–15, 133
Bradford, 162
Brahma, 190, 191
Brahmins, 190, 191–2
British Hawking Club, 68
Brodie of Forres, 42
Broxburn, 123
Bruce, James, 8th Earl of Elgin & Kincardine, 58
Bruce, Victor Alexander, 9th Earl of Elgin & Kincardine, 58
Buddhists, 182, 199
Budha, Gautama, 198
Budhism, 198, 199

210

Budowal, 122
Burdwan, Hon. the Maharajah dhiraja
    Bahadar, 72
Burgesses roll of, 12
Burj Gujran, 122
Burke & Hare, 14
Buxar, Victory at, 39

Calcutta, 39, 49, 87, 105
Calcutta Hindu College, 53
Caledonians, 5
Campbell, Colonel Charles, 41
Campbell, John, 74
Campbellpur, 60
Canada, 94, 104
Cape of Good Hope, 82
Caribbean, 162
Castle Cash & Carry, 176, 177, 178
Castle Menzies, 67, 68
Catholic Temperance Movement, 16
Celtic, 5
Central Region, 181
Chak No., 477 G.B. Kot, 136, 157, 176
Chak No., 482 G.B. Jagraon, 136, 157
Chak Mughlani, 120
Chamak, T. S., 155
Chanda Singh (Mrs), 160
Chilean Refugees, 174
Chileans, 180
China, 168–9, 198
Chinese, 172–4–5, 180, 181–2–7–9
Chinese Migrants, 168–9
Chinese sailors, 82, 169
Ching Ming Festival, 199
Christian Missionaries, 52, 55
Chung Yeong Festival, 199
Clive, Robert, 40, 41
Clyde, 15, 84, 132
Clyde district committee of the National
    Transport Workers' Federation,
    95
Cohan, Frank Israel (Councillor Glasgow
    District Council), 22
Cohen, Isaac (First Freeman of Jewish
    Origin), 20
Coltness Iron Company, 100
Commonwealth Immigrants Act, 1962,
    161, 163
Communist Party, 133
Constable Lady Winifred, 65
Constantinople, 37
Council of the Literary Association of
    Friends of Poland, 32
Cowcaddens, 141

Cromwell, 20
Culloden, Battle of, 54
Cumbernauld, 172
Cumming, Lt. Col. Alexander Penrose of
    Altyre, 73
Czarist Pogroms, 20

Dalriada, 6, 9
Dalrymple, of East Lothian, 42
Dass, Secundra, 83
Datta, Krishan Lal, 91
Delhi, 39
Denovars, 41
Dharamsala, 58
Dingwall, 142
Divali, 193
Diwan Tulsidass, 129
Dogras, 96
Doms, 62, 63, 81
Dragon Boat Festival, 199
Duff, Dr. Alex, 54
Duleep Singh, Maharaja, 65, 66, 68, 69
Dumbarton, 84
Dumfries, 22
Duncan, King, 7
Dundas, Henry, Viscount Melville, 47, 48
Dundee, 11, 20, 30, 33, 35, 49, 50, 56, 84,
    85, 88, 125, 126,
Dundee, Lord Provost of, 128
Durga, 190–3
Durga Puja, 193
Durie, James, Master of Ballantrae, 83
Dussehra, 193
Dyer, General, 79, 80

East Africa, 96, 104
East African Asians, 168
East India Company, 37, 38, 39, 43, 46,
    47, 49, 51, 55, 58,
Edinburgh, 8, 11, 14, 20, 21, 24, 25, 26,
    27, 35, 55, 65, 69,
Edinburgh Indian Association, 75, 78
Edinburgh, the Lord Provost of, 69, 72
Edinburgh, the University of, 70, 75, 76,
    78, 81, 123, 143
Edward I, King, 20
Egypt, 96
Eid–ul–Adha, 189
Eid–ul–Fitr, 189
El–Madina, S. S., 73
Elgin, 73, 126, 143
Elliot, Gilbert, 4th Earl of Minto, 59
Elliot, Gilbert, Earl of Minto, 55

Elphinstone, Mount Stuart of
    Elphinstone, 48
Elveden, 69
European Economic Community, 28
Eviction Acts, 12

Faisalabad, 136
Falkirk, 22, 26, 35
Farakh Siyar, Mogul Emperor, 39
Farangi, 43
Fascist movement, 26
Fasting, 186
Fateh Mohammed, 117
Fatehgarh, 66
Federation, 95
Fenian, 17
Fenian movement, 17
Fife, 181
Fiji, 94
Fort Munro, 60
Fort William College, Calcutta, 53
France, 33, 96
Fraser, William, 50

Galashiels, 35
Gandhi, M. K., 77
Ganesha, 190–3
Gardner, Alexander Houghton Campbell,
    51
Germany, 21, 23, 27, 33
Ghulab Singh, Rajah of Kashmir, 51
Ghulam Mohammed, 141
Gilchrist, John Borthwick, 53
Gillies, Josiah Dashwood, 75
Gladstone, John, 49
Glasgow, 1, 11, 13, 14, 15, 20, 21, 22, 24,
    26, 27, 35, 56, 69, 70, 75, 84, 85,
    88, 91, 92, 95, 99, 102, 103, 105,
    107, 108, 109, 114, 115, 117, 118,
    119, 122, 123, 124, 125, 126, 129,
    132, 133, 134, 137, 138, 140, 141,
    142, 143, 144, 146, 149, 150, 160,
    162, 172, 176, 178, 200, 202, 203
Glasgow City Council, 21
Glasgow Corporation Transport
    Department, 164
Glasgow Indian Union, 76
Glasgow Police, 89, 90
Glasgow University, 75, 76, 81
Glasgow, Shettleston Constituency, 133
Glasgow, the Lord Provost of, 70, 73, 96,
    152
Global Videos, 180
Glotian, village of, 114

Gobind Singh, Guru, 195, 197
Golden Temple, 195
Gorbals, 1, 132, 133, 137, 141, 150
Gorbals View, 1
Gordon, Jane Cumming, 74
Gordonston, 73
Grampian, 181
Grand Tully Estate of, 68
Ganges, 66, 191, 192
Grant, Charles M.P., 54
Granth Sahib, 195, 196, 197
Greece, 96
Greeks, 36
Greenock, 22, 26, 84, 91
Gretna Green, 130
Gulf Crisis, 201
Guru Singh Sabah (The Sikh
    Association), 150
Gypsies, 62, 63
Gypsy Kingdom of "Little Egypt", 62, 63

Hajj, 186–7
Hamilton, William of Dalzell, 39
Handingshawe, 41
Hanuman, 190
Hardie, Keir, 92
Hare, David, 53
Haripur, 119–120, 122, 146
Harvey, Rev. John, 1
Hashmat Ali (of Sher family), 177
Hastings, Warren, Governor General, 47
Hazara Singh, 141
Hebrides, 7
High Cost of Justiciary Glasgow, 113
Hinduism, 189, 190, 198
Hindus, 52, 139, 140, 141, 147,
    154–5–7–9, 160, 182, 191–2–3
Holi, 193
Holland, 21
Holyrood Palace, 69, 71
Hong Kong, 168–9, 171
Hookas, 43, 44, 52
Hope, Victor Alexander John, Marquis of
    Linlithgow, 59
Huddersfield, 171
Hume, Alan Octavian, 54
Hungarians, 36
Hungry Thirties, 133
Hunting the Barney, 15

Indentured labour, 93, 104
India, 1, 3, 4, 37, 38, 43, 47, 59, 60, 62, 81,
    141, 149, 155–
Indian Army, 59

INDEX

Indian Council Act of, 1909, 59
Indian High Commission in London, 80
Indian Home Rule, 71
Indian journalists, 96
Indian Mutiny of, 1857, 55, 57
Indian National Congress, 54, 71
Indian Oculists, 91
Indian Pedlars, 110–118, 123, 125, 126, 130–1,132–3–4–7, 144
Indian Seamen, 3, 63, 82, 84, 98, 125, 130, 169
Indian Servants, 3, 63, 86
Indian students, 75, 77, 78, 79, 118, 123
Indians, 61, 95, 164–5, 172, 174–180, 181–2
Industrial Revolution, 42
Internal Migration, 162, 168, 171, 175, 202
Inverkeithing, 123
Inverness, 40, 54, 72
Iran, 182
Iranians, 180
Ireland, 6, 9
Irish Home Rule, 18, 19
Irish Immigrants, 9, 26
Irish Labour, 10, 11, 95
Irish National League, 18, 19
Irvine, 26
Irvine Francis, 62
Islam, 182–3–5
Isle of Lewis, 142
Ismail, Mrs. M., 160
Italian Immigrants, 25, 27, 28
Italian Restaurants, 26, 27
Italians, 25, 26
Italy, 25, 26, 27

Jagannadham Dr. Pulipaka, 77
Jagraon sub division, 104, 110, 116, 119, 120, 123, 135, 140,
Jahangir Mogul Emperor, 37
Jallandher, District, 91, 104–5–115, 155
Jallianwala Bagh, 79
Jamaica, 8
James, Finlay, 49
James IV, 62
James V, 62
James VI, 37
Jamiat Ittehadul muslimin (the Muslim Mission), 150
Jammu, 51
Janamashtmi, 193
Jats, 96
Jedburgh, 42

Jewish Immigrants, 18, 20, 25
Jewish Pedlars, 22, 109
Jewish Refugees, 21
Jews (Eastern European), 21, 29
Jews, 21, 22, 24, 27, 29, 31
Jindan Kaur Maharani, 68, 69
Jodhpur, Maharajah of, 71
Johnnie Faa (Gypsy Monarch), 62
Johnstone, John of Westerhall, 41
Jordan, 66
Joshi, S. M., 146

Kaabah, 174, 186
Karachi, 157
Kartarpur, 121, 151
Kashmir, 60, 120
Kenya, 94, 167
Khair Mohammed, 114, 120, 142
Khalsa, 195, 197
Khan Jhulee, 87
Khan Roshan, 86
Khan, Wali Mohammed, 124, 125
Khatri, Girdharilal, 123–4
Kingdom of Oude, 55
Kiri, 122
Kirkpatrick, William James, 48
Kirlcaldy, 35
Kishanpura, 122
Koh–i–Noor, Diamond, 65
Kot (Mohammed Khan), 122, 136
Kot Badal Khan, 105–6–7–115–16–19, 122, 123
Kou, Chien Chih, 198
Krishna, 190–3
Kshatriyas, 190–1

Labour Party, 127, 128, 133, 152
Lahore, 65, 66, 67, 90, 105, 117, 129, 194
Lakshami, 190–193
Lakshmibai, Rani, 78
Lanarkshire, 30, 56, 178
Lascar colonies, 100, 101, 102, 106–7, 169
Lascar Labour, 100
Lascars, 82, 85, 86, 94, 101, 104–5–6, 118, 120
Lasswade & Duns, 56
Latvian, 30
Leith, 30, 49, 56, 84, 87
Liberal Party, 92, 133
Lithuania, 29, 31
Lithuanian Immigrants, 27, 30, 32
Lithuanian Jews, 30
Lithuanians, 29, 30, 31, 33

Liverpool, 169
Loch Tay, 68
Loch Kennard Lodge, 69
Lodhival, 122
Login, Dr. John, 53, 65, 66, 67, 68, 69
London Missionary Society, 74
Lord Cornwallis, 54
Lord Lansdown Viceroy of India
Lord Ormidale, 113
Lothian, 181
Lucknow, 53, 89
Ludhiana district, 104, 116, 127, 140, 155
Lyall, Sir James, Lt. Governor of Punjab, 130
Lyallpur, 136, 157, 176

Maan, village of, 107
Mansa Ram, 120
MacGregor of Glencarnaik, 42
Madarpura, village of, 116–12—122, 140, 157
Madras, 49, 54, 77
Madras, Christian College, 53
Mahabharata, 190
Makkah, 183–6–9, 194
Malabari, B. M., 70
Malawi, 167–8
Malaya, 94, 104
Malaysia, 182
Malaysians, 180
Malcolm, Sir John, 48
Malri, 122
Malsian, 122
Mathews, Father, 16
Mauritius, 94
McDonald, Donald, 11
McIntosh, Professor, 72
McLeod Road, 60
McPherson, Hamish McGregor, 50
McPherson, Sir John of Skye, 54
Meer Jan, 87
Mehadpur, 91, 122, 123
Mehwan, 121, 146
Melrose, 137
Menon Krishna, 128
Mesopotamia, 96
Mian Mir, 195
Mid Autumn Festival, 199
Middle East, 174
Midlands, 162–6–7, 172
Minto, Earl of, 48
Mirpur, 120, 135
Mirza, Abu Talib Khan, 64, 65
Moffat, 137

Mogul Empire, 38, 39
Mohammed Ali (of Sher family), 177
Mohammed Ali of Haripur, 119, 131, 143
Mohammed Bakhsh, 112–119
Mohammed Boota, 126, 129
Mohammed Hussain, 151
Mohammed Kaka, 137
Mohammed Shafi, 141
Molendinar, 15
Mongols, 63
Moolraj Dewan, 50
Moon Cake Festival, 199
Moorhead, Charles, 54
Morley, Minto Reforms, 59
Motherwell, 71, 178
Muhammed Bux (Royal servant), 88
Muhammed, The Prophet, 183–5, 194
Muller, Grace Maxwell, 129
Multan, 50
Munro, Sir Hector, 39
Munro, Thomas, 48
Murray, Peter, 42
Muslims, 52, 96, 139, 140, 141, 146, 147, 150, 154–5–9, 160,
Mysore, His Highness Yuvarava of, 70

Nabobs, 40, 41, 42, 44, 45, 50, 63
Naidu, Mrs. Sarojini, 71
Nakoder Sub–division, 91, 104–5–6–110–115–119–120, 123, 135,
Nana Sahib, 78
Nanak, Guru, 194–5–6–7
Nankana Sahib, 194
Naoroji Dadabhai, 92
Nathoo Mohammed, 105–6–7–8–9–110–11–12–13–14–15–16–17–18–19
National Rising – "The Indian Mutiny", 78
National Sailors & Firemen's Union, 98
National Union of Ship Stewards, Cooks, Butchers & Bakers, 98
Nawanagar, Col. His Highness the Maharajah of, 73
Nazis, 23
Nepalese, 180
New Zealand, 94
Noble Eight Fold Path, the, 198
Noon, Sir Feroz Khan, 73
Noor Mohammed (murder victim), 72, 112, 113, 119
Noor Mohammed of Salimpura
Normans, 7
Norsemen, 7

North West Frontier Province, 120, 135
Nur Mahal, 122

O'Dwyer, Sir Michael, 80
O'Hare Patrick (First Irish Catholic
    Councillor), 19
O'Shaughnessey, William Brook, 56
Oban, 70
Ochterlony, Sir David, 50
Okhai, Ibrahim, 168
Orkney & Shetland Islands, 7
Orissa, 39, 46
Ottoman Empire, 37
Outer Hebrides, 137, 181

Pabam, 120, 121
Paisley, 56
Paisley Pattern, 61
Pakistan, 1, 4, 60, 62, 81, 107, 141,
    154–5–7–8–9, 160–3, 171,
Pakistanis, 61, 95, 154, 164–5,
    172–4–5–180, 181
Pak Pattan, 159
Palestine, 96
Parker, Mr. (Lincolns Inn), 46
Parliamentary Elections, February,
    1974–, 173
Partick (Glasgow), 18
Parvati, 190
Patel, Hon. V. J., 71
Pathans, 120
Pebbles, 11
Pedlars Licences, 164
Peoples Republic of China, 169
Persia, 62
Perth, 11, 35, 84
Perthshire, 67
Peterhead, 126
Picts, 5, 7
Plassey, 40
Plassey, Victory at, 39
Poland, 20, 21, 33, 34
Poles, 32, 33, 34, 35, 36
Polish Government in Exile, 33, 34
Polish Jews, 32
Polish Refugees, 32, 34
Polish soldiers, 32, 33
Port Dundas Glasgow, 108,
    110–12–120–132–3, 141, 169, 202
Potato Famine, 17
Princess Anne, H.R.H., 178
Privy Council of the Kingdom of
    Scotland, 62, 63
Protestantism, 13

Prussia, 32
Public Park Trophies, 81
Pundit Nehemiah Goreh, 67
Punjab, 48, 51, 54, 58, 65, 91, 96,
    104–5–114–15, 121–126,
Punjab University, 53
Puranas, 190

Qadir Bakhsh, 120
Queen Anne, 38
Queen Charlotte, 65
Queen Elizabeth I, 37
Queen Victoria, 66, 70, 88,89
Quinn, Jane, 127
Quran, 184–5
Qutub Din, 112–114

Radha, 190
Rahmat Ali (of Sher family), 177
Rahmatullah, 130–1
Rajah Bhagwat Sinhjee, Thakore Sahib
    of Gondal, 69
Rajah Ajit Singh of Khatri, 70
Rajah Ram Mohan Roy, 53
Rajah Kumar Singh of Shakpura, 70
Rakhra, Mrs. K. S., 160
Rama, 190–3
Ramadhan, 186–9
Ramanavami, 193
Ramayana, 190
Ramdass, Guru, 195
Ramsay, James Andrew Broun, Lord
    Dalhousie of Coalstoun, 55,
Ranjit Singh, Maharaja, 51, 65
Ravena, 193
Ravi River, 195
Reekie, Miss Stella, 1
Renfrewshire, 56
Richardson Capt. David, 64
Rising, 1798 (Irish), 12
Roman Legionnaires (Black), 6, 7
Romans, 5
Roslin Place, Port Dundas, 132
Rowe, Sir Thomas, 37, 38
Roy, Gopal Chandra, 75
Rushdie affair, 201
Russia, 20, 32, 33, 34

Sabbath Laws, 27
Sadarpura, 120, 122, 159
Saggar Street, Dundee, 129
Saggar, Dr. Dhaniram, 128
Saggar, Dr. J. D., 126, 127, 128
Saggar, Dr. Karam, 128

Saklatvala, Shahpurji, 133
Salimpura, 120, 122
Salt market, 11, 15
Saluja, Dr. Gurudeo S., 131
Sardar Muhammed, 157
Sarsvati, 190
Scindia Steam Navigation Company, 73
Scots, 6, 7, 8, 9
Scott, David of Dunninald, 47
Scott, Sir Walter, 49
Scottish Banking Crisis of, 1772, 42
Scottish Business Insider, 179
Scottish East India Company, 38
Scottish Office Central Research Unit, 175
Scottish Polish Associations, 33
Scottish Polish Wives Society, 33
Selby, Mrs. Susan, 130, 131
Seraja Dowla, 46
Seran, Kartar Singh, 140
Shahab Din, 110–12–19
Shaik Roshan, 87
Sharif, Fateh Mohammed, 116
Sharif, Ghulam Mohammed, 120, 137
Sharif, M., 171–2
Sher Brothers, 177
Sher Mohammed of Tehara, 123, 124
Sher Kadir, 137
Sher Mohammed (of Sher Family), 136, 176, 177
Shinwell, Emmanuell (First Jewish MP), 23
Shiva, 190–3
Shivratri, 193
Sialkot, 51–114
Siberia, 34
Sidwan, 122
Sikh Kingdom of Punjab, 65
Sikhism, 66, 194, 196, 197
Sikhs, 96, 139, 140, 141, 146, 147, 154–5–7–9, 160, 182, 195,
Simon, Michael (First Jewish Elected Representative), 21
Sindh, 48
Singh, Hari, 114–15, 135
Singh, Jay, 81
Singh, Narain, 120
Singh, Santa, 146
Singh, Thakur, 120, 146
Sita, 190
Sitala, 190
Skinner, Lt. Col. Hercules, 48
Smith, Col. Richard Baird, 56
Somerville, Thomas, 42

South Africa, 94
Southall, 171
Springburn (Glasgow), 19
St. Andrews University, 75
St. Giles Cathedral, 69
Steel, Flora Annie, 54
Stirling, 26, 42, 84
Stornoway, 137, 142
Strathclyde, 181
Stroma, 137
Stuart, James Lt. Col. of Culross, 48
Sudan, 96
Sudras, 190–1
Sundhi Din, 107–8–110–12
Sutlej River, 104, 106, 116, 120, 135

Tain, 142
Talwan, 120, 121
Tanda Oora, 106, 121, 123
Tanda, Noor Mohammed, 98, 106
Taoism, 198, 199
Taoists, 182–199
Tayside, 181
Tehara, 122
Thurso, 137
Tilak, R. G., 71
Tipoo Sultan, 48
Turkey, 96, 182
Turks, 180

Uganda, 94, 167
Ukranians, 36
Union of Scotland and England, 170, 72
Upanishuds, 190

Vaisyas, 190–1
Vasco de Gama, 37
Vedas, 190
Vietnamese, 172–4–5, 180
Vishnu, 190
Vizianagram, Maharani of, 76

Wedderburn, Sir David and Sir William, Baronets, of Balindean, 54
West Indians, 175, 180
West Indies, 8, 94, 104, 163, 174
Wick, 137
World War I, 23, 26, 59, 71, 78, 95, 98, 105–7, 130, 169, 202
World War II, 24, 28, 32, 59, 73, 118, 124, 125, 147–9, 152

Yorkshire, 162–6–7
Young, William, 42

Zakah, 186